LANGUAGE AND LITERACY SE[RIES]
Dorothy S. Strickland and Celia [Genishi]
SERIES EDITORS

Literacy Events in a Community of Young Writers

YETTA M. GOODMAN
SANDRA WILDE
Editors

TEACHERS
COLLEGE
PRESS

Teachers College, Columbia University
New York and London

Published by Teachers College Press, 1234 Amsterdam Avenue, New York, NY 10027

Library of Congress Cataloging-in-Publication Data

Literacy events in a community of young writers / Yetta M. Goodman and Sandra
  Wilde, editors.
      p.   cm. — (Language and literacy series)
  Includes bibliographical references and index.
  ISBN 0-8077-3212-5 (alk. paper). — ISBN 0-8077-3211-7 (pbk. : alk. paper)
  1. English language—Study and teaching—Indian speakers. 2. English
language—Composition and exercises—Study and teaching—Arizona.
3. Indians of North America—Education—Arizona. 4. Indians of North
America—Arizona—Children. 5. Literacy programs—Arizona. 6. Writing
centers—Arizona. I. Goodman, Yetta M., 1931– . II. Wilde, Sandra.
III. Series: Language and literacy series (New York, N.Y.)
PE1130.5.A5L57 1992
372.65′21′08997—dc20   92-30734

Printed on acid-free paper

Manufactured in the United States of America

98 97 96 95 94 93 92   8 7 6 5 4 3 2 1

*To Alice Antone, Gabriel Cachora, Jr., Enna Hendricks,
Virgil Lewis, Ruth Romo, and Dwayne Valenzuela*

Contents

Foreword

Ofelia Zepeda

As a MEMBER of the same Tohono O'odham community as the children described in this book, and as a linguist whose work is the formal study of the O'odham language, I am interested in the role of language in the lives of our children: both the role of spoken language in our own traditions and the importance of the written language they learn in school.

THROWING WORDS

"Throwing words into the air." This is what O'odham say about talking, storytelling, praying, and singing, all of which make up the genre of oral tradition. The words are thrown into the air in the form of spoken word, song, oration, or invocation. Words, like other things that can be carried by the air, are at the mercy of the winds. The listener who happens to be on the receiving end of these words is also at the mercy of the winds. In O'odham, other than in the give-and-take of everyday conversation, protocol does not allow listeners the luxury of asking the speaker to repeat the words. If they do not catch the words as they were thrown, the listeners are left with questions and discomfort.

Some words that are thrown into the air are regular everyday words, but others are meant to invoke, to heal, to harm. But even everyday words, like the words that are meant to have special power, are embedded with their own strength. It is for this reason that so many believe in the power of words (Momaday, 1975) and believe that speakers must be careful of and responsible for what they speak.

SPOKEN O'ODHAM

The O'odham have a great deal of interest in their language, which has certain highly salient features for many speakers (Zepeda & Hill, 1986). The spoken language of the O'odham people has long been a consciously important part of their identity; in fact, regional dialect groups are an important social unit for the O'odham. In Jane Hill's and my work (1986) on regional dialects in O'odham, we note that ethnohistoric summaries suggest that these dialect groups were the basis for the formation of the eleven defense villages in which the O'odham lived during the nineteenth century, and they continue as the basis for the nine districts of the modern O'odham reservation. The importance of dialect-group membership was, and is still, expressed in joking, teasing, and competition among dialect groups.

Other observations about attitudes and practices in regard to spoken O'odham language are anecdotal. For instance, it is common for older speakers to forbid younger members of the community to mechanically record the former's speech, even with pencil and paper. They chastise the young listeners for being lazy, for not knowing how to listen in the way that *they* had to listen. They often retort, "If it is something important, you will remember it."

Still other speakers talk about the genre called "song and say," commenting that songs are "flowers for the ears"; that is, songs are stimulating and enjoyable in the oral medium in the same way that objects and experiences are stimulating to other human senses. Others talk of language as a commodity to be sold. O'odham speakers say "Sell my speech for me" when they require translation into English or Spanish.

Finally, speakers are acutely aware of the psychological power words can have. This power is different from that which is held by a select few, a trained few. This is the power ordinary people can have with words. There is the healing and nurturing power of words, but of course there is also destructiveness. O'odham speakers know the hurt they can impose on one another simply by an utterance or by denying one another words. One anthropologist has observed that the cruelest punishment an O'odham speaker can impose is to deny acknowledgment of another by not speaking to him or her. This is a way of saying that person no longer exists—certainly an unusual punishment. And it is for this reason that speakers must keep constant check on what they say, again being sensitive to the responsibility they have for the words they speak.

These are but a few examples of our growing knowledge about spoken O'odham. In contrast, attitudes and practices concerning written English language among the O'odham have evolved and been observed only very recently.

WRITTEN LANGUAGE

Scholars agree that the O'odham language is an oral language. It does not have a written tradition. Although it is true that certain ideas were "written" before contact with Europeans—as in petroglyphs, rock writing, calendar sticks, and so on—it is clear that the interpreters or the literate people of these writings were but a select few.

The study of children's writing presented in this book tells us three things. First, the children in the study learned how to carry out the task of writing. Second, the children also began to develop attitudes and habits about writing, many of which were influenced by their role models and peers. Third, and probably not as obviously, the children brought themselves and their world into their writing, making an extension into what I like to call the continuum of literacy. Here the students meshed the oral and the written traditions into one.

The writing activity as introduced by the teachers in the study was such that the students learned certain skills and applied them in their various writing assignments. Some of the students, of course, learned more than others, and some students applied their new knowledge more adeptly than their classmates, thus making clear their individuality as practitioners of writing in the English language.

The students, by responding to their teachers, their primary role models, began to develop attitudes and habits about writing. This is evident in the children's remarks on neatness, clean papers, spelling, and length or brevity of writing. Students saw certain qualities as pleasing to their teachers and to themselves. Eventually these attitudes will be reflected in their future writing experiences. Basically, the importance of the first two points mentioned above is that the students in this study learned in much the same way as all other students. The fact that they were O'odham students made little or no difference in learning about school expectations of writing.

However, what is unique about this population is what they chose to write about and how. These students' writings often gave the reader a small window into their world, the world of growing up in a special place, whether a village at the foot of a sacred mountain or a place where the whole village is an extended family.

I believe that it is at this level of the students' writing that the continuum of literacy joins up again the oral and the written. The students employed many traits of storytelling. They may have written about specific topics as assigned by the teacher, but at the same time they were gathering insights from their own experience, from their community, home, and family, to write what they felt made a good story. Also, as with the oral tradition, the writers played and in some cases experimented with the power of words. I find that in much of the students' writing they were tantalizing readers, especially the students who preferred to write brief pieces. They were using the power of words to tantalize readers by making them desire more. These students were, of course, oblivious to this power in their writing. Or were they?

Preface

IN THE AMERICAN EDUCATIONAL SCENE it is easy to focus on the failures of schools and of schoolchildren and their communities, because of our love affair with test scores, normal curves, and statistics. Because of the hypnotic nature of numbers, we have lost the view of the forest beyond the trees, the view of real children behind our statistical manipulations. Communities of parallel culture groups that are different from the mainstream and that represent ethnic and economic diversity often find that their children are viewed and defined by sets of numbers rather than by the experiences and activities of their daily lives. Ann Francisco, the principal of the primary school in the Indian Oasis school district, and I wondered whether we might uncover the knowledge Tohono O'odham children have about writing if we observed them as they wrote in the classroom and respectfully examined their compositions. Perhaps in this way we might discover the literacy learning potentials of these children and, at the same time, add to the growing information being disseminated by writing researchers studying other groups of children.

For many years I have dedicated myself to understanding the nature of the language learning of children who come from communities that often lose their humanity when educational researchers and practitioners attempt to paint everyone with the same brush. Through this search I have come to understand my own language and learning development. As a child, I also suffered from the critical attitudes and deficit views that are still prevalent toward the poor, the bilingual, the bidialectal, and others who reflect alternative views and life styles. By exploring the literacy learning of groups representing many cultures and languages, I hope to make their humanity visible so that teachers can understand the diversity in their classrooms and help all children reach their language potential.

The purpose of the research story told in this volume is to understand how writing was used by a community of learners in a classroom to construct meaningful learning experiences. The story shows how the writing of a group of Tohono O'odham children in particular was influenced by the classroom, their homes, and their community. We hope to introduce many of our readers to the Tohono O'odham people through the writing of their children.

The chapters of the book are organized to tell our research story and to introduce the children and their classroom community, with the first and last chapters acting as bookends.

In Chapter 1, I explore the influences of the community, the individual, and the text on the development of any literacy event. In the last chapter I return to these issues and explore their implications for classroom research and curriculum development. Chapter 2 provides an overview of the study. This chapter was compiled by Sandra Wilde and myself from the vignettes and writings of the whole research team. It relates the discoveries we made about the children and their writing and tells how the children's writing was gathered and analyzed. Chapters 3 through 6 explore specific aspects of the children's writing, reflecting the special expertise of the authors. Lois Bridges Bird reveals aspects of children's personal expression in writing, and Wendy Kasten examines the resources children used during their writing. Suzanne Gespass looks at the children's use of pronouns, and Sandra Wilde provides an in-depth look at their spelling knowledge. Chapters 7 and 8, by Sherry Vaughan and Sandra Wilde respectively, are case studies of two of the young writers. And in Chapter 9, Sherry Vaughan explores how research can be useful to teachers. These chapter topics were selected to reveal the complexity of the writing study and to interest a wide range of readers—teachers, teacher/researchers, curriculum specialists, writing researchers, linguists, anthropologists, and ethnographers, among others.

This book is for anyone interested in language learning. Teachers and researchers can relate the stories we tell, our descriptions, and even our statistics to their own experiences and searches for knowledge in order to explore how writing gives learners multiple ways to express their meanings. This book also allows educators to understand that communities of students in schools cannot be separated from the communities of their homes, villages, towns, and cities. The social history children bring to school represents the language, beliefs, and knowledge of their community, and affects both their writing and their views of themselves as writers. We can observe the similarities among all young writers and at the same time come to understand the unique individual and social differences among children and the communities in which they live.

YETTA M. GOODMAN

Acknowledgments

I AM GRATEFUL to the large number of people who made this story possible. The United States Office of Education funded this research project (National Institute of Education Project #G-81-0127), based on a proposal written with the help of Jay Walker.

We want to recognize all the children, community members, and school personnel for their contributions to our thinking and understanding. District superintendent Mike Ryan and the school board asked important questions about the nature of our research and were always cooperative and helpful.

We used pseudonyms in the original study and in all the articles we've written about the research (including the chapters of this book) because of agreements we made with the school board and the University of Arizona's Human Subjects Review Committee at that time. However, with the permission and encouragement of the 1992 school board, we express sincere gratitude for the support of the employees of the Indian Oasis school district and the Tohono O'odham people with whom we came into contact by using their real names in this preface.

Our work is dedicated to the six focus children whose writing we observed for two years and with whom we worked the longest: Alice Antone, Gabriel Cachora, Jr., Enna Hendricks, Virgil Lewis, Ruth Romo, and Dwayne Valenzuela. Three are now in high school and two are in college; one has chosen not to complete his senior year.

We also want to honor the other children with whom we worked. We focused on four additional students during the first year of our research. In addition, teachers encouraged us to observe, videotape, and interview other children in their classes so that they would feel involved in the project, and we did so whenever possible throughout the two years. The parents we contacted were always gracious and interested in our work, asking questions and providing information to show their concern and support for their children's learning.

The teachers Joyce Henn Juan, Chris Pray, and Sister Conchita Boyer, and the principals Ann Francisco and Sister Juliana Weber, provided us with important insights into classroom and school organization. Louella Martinez, a member of our research team from the Tohono O'odham community, worked with us to maintain contact with the children's parents and to aid us in observing and collecting the children's writing. Over the two years Frances Miguel and Phyllis Ventura also had on-site responsibilities, and we are indebted to them as well.

As we came close to the publication of this book we decided that in addition to the children's stories, it would be illuminating to our readers to have visual images of Tohono O'odham children writing in their classrooms. We had video and audio tapes of the young writers in our study but no photographs, so we illustrated the chapters in this book with photographs of current Tohono O'odham third and fourth graders, whose names appear on page xvii. Joel Brown was the photographer of this next generation of Tohono O'odham writers.

Special thanks go to the research team, most of whom are authors of chapters in this book. Sandra Wilde, my coeditor, has been an important influence on my own thinking, in the direction of the research, and in the development and completion of this volume. With Sandra, the research team included Lois Bird, who was the first project director and who organized the original research procedures, Suzanne Gespass, Wendy Kasten, Sherry Vaughan, and David Weatherill. At the time of their involvement all of them were doctoral students. Now they are involved in successful careers of their own. This study could never have been completed without the untiring efforts of these researchers. During our regular meetings, the debriefings we held in the 90-minute rides to and from the schools, and our informal interactions, we influenced one another's thinking, knowledge, and attitudes. Together, we all learned much about children and the writing process. We built relationships with the children that helped us gain even greater insights into the children and their language learning, relationships that were often reflected in the children's writing.

We thank Nada Spencer and Diane Barajas Ybarra, who typed transcripts and performed a variety of secretarial duties. Ron McConeghy gave us important computer help. The work of the secretaries and computer programmers was basic to our data analysis. Kathryn Whitmore, Prisca Martens, Rick Meyer, Louise Lockhart, and Karen Wahl worked conscientiously during the editing process. This involved not only reading for meaning but preparing charts, figures, and samples of children's writing.

Ofelia Zepeda, who wrote the foreword to this book, and Peter Fries were often called on to provide insights into the linguistic issues we were considering. Sue Hawkins and Bonnie Chambers, visiting scholars to the University of Arizona, were additional resources we called on to help collect information in the classroom, observe the children, and add to our growing insights.

We are also grateful to our editors at Teachers College Press: series editors Dorothy S. Strickland and Celia Genishi, acquisition editor Sarah Biondello, and production editors Faye Zucker and Linda J. Lotz, who helped us make our findings available to a wider audience.

A research study and a book telling the story of such research involves discussion with many people. We talked about our work and raised questions with Don Graves and Lucy Calkins. We thank them for their inspiration. Each of the authors in this volume has had countless conversations with students and colleagues. We thank them all and as one third grader wrote in the dedication of a book she wrote: "I AM SORRY IF I MISSED ENYONE ELTS IF I DID FORGET YOU PLEAS CONGRATULAT YOURSELF."

As I conclude this glimpse of the people who influenced this work, I also have to say thanks to Ken Goodman, who is always there to help me reflect and wonder.

Y.M.G.

IN ADDITION TO echoing Yetta Goodman's words of appreciation to everyone, I'd like to give special thanks to the students of Fort Alexander, Manitoba, Canada, who taught me so much in my first three years of teaching, and to Vaughn Huff, David Northway, and Dr. Donald Marvel.

S.W.

COVER AND TEXT PHOTOGRAPHS BY JOEL BROWN.

THOSE PICTURED ON THE COVER: *Front row:* Michelle Porter, Denise Martinez, Gerilyn Johns, Crystal Mendez, Nicole Juan. *Back row:* Maria Ramon, Ed Tas Galvez.

THOSE PICTURED IN THE TEXT: *Chapter 1:* Brandon Lewis, Brandon Shaw. *Chapter 2:* Melody Antone, Natalie Anissia Mattias. *Chapter 3:* Elijah Garcia. *Chapter 4:* Nicole Juan, Lisa Garcia, Delcine Sam (back row). *Chapter 5:* Maria Joseph Ramon. *Chapter 6:* Sharon Padilla. *Chapter 7:* Maria Antonio. *Chapter 8:* Faron G. Moreno. *Chapter 9:* Ronald Pablo, Donahue Queentaria. *Chapter 10:* Christina Moreno.

Literacy Events in a Community of Young Writers

CHAPTER 1

The Writing Process

THE MAKING OF MEANING

Yetta M. Goodman

IN THE BEGINNING THERE WAS A QUESTION: In what ways would children in a public school in a Native American reservation community develop as writers in a classroom where daily writing was an ongoing part of the curriculum? Along with Ann Francisco, a dedicated educational practitioner who was the principal of such a school, we began to formulate a proposal to try to answer that question and others, and the story to be told in this book began to unfold.

> Dear Pen Pal,[1]
> My name is Dana. I go to school at Topawa. I got one sister. My favorite sports are basketball and baseball. I live in Crowhang. I have lots of friends. My best friends are Harrington and Cody. Everytime it is fun here and hot. How is it over at your place?
> Sincerely yours, Dana

Just as Dana sketched a profile of himself for his pen pal, I will provide a backdrop for the (re)search we did to answer our questions. Dana was one of a group of Tohono O'odham students from southwestern Arizona that the authors of this book observed on a fairly regular basis. (The names of all students and teachers have been changed to protect their privacy.) We became fascinated with the collaborative nature of writing, reading, and learning in the classroom. We interviewed students about what they knew about their writing, what they liked about it, and what they believed were their teachers' perceptions of their writing. We observed the teachers as they were giving assignments and leading discussions about writing. We observed the settings in which the children wrote. We became aware of the influence of what was placed on chalkboards, walls, and bulletin boards, and of what books and other print materials were available and accessible to the students. It became obvious that our own interactions with students and teachers were influencing the students' writing, so we noted our involvement with the literacy community.

This research employed naturalistic techniques, imposing minimal control on the setting in which the data were collected. Such techniques seem especially appropriate when the object of study is to focus on the process as well as the products of writing:

> As a general premise, it is probably safe to assert that the best way to study process is to observe it directly, rather than to infer its nature from the known input and the observed output. When process is the issue, naturalistic inquiry seems to offer a more useful means for its study than does the experimental model. (Guba, 1978, p. 25)

As a team of researchers, we interacted with two grade levels, three class-rooms, three teachers, several classroom aides, two principals, approximately seventy students, and some of their parents, although we worked most closely with ten children the first year of the study and six of those children the second year.

The story of our research begins with a profile of the complex transactions that we now believe make up every literacy event in the classroom setting. One of the most striking conclusions that emerged from our study has to do with the social nature of writing. Writing is strongly influenced by societal views about literacy, by the nature of the social community within and outside classrooms, and by the ways in which schools and classrooms are organized. These social influences strongly impact the personal writing history of every student in the classroom.

Our profile of the social nature of composing emerged over the two-year period and generalizes what we learned about the writing process as we carefully observed young authors engaged in the making of meaning through written language. In the chapters that follow, we present specific aspects of the study, analyze texts that the students wrote, and describe the development of individual students.

In this chapter, I provide an overview of the complex influences on the writing development of the third and fourth graders we studied. It is by un-derstanding this complexity and by valuing all students as makers of meaning that teachers and curriculum developers can organize schools and classrooms for students to make the most beneficial use of the literacy community as they write. Our purpose is not merely to understand the influences on the writing of these particular children but also to suggest how all children learn to write, learn through writing, and learn about writing (Halliday, 1980).

This research narrative starts with a question about Tohono O'odham children as young authors in school. It includes characters such as researchers, teachers, paraprofessionals, principals, elementary school students, and par-ents participating in plots and themes influenced by their languages and cul-tures, which changed and developed over a two-year period. Old questions were answered and new ones raised. We began to see patterns in all this ac-tivity, to discover myriad transactions that made up the literacy events that are at the heart of this narrative. Every piece of writing produced by the children resulted from a complex literacy event represented by the diagram seen in Figure 1.1. The diagram reveals the complexities of the processes involved during composing, which is a dynamic transaction among a variety of con-straints and influences that can be organized into three broad categories to highlight their significance: the literacy community, the writer, and the writ-ten text.

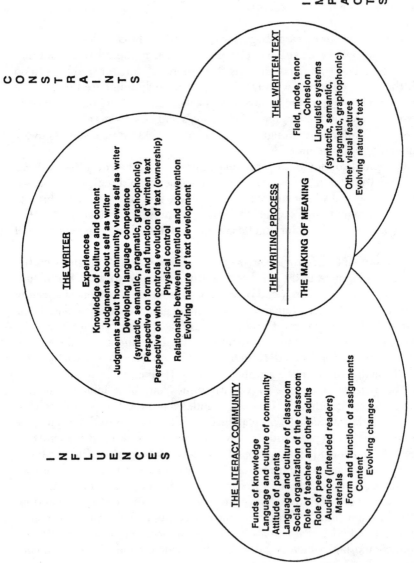

CONSTRAINTS

IMPACTS

INFLUENCES

THE WRITER

Experiences
Knowledge of culture and content
Judgments about self as writer
Judgments about how community views self as writer
Developing language competence
(syntactic, semantic, pragmatic, graphophonic)
Perspective on form and function of written text
Perspective on who controls evolution of text (ownership)
Physical control
Relationship between invention and convention
Evolving nature of text development

THE WRITING PROCESS

THE MAKING OF MEANING

THE WRITTEN TEXT

Field, mode, tenor
Cohesion
Linguistic systems
(syntactic, semantic,
pragmatic, graphophonic)
Other visual features
Evolving nature of text

THE LITERACY COMMUNITY

Funds of knowledge
Language and culture of community
Attitude of parents
Language and culture of classroom
Social organization of the classroom
Role of teacher and other adults
Role of peers
Audience (intended readers)
Materials
Form and function of assignments
Content
Evolving changes

FIGURE 1.1: The Literacy Event

THE LITERACY COMMUNITY

The writing of these third and fourth graders took place in the social context of the classroom: the classroom literacy community. At the same time, each member of that classroom community was also a member of family and cultural groups, a broader literacy community. The classrooms that we studied were part of the Indian Oasis school district, located on the Tohono O'odham Reservation about 70 miles west of Tucson, Arizona. At the time of our study and today, eighty-five percent of students are bused to school, some as far as 50 miles. Approximately 50 percent of the students live in or within ten miles of the largest town on the reservation, site of the elementary school where we first conducted the research. Other students live in villages scattered throughout the reservation. Villages may be as far as 20 miles apart, with homes within a village often separated by one to five miles. Two languages are used in the community. At the time of our study, the Tohono O'odham language was generally spoken fluently by the schoolchildren's grandparents, who in some cases spoke little English. The children's parents were typically bilingual in Tohono O'odham and English, and many of the children were primarily English speakers, although they did have varying amounts of receptive understanding of the O'odham language. The majority of the community are practicing Catholics as well as active participants in Tohono O'odham religious and cultural events. This community has many informal networks through which knowledge of the community and culture is shared and passed on to the children.

Every time the children wrote, their language and culture, formed by multiple influences, were reflected in their writing. These children called on their language repertoire as members of varied linguistic and social groups. Their writing reflected aspects of the English spoken by the Tohono O'odham, the English spoken by the dominant, mainstream population of the region, and also an awareness of the kinds of language appropriate to different kinds of writing. Although the children heard the Tohono O'odham language spoken with varying degrees of frequency by parents and grandparents, it never appeared in the compositions we saw, probably due to its out-of-school association and oral language form.

Culture was also reflected in the children's writing. Their writing revealed that they were part of the Tohono O'odham and at the same time members of the culture of all eight- to ten-year-old North Americans who are influenced by television, movies, and the school curriculum. Darren created an episode in which the movie character E.T., popular among all third and fourth graders at the time, received his powers from E'etoi, the deity and protector of the Tohono O'odham (see Chapter 3).

Children represented their personal histories—their language and the worlds of their homes and communities—in their writing. Teachers' writing assignments and the extent of choice within those assignments also had an impact on the children's writing. During the first year of the study, the research was conducted in a single third-grade classroom. In the second year of research, the same children were in two classrooms in two different schools. Each of the three teachers had her own individual style and philosophy about teaching writing; the main common ground was that all provided for writing on a regular basis (see Chapter 2). Because of both choice and circumstance, we focused on examining the writing process as it was organized by the teachers in their classrooms rather than on trying to change those environments. Therefore, although we responded to the teachers' questions and talked with them frequently about the students, their writing, and the classroom curriculum, we did not systematically attempt to influence their instructional practices. By observing different classroom practices, we were able to conclude that constraints and freedom in areas such as assignments, scheduling, and organization certainly affect writing.

Although we agree with Donald Graves (1983) that assignments often narrow what and how children write, some good writing was done in response to assignments. Both narrative and expository topics were assigned, although the latter tended to be more highly constrained. In most cases, the narratives the children wrote were more engaging and interesting than their attempts at report writing, although the students did not always keep these two genres in neat categories, especially when writing reports. Marian, for instance, showed a blending of genres in her assigned social studies report on the state bird:

> One day the state bird is going to get a worm. He's going to eat the worm and he wants to get some more of the same worm. He's going to eat lots of it, lots of the worm. He likes worms. The End.

Our examination of genre in the children's writing raised the question of whether young children's writing can be categorized as neatly as the traditional genre classifications used to discuss literature.

We found that classroom scheduling also strongly influenced the developing text of a writer; children's writing reflected the amount of time they were given to write. When they had only a specified short writing time daily, with the expectation of a finished product at the end of the period, story endings were often quickly conceived:

> One day when I was at the circus a man was whipping the lions so they would jump through the circle that's on fire. After the circus was over

the lion's trainer asked me if I wanted to be a trainer like him. I said,
"O.K."

When the students were asked to write about what circus act they would
like to be, Gordon was able to create an exciting image in his story. Needing to
finish in 20 minutes, however, he didn't have time to elaborate on his response
to the lion trainer. Although the teacher didn't impose a time limit, the children assumed that a piece of writing had to be completed within one 20-
minute writing center period; it didn't occur to them that they could continue
the next day. So if a classroom is organized to provide time to finish writing
later in the day, if students are encouraged to continue writing as other activities take place, or if writing is seen as an ongoing process that continues
from day to day, students will have time to think about the ending of a piece
and to shape it appropriately.

Classrooms can be organized to include opportunities to interact with
peers and teachers during writing episodes. Even when interactions seem to
be boisterous, students gain a lot from questioning teachers and peers, listening to one another read aloud, answering each other's questions, thinking
aloud, and discussing pieces of writing. One writing episode provided a
glimpse into the impact of classroom organization on the writing community.
Walter, Dana, Carl, and Vincent were all writing at the same table. The researcher was observing Dana's writing and taking notes meticulously. Walter
asked Dana the spelling of a word; Dana responded appropriately. Dana then
wrote the last sentence of his story and said, "I'm finished." The researcher
asked Dana to read his story onto an audiotape. Vincent, who was sitting next
to Dana, interrupted his own writing, crawled onto the desk, and listened in-
tently to Dana read his story. Then he also listened to Carl read his story. By
this time, the rest of the class had lined up for lunch and gone out the door, but
the group at this table did not break up; they were too immersed in sharing
their writing and talking about their stories. This event was made possible by
both the seating arrangement and the students' freedom to get out of their
seats and move about the classroom.

The classroom literacy community provides an audience for the writer's
evolving text as well as for the completed version. The impact and expectations of various audiences and the ways in which those audiences interact with
the writer all have their influences and can support the construction of text, as
it did in the following example. Gordon was deciding how to spell *butterfly*.
He looked at the dictionary Anna was using; he then went over to the book-
shelf and examined another dictionary but still didn't find the word. He looked
in yet a third dictionary for a while and then brought that dictionary back to his
table and said *butterflies* out loud as he wrote the word. During this time Gordon also gave Ann an eraser, told her how to spell *dragon*, helped David find a

word on the wall chart, helped Mark with a spelling, talked with David about playing drums, and chatted with the researcher about her trip out to the school. The other children knew that Gordon was a good person to ask for help with spelling and dictionary use, and most of his assistance came about because he was tuned in to the needs of the others and eager to help them. Not all his activity was directly related to writing, but his attention always returned to his text.

This vignette featuring Gordon helps explicate a concept being explored by Luis Moll and his associates (1990). The concept of "funds of knowledge" suggests that within any community there are members who are recognized as experts with special knowledge in specific contexts. As we studied these classrooms, we observed Gordon as a spelling and grammar expert, Vincent as an expert about the traditional life style of the Tohono O'odham, Anna as an expert on modern life on the reservation, and so on. As teachers understand more about the funds of knowledge that exist in a classroom, they can help support the insights that students build about their personal abilities and those of their classmates. This is how a community of writers (or readers, or learners) in a classroom becomes a force to enhance everybody's learning.

There are dramatic differences between classrooms. Some classrooms are exciting literacy communities in which reading and writing represent important parts of children's daily world. Children are involved in what they are writing about; they know why they're writing and what purposes it serves. Children see their writing as authentic experience, important to their personal lives, and they take their work seriously. In other classrooms children see reading and writing as instructional: assignments that must be completed at a particular time and in a particular way in order to get an appropriate grade.

The decisions made about the kind of writing environment to establish will depend on how teachers and administrators view the impact of classroom organization and accessibility of resources on children's writing. It will depend on the values school personnel place on student interaction or on silence. Such decisions, which are based on beliefs about the empowerment of teachers and learners, significantly affect children's writing development.

The opportunity to move around the classroom and the availability and accessibility of appropriate writing materials and resources invite writers to "live off the land," a metaphor Donald Graves uses to describe how writers make use of a rich classroom environment. Such an environment provides opportunities and resources for children to think about, read about, talk about, and extend their composing. The freedom to use reference books and dictionaries and to stare out the window or at the ceiling, as well as to interact with teachers, peers, paraprofessionals, and others who participate in the community life of the classroom, dynamically influences children's writing (see Chapter 4).

THE WRITER

Every time we watched a child write, we saw evidence of the strengths of a writer who was developing as an author. The young writers brought their personal histories, including their background and experience, to their writing (see Chapter 3). They reflected in their writing their unique experiences as individuals as well as experiences shared by their peers in school or by other children of the same age throughout the United States.

All the students we examined in depth were native speakers of English, competent oral users able to communicate appropriately with both their peers and adults. Both oral interviews and writing samples revealed the children's control over the major linguistic features of English, even though the students had a range of abilities. They produced the syntactic structures of English in many appropriate variations. They wrote dialogue, questions, and imperative and declarative sentences. They showed an intuitive knowledge of linguistic units such as words, phrases, and clauses and of genres such as stories, letters, narratives, and reports. They used the first person to reveal themselves as speakers in a story or letter, and in their third-person narratives they used pronouns to refer to appropriate characters and objects. They provided evidence of the dynamic ability of humans to invent written language forms for a variety of purposes and functions (as seen, for instance, in Chapters 3, 5, and 6).

Every writing episode involving our subjects showed that the writers knew that they could produce a written message that others could read. They wrote about personal concerns, real events, and imagined experiences, embedded in descriptions of the cultures in which they lived. They wrote about Native American legends that they had heard at home, about becoming medicine men and going to rodeos, about playing PacMan at the video game arcade and going to the Arizona State University Sun Devils football game. They were aware of audience expectations. In their letters, narratives, and expositions, they used different types of language appropriately, showing insights into the pragmatics of different genres and audiences. They exploited different written forms for letters or stories or lists. Dana showed in his letter at the beginning of this chapter that he knew how to introduce himself appropriately. He told about himself, asked his pen pal a question, and used "sincerely" in this formal first letter to someone he had never met before—a form of language he would never use in any oral setting, and that he changed in subsequent letters to "your friend."

These young writers were very sensitive to one another and to the daily social interactions of a classroom. They were able to discuss what they were writing with their classmates and to suggest ideas about writing to others. They had reasons for why they liked their own writing, why they believed they were good or bad writers, and which of their writings their teachers would appreciate the most. Their reasons reflected their knowledge of the expectations of the school and community.

Gordon illustrated some of these attitudes. To Gordon, writing was fairly straightforward and uncomplicated: "I just sit there and then I think and then I write it." When asked why he chose some of his stories as being better than others, he usually referred only to the interesting parts of the content, such as "the parrot got to talk." But he was also able to give a global assessment of why he liked a story: "It's the words, and the letters, and how it sounds." He knew how to tell if someone was a good writer, because "their stories are sometimes funny and sometimes sad." According to Gordon a good writer "writes straight . . . and never makes no mistakes. A good writer doesn't write sloppy or crooked," in contrast to bad writers who have messy papers when they erase, which "makes black marks and tears the paper." He also believed that his teacher would prefer his longer stories, because he had learned through his varied school experiences that length is an important measure of a story's worth. He saw these surface aspects of writing as important for success in the adult world. Spelling was important because "if you're like a police then you're going to learn better . . . if they don't write straight and it doesn't look good . . . they just throw it away and start on another copy." Other adults had to deal with forms, where "they have to fill out all the blanks," and "if words are misspelled, he'll give it back to you." In contrast, Gordon believed that in writing a personal letter, spelling wasn't important because "it's your writing."

The writers in this study wanted others to read what they wrote and appreciated the questions and responses they received from their peers, the researchers, and their teachers. They used their interactions to edit and revise when they had the opportunity to do so. However, like Gordon, they were especially concerned about how their products looked, so that the majority of the editing they did was really proofreading, making their papers look neat or correcting their spellings (see Chapter 4).

They sometimes asked others about topics and looked for topics on lists and in books. They selectively asked others to verify their spellings and appropriate language use, depending on the degree to which they wanted to control conventions for a particular piece of writing. They used information in dictionaries and books and on charts, chalkboards, and wall charts to help them with vocabulary and conventional spellings. They showed that they knew that some dictionaries had easy words and that others included words with a wider range of difficulty.

All these strengths were evident in the very first writings the subjects produced. Although they didn't control this knowledge according to adult conventions, they showed in various ways that they were moving toward control and understanding of the social conventions of writing. An analysis of the data collected over two years revealed development across many features that can be measured quantitatively (see Chapters 2, 7, and 8). It is easy to show quantitative growth in areas such as conventional spelling, punctuation, embedded clauses, longer and more cohesive texts, and exploration of a greater variety of topics. But this development does not follow a straight ascending line from one writing episode to the next. As Wilkinson says, "Development obviously takes place, but does not take place obviously" (Wilkinson, Bornsley, Hanna & Swan, 1980, p. 2). However, development does not mean simply doing something better according to an adult standard. Rather, development must be seen from the writer's perspective. Development reflects the growing experience of writers and their personal histories within a specific cultural context as they begin to control written language to express their meanings (Vygotsky, 1986). Even for professional writers, their latest work is not always their best.

In discussing development, it is important to include the writer's willingness to wade into uncharted waters and to take appropriate risks. Development in writing means using more complex language and expressing more complex ideas, resulting in written texts that sometimes look on the surface as if control over some aspects has been lost (for instance, spelling may be less conventional). However, these controls usually return later in the student's writing, often with greater sophistication.

In January of the second year of the study, Elaine wrote a story called "The Day the Sioux Came to Town" that helps to illustrate the complex nature of development in writing[2]:

> One day the Sioux came to TONW [town]. BECUES [because] they were dancing . . . and she was a good dancer. They live way out in the DESTX [desert]. . . . The men WAR [wear] MOUCSNS [moccasins].

This was just the beginning of a four-page composition, Elaine's longest ever. She participated in the class unit on Native American peoples by selecting a picture of a man and woman in the traditional dress of the Plains Indians. She was excited about writing a story based on the picture. She had never written such a description before and referred constantly to the picture. She had few interactions with those sitting near her. She showed little concern for conventional spelling (contrary to her usual pattern). Because she made many exophoric references—references to material outside of the actual written text (in this case, to the picture)—the writing was not always internally cohesive. In other words, in order to fully understand Elaine's pronoun references it was necessary to refer directly to the picture she was writing about. Elaine selected this story as one of her favorite stories of the year, and her mother reported that she had a photocopy of the picture hanging in her room four months later. This story had the most complex syntactic structure of any story she wrote in two years and also had the lowest proportion of conventional spellings.

Periods of intense growth for a writer are often not reflected in the product, or are reflected in only one aspect of writing. New processes need to be explored and experienced many times before they become integrated and can be used often and easily. As a writer attends to a new concern in composition, energy and attention are often directed to that new problem, and writing conventions that the writer usually controls seem to fall apart. The result is a written text that may look much less sophisticated than an earlier piece. This view of development is in keeping with Heinz Werner's notion that development is discontinuous, with highs and lows, leaps and descents, rather than being a simplistic process of gradual ascending transitions in neat and orderly increments (Werner & Caplan, 1950).

This developmental view of the writers in our study is grounded in a focus on strengths, building on the social and historical experiences of the child in the context of a literate community. Another view of development might have focused on "problems." Spellings were not 100 percent conventionalized, grammatical structures were not always complete, antecedents were not always clear, narrative and expository forms often appeared in the same composition. These patterns will be addressed in more detail in subsequent chapters. The point here is to appreciate that such "problems" reveal the abilities of young writers. They must have knowledge about literature in order to mix genres, they must understand aspects of the English alphabetic system in order to invent spellings, they must control aspects of cohesion in order to produce ambiguous references. If we understand this view of development in writing, schools and curriculum can be organized to help students become better writers, and teachers can organize their classrooms to be developmentally supportive writing environments.

In considering the role of the learner in written language development, Kenneth Goodman and I (Y. Goodman & K. Goodman, 1990) have explored a learning concept regarding the role of personal invention of language by the individual, in tension with social language conventions of the society, as part of a social view of language development. We see language development as influenced by both invention and convention. Language is developed by people (including children) individually to express new experiences, feelings, and ideas. At the same time, socially shared language forms and functions constrain language inventions. Language is social, and in written language as well as oral language there is an audience to be considered.

> There is almost an explosive force from within children that propels them to express themselves, and at the same time there is a strong need to

communicate that pushes the direction of growth and development toward
the language of the family and the community. (Y. Goodman & K. Goodman,
1990, p. 232)

This research, as well as research on miscue analysis and other aspects of language learning, have helped explicate the notion of personal invention and social conventions. It helps us be confident that children are always learning language, inventing forms and functions; but at the same time, because they want to be understood by their social communities (their peers, their families), they keep balancing their need for new language uses and forms with what they know about how language is used and formed in the world at large. These social forces strongly influence and/or constrain the personal literacy development of learners. The home, the school, and the community are crucial social sites where written language learning occurs.

THE TEXT

The third influence and constraint in the making of meaning is the most visible and permanently available for continuous scrutiny: the author's text. The text includes both the evolution of what is being composed and the author's final text. Both are important in understanding how the composing process develops in writers.

Halliday and Hasan (1976) define text as "the basic semantic unit of linguistic interaction" (p. 295). It is through the written text that writers express their meanings to their perceived audiences. Although the written text is an act of creation, authors learn that in order for their expression to be meaningful to others, they must conform to certain conventions based on the expectations of their audiences. These conventions in turn constrain the production of the text. Our young authors showed that they understood these constraints.

Every written text is part of a larger context of situation, and the students in this study reflected their awareness of this through their use of the various linguistic systems they controlled, as well as the form their writing took, as represented by a variety of visual text features. The students' writing reflected their understandings of field, tenor, and mode within the context of a particular situation—the social community of the classroom (Halliday and Hasan, 1976, p. 22).

The children's texts showed their awareness of the *field* in which the writing took place. The concept of field refers to the subject matter, the events, and the experiences that the author brings together to create meanings. The students' writing reflected the assignments given by their teachers and discussions among both the whole class and smaller communities of young authors who often sat together and talked about their writing—discussions that also included the important news of the day within the classroom community. Rodeos, trips within or outside the reservation, television programs, movie and rock stars, suicides, accidents, and the lives of their teachers and friends appeared in their writing either explicitly or implicitly (see Chapter 3).

Tenor refers to the relationships between the writer and her or his perceived audience. Tenor was represented by the relationships among characters within the narratives themselves, reflecting the cultural relationships in the lives of the children, but it was also shown in the relationship between the author of a piece and its various audiences: peers, teachers, researchers, paraprofessionals, pen pals, and others. For example, when letters were written, the recipients influenced the creation of the text. A letter to a known pen pal or a relative would be signed appropriately with "your friend" or "your son." A letter to an unfamiliar or important person would have a more formal closing. When Vincent was writing to Jamake Highwater, an author he admired greatly, he spent a long time thinking through an appropriate ending, then finally turned to the researcher and asked, "how do you spell *sincerely?*" The language in the body of the letter also reflected the relationship between the writer and the person to whom the letter was being sent.

The field and tenor constrained the *mode* and resulted in the choice of the language and form of the composition. The concern for appropriate content and form was represented in both the writing conventions used by the students and their oral interviews with the researchers. They were quite confident about what they believed to be the views of the school and business communities toward writers and writing conventions. They believed that teachers liked neat, perfectly spelled, and long compositions. They understood that various people such as nurses and police officers needed to spell accurately and write carefully in order to function properly in society.

Whenever these young writers wrote, they provided evidence that they were aware of the cohesion of a text. Although they were not always successful in providing all the necessary cohesive ties for the reader to make the most appropriate inferences, as shown earlier with Elaine's piece, their distinctive types of cohesive tie did not spill over from one kind of text to another. In other words, sports stories maintained the language appropriate to those kinds of texts, and folktales had many of the appropriate features that enabled readers to recognize that genre. The language of the story a child was working on stayed within the boundaries of a particular text. When a new composition was begun, new cohesive ties were introduced and maintained in the new text.

Of course these young writers did not control all the necessary features of a text, but they controlled many of those features even from the very beginning of the time we observed them and developed greater control over various textual features as they wrote more and varied texts over the two-year period (see Chapters 7 and 8). Most of the texts we analyzed in this study were first drafts that were not revised after their initial production, although the students did revise various aspects of their compositions as they were writing them for the first time (see Chapter 4).

CHANGE, DEVELOPMENT, AND THE EVOLVING NATURE OF TEXT

The dynamic nature of change must always be considered whenever researchers are involved in responding to and analyzing any literacy event. Each of the intersecting categories I have been discussing is in flux even during the act of one literacy event, let alone across the many literacy events that occur daily and weekly in the classroom. The literacy community is always recreated as teachers, peers, and nonhuman resources change, move, and develop over time. The writer is also developing, growing, and changing. The text itself also evolves as it is written. These changes may not always result in better written productions or better writers. These complexities can have either positive or negative influences on writers.

It is necessary for teachers to understand the influences and constraints that the schooling community has on their students' writing development. Curriculum is often organized without consideration of the dynamic nature of the classroom. There is a tendency to point to good instructional practices when students produce well-written compositions and to subtly blame students when writing is less than successful. I believe that certain kinds of instructional practices in sterile and rigid settings develop writers who produce compositions that are less than adequate. In other words, instruction can result in teaching people to write ineffectively.

This profile and discussion of the many factors involved in any literacy event reveal the complexity of the writing process. Every literacy event is influenced by many factors that teachers and researchers must consciously take into account whenever writing research, instruction, or evaluation is undertaken. In order for writing research to be meaningful it must consider the dynamic nature of these transactions. Curriculum developers and teachers must acknowledge these complexities to facilitate writing for students. There is enough evidence from this study and many others to know that in order for children to write well and develop confidence in their writing, they need to be free from classrooms where they must stay in their seats quietly writing in response to a single narrowly conceived assignment with little purpose or meaning for the author. Teachers who know how to exploit the richness of the literacy community and to value the evolution of written text and the development of the writer take into consideration the complexity of every writing event, including the strengths and knowledge inherent in every writer.

Now that I've provided a picture of the complex nature of the making of meaning through writing, we will look more specifically at the many aspects of the research story. We present the context of the research and our findings in a general sense. We look at what the children wrote about and at what they did as they wrote in the classroom. We examine the development of specific linguistic features and we take an in-depth look at two of the children. These all emerge and merge to provide a rich profile of the writing process as it occurs in classrooms.

NOTES

1. In most cases, we have edited the students' spelling and punctuation.

2. We have used upper-case letters throughout to represent students' invented spellings.

CHAPTER 2

The Research Story

CONTEXT, METHODOLOGY, AND FINDINGS

Sandra Wilde[1]   *Suzanne Gespass*
Yetta M. Goodman   *Wendy C. Kasten*
Lois Bridges Bird   *Sherry Vaughan*
David Weatherill

WHEN WE THINK BACK on the story of our research, we remember a collage of many different kinds of moments:

- Driving through 70 miles of desert at 6:30 in the morning on our way to the children's schools;
- Enjoying the children's interactions as they talked about their writing;
- Watching a teacher conference with children about their texts;
- Interviewing parents about their children's use of literacy;
- Debating how to analyze children's writing, and spending many hours computer coding it;
- Getting excited about patterns and themes that emerged from the children's writing;
- For some of us, taking a deeper look at one aspect of the writing for our dissertations.

All of us who worked on this research project have similar memories, and in this chapter we communicate some of the flavor of how we went about our research as well as an overview of what we found out. Then, in the chapters that follow, we go a little deeper, focusing in depth on one aspect at a time.

The first part of this chapter focuses on *where* the study took place (the community and classrooms), *who* we learned about (the six children who were the main focus of our work), and *how* we went about doing our research (data collection and analysis procedures). The remainder of the chapter explores *what* we found out, moving from a broad focus to a narrower one as we touch on how students interacted with the classroom environment while writing, what influenced students' creation of meaning, and the ways in which young writers used linguistic systems. As described in Chapter 1, any literacy event is a complex process. In this research, we observed literacy events in that rich, contextualized complexity and then pulled out parts of them to examine more closely, as a way of enriching our understanding of the complexity of the whole.

THE TOHONO O'ODHAM CULTURE AND COMMUNITY[2]

Today, the O'odham *himdag* (culture) is shaped by two forces: the ways of the old and the ways of the new. The old way is to accept things as they are (Blaine, 1981), to accept a sometimes harsh existence in the Sonoran desert where the Tohono O'odham have made their home for centuries. The new way is to accept and adopt more and more of the culture of the surrounding United States. Today, the Tohono O'odham, both the adults and the children, live increasingly with the tension that arises from the encounters of the two cultures and with the changes, both positive and negative, that have resulted.

The main Tohono O'odham Reservation is located in the southernmost portion of Arizona, with its eastern edge 15 miles from Tucson. It borders Sonora, Mexico, to the south for 64 miles. It covers an area of 2 million square acres, or 3,000 square miles, making it second in land area only to the Navajo reservation, the largest in the nation. The Tohono O'odham live in over 50 villages and in Sells, a community that has grown up around the tribal government and federal Bureau of Indian Affairs offices and is today the reservation's largest town.

The reservation encompasses the northern portions of the Sonoran Desert, an area ringed by rugged mountains. Baboquivari (7,730 feet) is the most prominent peak, visible from everywhere on the reservation. For this reason, perhaps, Tohono O'odham consider Baboquivari the center of the universe. E'etoi, or "Elder Brother," the deity responsible for bringing the Tohono O'odham into the world, is said to live in a cave on Baboquivari, where to this day he watches over his people, "grant[s] children luck, and provide[s] medicine men with the healing power they request" (Nabhan, 1982, p. 14). Although the word *desert* often brings to mind images of sunbaked sand dunes and endless stretches of barren land devoid of any vegetation, the Sonoran Desert the Tohono O'odham inhabit is, in fact, one of the most ecologically rich and varied zones in the region. After the rains, which usually come in July and August and again in December and January, the desert floor is alive and green with millions of annual plants.

In years past, Tohono O'odham reaped the fruits of the natural desert harvest: mesquite pods, palo verde and ironweed beans, saguaro seed and pulp, cholla, cactus buds, prickly pear pads and fruit, greens, chia and tansy mustard seeds, underground stems, roots, and bulbs (Nabhan, 1982, p. 105). Wild game (rabbit, game birds, deer, peccary) was also a plentiful source of food. Today, the old ways of hunting, gathering, and farming have been largely replaced by the new ways, especially modern technology. Although farming is still practiced by some, and there are those who know where to gather wild mustard greens and when to pluck the tender cholla buds, few Tohono O'odham live off the land today. Instead, many buy and eat large quantities of lard, white flour, and sugar. This change from the healthier traditional diet has exacerbated a genetic predisposition to diabetes, whose incidence in this community is among the highest in the world (Bird & Gollasch, 1979).

With the passing of the old ways, the Tohono O'odham diet is not the only aspect of life that has changed. No longer self-sufficient on the land, the O'odham are forced to turn to outside jobs that are all too scarce. The annual per capita income is approximately $2,500. "Cattle raising is the largest productive industry, but eighty percent of the cattle are owned by fewer than twenty percent of the tribal members" (Fontana, 1981, p. 90). Some Tohono O'odham work in the copper mines on the reservation. Other employers include the hospital, the school, and the tribe itself. Separated from the traditional Indian ways, and not a viable part of the American mainstream society, the economic survival of the reservation depends primarily on the support of federal funds. Frustrated and depressed by what sometimes seems like a colonized status, some O'odham turn to alcohol and even suicide for escape.

Family life is a central feature of present-day Tohono O'odham culture. Life on the reservation revolves around the extended family, which is likely to include a mother and father and their unmarried children, as well as any married children and their families. The close family ties are reflected in kinship terms; cousins are referred to as brothers and sisters, and children consider both the siblings and the cousins of their parents as aunts and uncles. Traditionally, all family members lived together and supported one another both economically and socially. Although this may have changed somewhat in recent times, most Tohono O'odham children still grow up surrounded by the love and support of not only their immediate family members but grandparents, aunts and uncles, and cousins as well. Children are viewed as integral members of the group and are regular participants in such "grown-up" activities as dances and ceremonies. In fact, the rigid divisions that separate various age groups in the mainstream American society do not exist in O'odham culture.

In the past, the education of Tohono O'odham children was accomplished within the family primarily through modeling, storytelling, and verbal chastisement. Children received a broad education in everything from agriculture to religion and learned the skills and knowledge necessary for survival and citizenship in their physical and social environment. Formal education was limited to off-reservation boarding schools, which were not positive experiences for most tribal members who attended them. Boarding schools were largely avoided by the Tohono O'odham, since the "basic goals of these schools were to 'civilize' the students and replace their 'Indianness' with 'whiteness'" (Papago Education Committee, 1982, p. 13).

To some extent, mainstream American values and curriculum content continue to dominate Indian education. Recently, however, in keeping with both federal and tribal policies of self-determination and self-sufficiency, the local tribal council and education committee have been taking steps to regain control of many aspects of O'odham community institutions, including education. Indeed, the tribe's action in 1986 to officially change its name from Papago to Tohono O'odham was one important symbol of this policy shift. The former name had been given to them by the Spaniards and means "bean eaters"; the latter is the traditional name for the tribe and means "desert people" in their language. In addition, the tribe has developed a language policy sanctioning O'odham as its official language and has developed educational standards requiring meaningful incorporation of the language and culture in the children's education. These efforts have reinforced O'odham values and culture in the schools and helped students learn to function in different cultures—the O'odham culture and mainstream American society in particular. In this way, the Tohono O'odham people hope to overcome many of the problems introduced by outsiders that have plagued their educational system.

Despite these comprehensive educational efforts, the effects of cultural contact and change have meant that the Tohono O'odham language is becoming increasingly unfamiliar, especially among the young children. In the school halls and on the playground, one is unlikely to hear the native language being spoken, no doubt partly a consequence of the fact that in the past, community members were punished for speaking their language in school. However, there are still many strong native-language communities on the reservation, especially in small villages in the interior regions. At the time of our study, Ann Francisco, principal of the reservation's primary school, estimated that Tohono O'odham, or a combination of O'odham and English, was spoken in the homes of about 80 percent of the students (Bird & Gollasch, 1979, p. iv).

Present-day life on the reservation is a blend of the old and new. Traditional ramadas built of ocotillo and saguaro ribs adjoin prefabricated homes and double-wide trailers. The tribal council, made up of elected representatives from every village, meets in the cool, air-conditioned comfort of the newly constructed tribal building. Tohono O'odham adults visit and chat while their children twist and turn to the rock music blaring out of a radio turned up full volume. Acculturation is inevitable; yet, to a large extent, the Tohono O'odham have taken the new ways and made them their own.

THREE CLASSROOMS

This study took place in three different classrooms: one third grade, one pre-fourth grade, and one fourth grade. Each teacher had her own individual style and philosophy about teaching and writing; the commonality is that all provided time for writing on a regular basis, and all were hardworking and caring teachers. Although the researchers had many informal interactions with the teachers about writing curriculum and instruction, we were mainly observers in those classrooms, accepting what we found and making few attempts to influence instruction or to impose ideas about the writing process. Since the major objective of this research was to understand how third- and fourth-grade children learn to write in classroom settings, our focus was on the children—not on the classroom, the teacher, or writing instruction. We made this focus clear to the teachers. The classroom descriptions, therefore, are nonjudgmental in intent. We are neither endorsing nor disavowing the teaching practices or the environments in which they occurred. That was not our purpose.

We are grateful to Linda Howard, Sister Susan Caldwell, and Darlene Pagett (pseudonyms) for allowing us into their classrooms on a regular basis. Our discussions and interviews with them were always helpful as our research unfolded. Because of our focus on the children and the 140-mile round trip of each visit, we responded to the teachers' questions and requests but rarely had extended discussions about writing process and instruction with them. We know that they made some changes to their instruction based on our discussions about the children and their writing. We also learned a good deal from the teachers through our discussions and from the time we spent in their classroom learning communities.

The first year of the study took place in the district's primary school, located in the town that is the administrative center of the reservation. All the kindergarten through third-grade classes for the whole district were located there, with about three classrooms at each grade level. Some of the teachers lived in the community and some commuted daily from Tucson, some 70 miles away. The principal had lived and worked in the community for many years.

Linda Howard's Third-Grade Class

Linda Howard, the teacher for all our subjects during the first year of the study, knew and respected all her students as individuals with special needs and strengths. She was a hardworking and creative teacher and spent hours designing elaborate thematic units as well as bulletin boards and other instructional materials. She believed strongly in the value of writing as an instructional tool and integrated writing across the curriculum.

Linda set up her instructional program using 20-minute work periods. Students spent time at learning centers during the morning and part of the afternoon, leaving the rest of the afternoon for sustained silent reading, special projects, and other activities. In most cases the children worked in groups on assigned tasks that they completed in a specified time period. After roll call and lunch count, a typical day began with a teacher-directed whole-group discussion of the day's activities and lessons. During this time, Linda often conducted special whole-group lessons or showed filmstrips and movies.

Linda divided the students into six groups. She explained to the children that they were grouped not on the basis of ability but because they "worked well together." The students moved, as designated groups, from center to center until they had visited each center. Every 20 minutes a bell rang, alerting the children that they had five minutes to clean up and move on to the next center. At the writing center, students developed a sense of how long 20 minutes was and geared their work to this time constraint. Sometimes when students wanted to complete a story before the time was up, they wrote quick conclusions rather than putting away an unfinished story.

Almost all classroom writing was assigned, related either to holidays or to instructional thematic units. Thus the children wrote stories connected with each of the major holidays (Halloween, Thanksgiving, Christmas, Valentine's Day, and Easter) as well as with special events such as the rodeo and carnival.

Linda built writing into her entire program, so that the children experienced writing in social studies, science, language arts, and health. The social studies units during the year of the study included the 50 states, early Tohono O'odham life, life in Switzerland, and ancient Egypt. The major science unit centered on space and the nine planets, and the language arts units included fairy tales, tall tales, just-so stories, and poetry. In addition, there was one health unit concerned with fire and bicycle safety. The genres assigned in Linda's room ranged from narrative stories to letter writing to expository reports. The children were also asked to write in journals, but due to a lack of time these were not continued. In addition, the children wrote haiku during a Japanese poetry unit.

As a rule, Linda introduced a new writing assignment with an example. For instance, during the tall tales unit she read the students stories about Paul Bunyan, Pecos Bill, and John Henry and then encouraged them to write similar stories about their favorite tall tale heroes. On another occasion when the class was studying the nine planets, Linda told the children about an imaginary trip she had taken in her spaceship and what she had seen out her porthole once she landed. She then requested that they write a similar story using her story as a model.

After the initial introduction to a writing activity, the class as a group generated possible story titles that Linda wrote in black letters on large sheets of tagboard. She then hung these on the wall near the writing center. When the children arrived at the center, they usually took a few minutes to scan the list of titles before choosing one and settling down to write a story to fit. For some of the units, Linda made elaborate bulletin boards and tagboard folders with pictures and lists of questions designed to stimulate the students. During the circus unit, for example, she created folders of colorful circus photographs with a caption under each picture, such as "You have run away from home to join the circus. Which circus act are you going to be?"

Once, based on our suggestions, Linda did encourage the children to write about a topic of their own choosing. However, since her instruction as a whole was so intimately tied to writing, she believed that it was necessary to assign topics that were related to the unit the class was presently studying. She also believed that assigned topics helped children become better writers.

Linda instructed her students to bring their completed first drafts to her for editing. Time permitting, she usually asked them to read their pieces to her first. Then together she and the child went back over the piece; Linda usually discussed and circled all misspelled words, incorrect syntax, punctuation problems, and so on. On occasion, Linda also spent an editing session helping a child express meaning more effectively. Toward the end of this first year of the study, she allowed some of the more capable students to handle their own editing. Once the editing was completed, the children knew they were expected to copy the corrected first draft over on a new sheet of paper. Some stories were made into bound books.

Linda had a specified grading policy. Students were given a weekly grade for writing; at the beginning of the school year, the children had to produce a minimum of three stories and one bound book in order to obtain an "outstanding" grade that week. About mid-year, after Linda decided her original policy was too demanding, this policy was changed to two stories and one book per week.

Sister Susan Caldwell's Pre-Fourth-Grade Class

Three of the study's original subjects were in Susan Caldwell's pre-fourth-grade classroom in the second year of the study. (We usually refer to this class simply as "fourth grade.") They were in the same school as the year before, which usually contained only grades one through three; fourth graders normally went to the intermediate school eight miles away. Sr. Susan's pre-fourth grade of 21 children consisted of those children whose third-grade teachers felt they weren't ready for the more rigorous academic demands of fourth grade in the intermediate school. The plans were that all the children would be in a regular fourth grade the next fall.

Sr. Susan's schedule consisted of several major types of activities that remained fairly consistent throughout the year. Every day, either at the beginning of the morning or after lunch, there was a free reading period of 20 minutes or so. The children spent this time reading silently or reading aloud to one another in small groups. The class worked as a whole group for mathematics and writing. A large chunk of the day was spent in small groups that moved every half hour among four learning centers. Since a major purpose of the groups was to provide for reading time with the teacher, the children were grouped according to reading ability. The centers varied in content depending on what aspect of the curriculum was being covered. One group worked on reading with the teacher, one group worked with the classroom aide, one group usually did some form of writing, and one group was involved in some other non-teacher-directed activity. The group activities ranged from reading instruction to theme-related activities to language pattern activities. Expectations for the groups working independently were made clear, and these sessions operated very smoothly. The schedule as a whole was a flexible one that provided a predictable framework for a variety of activities but changed somewhat depending on the curriculum and the children.

Since Sr. Susan viewed the children in this specially organized pre-fourth-grade class as having special needs and problems, her primary goal for the year was to get her students to work well together as a class unit. As she felt that this goal was being accomplished, she devoted increasingly more energy to her second goal, that of getting the children "up to fourth-grade level" in all areas of the curriculum. Another important goal, which was obvious in everything she did, was to treat the children with affection and respect. The children were assumed to be interested in learning and, in fact, they did feel that they were partners in learning with the teacher.

Sr. Susan believed that her students were very interested in writing, and she took advantage of this. Children usually wrote twice a day. In one of those time periods, the whole class wrote on self-selected topics. They first spent half an hour drawing and coloring pictures and then wrote four accompanying sentences. However, as the year progressed, Sr. Susan believed that the picture stimulus was no longer necessary, so that step was eliminated in November. The writing time was virtually always followed by a sharing time when many (and often all) of the children read their stories to the class. One goal of this activity was to help the children feel more comfortable speaking in front of a group. The time allowed for writing and sharing was about an hour, but ran longer if necessary. The sharing time was also used by Sr. Susan to answer student questions, suggest new directions for their writing, and conduct planned instruction related directly to perceived needs in the children's writing.

The group writing time was a lively one, filled with a good deal of informal interaction. As a result, the children got many ideas for topics from one another. For example, during September many of the children drew and wrote about the desert for days on end. PacMan and E.T. also emerged as popular topics in the fall.

Most days the children also wrote in a "creative writing" center. When Sr. Susan was discussing the day's centers with the class, she often mentioned what they might choose to write about. Some days there were pictures or story starters available; on other days she suggested that they write about a content-related topic. They always had the option of writing on a topic of their own choosing. Again, if children had no ideas at first, they often got them from the small group interactions.

Most of the children's stories remained in first-draft, unedited form. Some editing occurred on an episodic basis. For instance, if several children were having problems with capital letters, the teacher might call them together to work as a group. Sr. Susan also occasionally met with small groups to suggest what changes should be made in order to make a story into a book or to lead a few sessions of peer editing, where she guided groups in learning to be effective respondents to one another's work. Sr. Susan's use of writing in the classroom could be characterized as informal in tone although directive and purposive. The informality was evidenced in the children's freedom to choose their own writing topics (with teacher support and suggestions when necessary) and to interact freely while writing. Sr. Susan's direct involvement in the children's writing was also informal but reflected very definite goals. She was skillful in taking advantage of naturally arising opportunities for learning, some spontaneous and some planned, but all growing out of a sense of the children's capabilities and interests. Writing instruction in Sr. Susan's classroom was always directly related to the children's own work; she was never observed conducting a formal, out-of-context writing lesson.

Darlene Pagett's Fourth-Grade Class

Three of the subjects from the first year of the study were promoted to Darlene Pagett's fourth grade; she taught in an intermediate school that was eight miles from the primary school and served grades four through six for the entire district.

A typical morning in Darlene's class consisted of a math lesson for the entire class followed by the students working on up to four assignments that were listed on the board. One of the assignments was typically a follow-up to the math lesson. Others included dictionary skills, an English or social studies lesson, and a writing assignment. Students could choose the order in which they would complete the assignments, aware that they all had to be completed by lunchtime. For students who did not complete their work, recess time was set aside.

Students were encouraged to raise their hands if help was needed. They were expected to talk as little as possible and to remain in their seats, although quiet talk and interaction were condoned and seldom interrupted.

Whole-class activities were the usual mode of instruction. Plants grown from seeds, weather pictures, and model volcanoes were displayed at various times during the year. Molds were grown, carefully dated, and labeled. One social studies lesson focused on the southwestern United States. Darlene also read children's novels to her class. Assignments reflected Darlene's recognition and appreciation of the significance of Native American heritage and culture, and included writing and reading Native American legends and stories with a focus on the Tohono O'odham. Darlene occasionally played a traditional native game, similar to soccer, with her class. Physical fitness was encouraged during recess, including a regular one-mile run in which Darlene participated with the class.

All class members maintained correspondence with pen pals from another small Arizona community. Almost all writing was teacher assigned, including retellings of films shown to the class, creating stories from pictures, and coloring imaginative designs with accompanying stories. The assignments were designed to give the students varied experiences in writing. Occasionally some of the assignments were edited and proofread, such as stories the class wrote in preparation for a writing conference. Although Darlene was personally interested in and committed to writing, she frequently stated that her curriculum during the year of the study was hampered by discipline problems early in the year. She never engaged her class in some activities that she had originally planned, including journal writing and conferencing, due to these perceived problems.

Summary

We were fortunate to have the cooperation of three different teachers during the course of the study. Although there were similarities, each teacher had a different curriculum focus for the year. Linda Howard developed units that introduced students to a wide variety of content, Susan Caldwell emphasized self-concept and social interaction, and Darlene Pagett stressed the land and culture of the Southwest. Although none of the teachers was knowledgeable about writing process curriculum in the manner of Graves (1983) or Atwell (1987), all three provided regular time for writing, each using it in a way that suited her curricular goals and teaching style. We were thus able to observe children's writing in a variety of contexts.

SIX CHILDREN

Six children were the primary focus of our study. At the beginning of the first year we chose ten students (to allow for attrition), half male and half female, representing a range of development as writers. We followed six of them into a second year and focused on those six in our analysis. Although other children's names will appear throughout this book, the six referred to most often are (in alphabetical order) Anna, Dana, Elaine, Gordon, Rachel, and Vincent. (These pseudonyms were validated with community members as culturally appropriate.) The following capsule descriptions of them have been adapted from passages written about each child (in Y. Goodman, 1984) by the researcher who worked with him or her most often (Wendy Kasten for Vincent and Dana, Sherry Vaughan for Anna, David Weatherill for Rachel, and Sandra Wilde for Elaine and Gordon), as well as from interviews with one or both of each child's parents.

Anna

Anna was a dark-eyed child who lived with her parents, an older brother and sister, and a younger brother in a village southeast of town. Her father worked as a laborer and her mother worked as an instructional aide at the elementary school. Her parents spoke both English and the native language in the home, and her parents said that Anna understood Tohono O'odham but spoke only a few words of it. When the children were infants, their mother had made a conscious decision not to teach them her language because of her own bad school experiences, but she later regretted that decision.

According to her mother, Anna had never been an avid reader; in fact, her mother believed that she had only begun to really enjoy reading in third grade. Earlier, her parents had taken Anna on frequent public library trips, but she loaned her books to friends who lost them, resulting in hefty library fines and the elimination of the library trips. Her mother mentioned that Anna enjoyed writing more than reading. For several years she had a sponsor from New York (through a charitable organization) who took her on numerous trips and wrote to her regularly. Anna wrote back to her, as well as writing letters to a friend in Wisconsin and notes to children in the neighborhood. She also wrote frequently in the car on weekly hour-long drives to Tucson. During the two years of our study, Anna brought home several books and stories that she wrote at school, which her father especially enjoyed reading. Her younger brother also read her work, and they sometimes worked together at the kitchen table, Anna writing and her brother reading what she had just written.

During the two years that we observed Anna, she moved from being a shy, restrained, reticent child to one who was a confident organizer, mediator, and caretaker in her classroom. She often took care of housekeeping duties, settled disputes between classmates, and looked after those who had special needs on any given day.

Dana

All of Dana's shirts for school were decorated with the insignia of a basketball or baseball team; Dana loved sports, which was reflected in many areas of his life. He often chose to write sports stories when he was given the opportunity to choose his own topic, and talking to Dana revealed his considerable knowledge of football and basketball leagues as well as specific information about teams and favorite players. His mother reported that he regularly followed sports articles and scores in the newspaper and on television. A second interest of Dana's was science fiction, "Star Wars," and space exploration. He often asked to stay home to watch space launches on television when they occurred. He liked to play video games, and his favorite one, "Tron," was space related.

Dana lived in one of the many small villages on the reservation, a long distance from the town where he went to school, but relatively close to Tucson. Dana had one sister, three years younger. His father worked for the tribal government and his mother worked at home. Both languages, English and Tohono O'odham, were present in the home, although English was used most. His mother spoke the native language when conversing with Dana's grandparents, who didn't speak English. Dana said that he did not know much about the O'odham language, but interactions with him suggested that he probably knew more than he realized, especially in his ability to understand when he heard it. He did not normally attempt to speak the language, according to his mother, but had occasionally shown some interest in knowing how to express particular meanings. Dana's knowledge of O'odham culture and its stories came primarily from contact with a great-grandparent when he was younger and from what he had learned in school. (His mother said that she often learned about O'odham culture from her son.)

Dana's mother reported having read to him from an early age; he was interested in books early and loved to read, play school with his older cousins, and spend hours filling in old workbooks. When the family went shopping together, Dana often asked his parents to buy him books, including comic books, and would read each new acquisition all the way home in the car. His mother also related that Dana would beg his father to buy the newspaper when they were out, and that Dana read various parts of the newspaper, the sports section most thoroughly. Dana wrote at home, often about the sports events he had seen on television, sometimes keeping track of the playoffs. One year, Dana kept a diary on a regular basis. He also wrote letters to his mother and informational pieces about space.

In school, Dana was close to an ideal student; he enjoyed the routine and the work of the classroom and was careful and precise, always handing in neat and well-done papers. Dana erased frequently in an effort to be correct and shuddered at the thought of having to redo a paper. In fourth grade, Dana received the class academic award.

At recess, Dana was somewhat reserved. Although he seemed to be well-liked and well-respected by his peers, Dana seemed more like a "loner" than someone who had strong group attachments and thrived on group membership. Dana's mother shared with us that she felt that he liked school and was bored at home on vacations when he couldn't see his friends.

Dana was likely to continue to be successful both as a writer and as a student; he enjoyed the school milieu and the tasks associated with it, was self-confident and flexible, and maintained a strong sense of self.

Elaine

Elaine was a sociable and affectionate child who enjoyed the personal interaction of school. She relished the personal attention she got from the writing project researchers and as a result was always eager to work with us. Elaine lived with her mother, one older sister, and two younger brothers. Her mother was a secretary at the school district office, located close enough that Elaine could (and did) visit with her during the school day. Elaine's first language was English, but she also understood a limited amount of Tohono O'odham. Her mother stated that Elaine could speak a few individual words of the language but could not produce whole sentences or carry on a conversation. Elaine didn't read much at home but did a fair amount of writing; during the first year of the study most of her home writing was notes to her mother and sister, but by the second year she wrote stories at home as well. Her involvement in writing at home was shown by the fact that she got annoyed when she couldn't find a pencil or when her little brother interrupted her. Elaine's mother enjoyed her writing and was happy with her progress.

Elaine's year in third grade was one of mixed success. Although Linda Howard believed that Elaine had made some progress, she also disciplined her for cheating and other misbehavior several times. Elaine, in turn, was somewhat lacking in self-confidence and felt that the teacher would say she was cheating no matter what she did. At the end of third grade, Linda decided that Elaine should go to the school's new pre-fourth-grade class rather than regular fourth grade. At the beginning of the second year of the study, Elaine's mother placed her in a private "back-to-basics" school in the area. We thought we had lost her from the study, but in early November she appeared in the pre-fourth-grade class and remained for the rest of the year. (Elaine's mother didn't volunteer any information about why she had originally enrolled her in or why she had taken her out of the back-to-basics school.) After a brief period of social readjustment, Elaine had a good year in Susan Caldwell's class. Her confidence increased and she progressed academically.

Gordon

Gordon was a lively, sociable, and creative child who provided a good deal of pleasure and laughter during the course of the study. He enjoyed being part of the research and often went out of his way to provide the researchers with data about himself. Gordon's progress in third grade was satisfactory but not outstanding; at the end of that year a decision was made to put him in the elementary school's pre-fourth-grade class rather than promoting him to fourth grade in the intermediate school, in large part because he seemed socially less mature than many of the other students.

Gordon was well-liked by his peers, who enjoyed his energy, enthusiasm, and quirky sense of humor. He spent a lot of time interacting with other children in school, some of it related to schoolwork and some of it purely social. Particularly in the second year of the study, other children became aware that Gordon was often a valuable writing resource for them; he was often able to help them think of an idea, figure out how to spell a word, or use the dictionary. He was especially helpful with Mark, a friend of his who was very insecure and inept as a writer. Gordon often sat with Mark during writing time and gave him moral support and just the right amount of help.

Gordon lived with his mother during part of the period of our study, but had moved in with his father by the time of our parent interviews. When Gordon's father was interviewed, he reported that Gordon could generally understand the Tohono O'odham language but spoke very little of it, although he wanted to learn more. Gordon's sister had been learning to write in the native language in the intermediate school, and the father felt that Gordon would learn to do so too when he got there. Both Gordon and his sixth-grade sister read and wrote a lot at home; Gordon wrote stories every night and also brought home his writing from school. They had a big dictionary at home and Gordon used it frequently; his father said that the dictionary was very helpful for Gordon's writing. When the researcher remarked on the variety of print and evidence of writing in the father's office (where he ran the reservation school-bus operation), he mentioned that he often took written work home (such as report writing) and that Gordon was very aware of it. Gordon's father was struck by the improvement in Gordon's story length and quality, handwriting, and spelling over two years. He was obviously very proud of Gordon's work and enjoyed his imagination.

Linda Howard, at the end of Gordon's third-grade year, commented on Gordon as a person and as a writer:

> He seems to enjoy writing even when it's not an assignment. He writes at home and he writes me letters frequently. He's a generous little boy and he's very aware of what's happening with other people. When I was sick he sent me a get well card with a little story on it to make me feel better, so he uses his writing in his everyday life. He's very aware of writing as communication and I think that shows when he's writing for an audience. When he knows that someone else is going to read it, his writing is to the point and he has a lot of information.

Rachel

Rachel used the writing process both in and outside of school, writing regularly to three grown sisters in Colorado. When she decided she needed to use a typewriter, she taught herself to touch-type fairly rapidly.

Rachel worked fairly quietly in the classroom, talking to her cousin and other children around her while working, often stopping her work to talk about something outside the classroom context. Rachel was a quiet child, speaking to her teachers usually only when they asked her direct questions, and was considered an average student.

Rachel did not really seem to enjoy writing at school, and what she wrote was greatly influenced by her mood as well as by the type of assignment. One day, Rachel was observed with a list of assignments from the teacher, which included a spelling exercise, a mathematics ditto sheet, an exercise on dictionary words, and a writing activity. She put the activities in a pile, with the writing assignment on the bottom, and worked her way through, placing each finished piece in the appropriate basket. The writing activity involved completing a scribble picture by turning it into a creature and writing a story about it. Rachel wrote four sentences and neither revised nor reread. Rachel's sense of story was closely related to how she conceived a writing activity. When she was more deeply involved, Rachel produced meaningful and well-organized pieces. When the writing experience was less inviting, Rachel tended to produce minimal statements, with little attention to making sense overall.

Rachel's mother was Navajo and her father Tohono O'odham, so they used English in the home setting. Rachel's younger brother, who was both physically and mentally handicapped, died during the period when we were working with Rachel (in 1982), which had a severe impact on her. After his death, she was the only child left at home. At home Rachel assisted with the cooking and cleaning since both of her parents had physical disabilities. Rachel's mother read a great deal and had many books in the home, but Rachel didn't read very much at home. Most of the time she watched television and had her own set in her bedroom.

What happened at school was rarely discussed at home. Rachel occasionally brought home her stories or work and talked about them with her parents, but she didn't like doing homework and would rather be outside playing. Her father was trying to interest her in the native language. He had a paperback reader written in both Tohono O'odham and English that he had been studying himself, and he would have liked Rachel to learn to read the language.

School days were long for Rachel, who lived 20 miles from the school; she was on the school bus at 6 a.m. and arrived back home at 4 p.m. The bus arrived at the school just a little after 6:30, giving Rachel an hour and a half to fill in before the start of school. After third grade, Rachel was promoted to the regular fourth grade and moved to the intermediate school in the district.

Vincent

The researchers first came to know Vincent through his intense interest in and continuous questions about the research process. In the early days of the study, as we were observing and describing Vincent's writing, he had to know what we were writing down, what the different symbols meant, and why it was all being done.

Vincent had a quiet curiosity about the world and a serious, reflective approach to life. In his world, adult approval was not particularly important. He preferred the pursuit of his own agenda in order to develop his own understandings. Since Vincent did not view most schoolwork as important, he found little satisfaction in getting assignments in on time or at all. This did not make Vincent immediately popular with his teachers, although they eventually learned to appreciate him for his other virtues.

Vincent spoke often of his mother and what they did together and from time to time mentioned his three older sisters. He liked to write stories about his family experiences; for example, he related his involvement in collecting the fruit of the saguaro cactus, which for centuries Tohono O'odham women and their children have collected and cooked into syrups and jams. Vincent's father, a laborer, also lived at home.

Both of Vincent's parents spoke Tohono O'odham. Vincent had good receptive control of his Native American language and had recently begun to take an interest in learning to speak it. Vincent was intensely interested in the lives of some of the tribe's medicine men, expressing a desire to become a medicine man when he grew up, which would require him to be fluent in Tohono O'odham. He had asked his mother questions about becoming a medicine man, and she had suggested which tribal members he might seek out to learn more about it. During the course of the study, Vincent occasionally spoke with wonder and awe about some of his uncles who were medicine men and some of their activities that he had witnessed or heard about.

Vincent told the researchers that after school he spent most of his time playing outside. Occasionally, however, he would sit at the table and write while his sisters were doing homework. He sometimes read at home and brought stories from school to read.

Vincent seemed to get along with his peers at school, but he preferred somewhat older children as his close buddies. Although he lived in the main town on the reservation, near where the schools were located, Vincent was frequently absent in fourth grade, saying that he'd missed the bus. Vincent talked about episodes of staying up late watching television, which was why he got up late and missed the bus on so many occasions. Vincent seemed particularly vulnerable and sensitive to the classroom climate, displaying his more than usual seriousness when things went wrong. His occasional succinct but accurate expressions of feelings about events or people revealed a quiet, understated affect of hurt or even anger. It was not unusual to see Vincent fulfilling a task as punishment for some prior misdemeanor or to see his desk removed from the classroom arrangement to a place by the chalkboard or by the teacher's desk. Vincent spent many recesses indoors completing assignments.

Vincent's wonderings, displayed through his thoughtful questions, revealed an insatiable curiosity about life. And yet he seemed to have little desire to please teachers and a general unwillingness to play the school game in order to succeed.

HOW WE COLLECTED AND CODED OUR DATA

We spent two years watching children write and analyzing their writing as well as the settings and personal interactions in which their writing emerged. As a result, we developed a picture of the writing process as encompassing a child's production of written language with layers of activity taking place before, during, and after the actual act of writing. This profile of the act of writing or composing takes a time-expanded view of writing as more than just the mere setting down of words at one point in time and more than just a child's final product. The writing process includes:

- Children's choosing or being given a topic;
- Children's thinking about that topic through conversation, drawing, or outlining;
- The many interactions children engage in during writing;
- The many literacy resources children use to support their writing;
- The problems children solve and the strategies they use while composing;
- Children's examination of their product after writing; and
- The language and concepts children use to discuss their own writing and the nature of writing in general.

Our methodology was an attempt to capture this complexity. The core of our data collection was the field notes we wrote as we observed children writing, but we also conducted interviews with students, teachers, and parents and kept other relevant written records.

We collected writing samples frequently from each subject. Each writing episode was observed by a researcher using an instrument we called the manual observation form (adapted from Graves, 1975; see Figure 2.1, page 36, and Figure 2.3, page 49) that served primarily as a format for collecting field notes about what the children did as they wrote. Codings such as "revision" and "re-reading," defined later in this chapter, were used to provide a basis for future categorization and were accompanied by detailed descriptions of the activity whenever possible. The category system was revised over the two years in ways suggested by the data. Many texts were read by the writer onto an audio-tape at the end of the observation period to be used for later clarification. We also videotaped three or four of each child's writing episodes.

Two different kinds of interviews were carried out with all the subjects at regular intervals. (Some aspects of the interviews were adapted from pro-cedures used by Graves, 1975.) About three times each year, interviews were conducted with the subjects to give them a chance to discuss their own writ-ing. During these writing assessment interviews, we asked the young writers to reread their most recent compositions and rate them from best to poorest, stating a rationale for their ratings. The subjects were then asked to rate the papers as their teacher might, again stating a reason for their hypothetical rankings. At the beginning and end of each year, another interview, focusing on concepts about writing, was held with each subject; these included ques-tions about the composing process, handwriting, spelling and punctuation, audience, genre, and characteristics of a good writer. The purpose of these interviews was to gain insight into the students' developing knowledge and attitudes about written language.

Periodic interviews were also held with each teacher. The teacher read through the written work of each child and was asked to rank order the pieces. Once the rating was completed, the teacher was encouraged to talk about each piece, sharing background information about the purpose for the assignment, her personal reaction to the piece, and her insights into the student's writing ability and development.

Parents were interviewed at the end of each year of the study in order for us to share with them our experiences with their children and to develop a more complete picture of the literacy-related and other activities that the chil-dren engaged in at home.

The researchers also recorded any relevant observations about the class-room activities after each session (usually in discussions during the 90-minute car trip back to the university), including descriptions of writing curriculum and instruction.

The data collected over the two years (for ten subjects in the first year of the study and six of those ten in the second) consisted of:

278 texts (with accompanying field notes)
63 videotapes
46 writing assessment interviews

(rev. LH 3-29-82)

CODES —
/// = erasure   RR = rereading, silent or oral
DR = drawing   RV = revision (change in text)
IS = interruption solicited   ST = stop and think
IU = interruption unsolicited   SV = subvocalizing
R = resource use   T = teacher involvement
RT = related talk

Subject __Gordon__
Researcher __Sju__
Context __unassigned__
Date __11/16/82__ Page __1__ of __4__
Starting Time __8:45 am__

Video tape # _____   Audio tape # _____

Number	Code	Observer Text	Subject Text
1	15	gets up to change date on calendar, puts calendar cards in order (2-3 minutes)	One$_1$ night when$_2$ I was coming$_3$
2	—	Gregory's making a lot of noise - Gordon ignores	home$_{4,5}$ from a foot$_6$ ball$_7$ game some-$_8$
3	RR	whole thing - silently	
4	RR	whole thing - silently - 3 or 4 times	
5	RT	"Does coming home from the football game mean that you were going home from the football game?	thing$_9$ threw$_{10}$ a rock at me and$_{11}$ the
6	RV	Erases "foot", rewrites for neatness	
7	RT	"Does football game go together?" "What do you think?" "Yeah." Then decides there should be a space between "foot" and "ball" but smaller than between words "because they're together."	
8	15	looks up, whistles (I think he's trying to get my attention to see he's wild hyphen)	
9	15	sings "thing, thing, thing"	
10	15	looks at Guinness Book of World Records with Gregory and Sharon	

FIGURE 2.1: Manual Observation Form

32 concepts of writing interviews
9 teacher interviews
13 parent interviews

The primary tool of data analysis involved putting information about each story into a format suitable for computer manipulation. Each text was coded for invented spellings and other orthographic features, the boundaries of syntactic units, and the child's observable behavior during the writing of the story. A computer program was developed to reorganize the data in ways suitable for further analysis. The frameworks developed for looking at each type of data were based on previous research, linguistic concepts, and categories that emerged from the data themselves. They will be discussed in the appropriate sections of this book.

WHAT WE FOUND OUT

Although what we found out is the subject of this book as a whole, this chapter provides an overview of some of the major findings and themes that emerged from the research, focusing on the children's activity while writing, the creation of meaning, and the use of linguistic systems.

Children's Activity When Writing

When students write in a classroom, a number of activities accompany the actual writing and form a dynamic part of the literacy event. We collected information on the activities or behaviors that accompanied writing and defined, categorized, and analyzed them. From the beginning of the study, the field notes collected on the manual observation form included coded indications of the specific points in the text where various types of activity occurred. The categories provided a way of organizing a complex variety of data. Nine categories were eventually settled on, which encompassed virtually all the children's activities during writing:

1. *Drawings:* any graphic design not part of the language.
2. *Interruptions:* overt verbal or nonverbal interactions that did not seem directly related to the composition. These include solicited interruptions, which were initiated by the subject, and unsolicited interruptions, initiated by the teacher or peers and including such distractions as bells ringing or classroom commotion.
3. *Resource use:* solicitations by the student of story ideas, word spellings, or any other information related to the composition. Resources were ei-

ther inanimate, such as dictionaries, pictures, and writing on blackboards, or human, such as classmates and teachers.

4. *Rereadings:* silent or oral readings of any part of the composition initiated by the subject at any time before being asked to reread by the researcher at the end of the writing episode.

5. *Related talk:* comments or conversation (other than resource use or teacher talk) related to the writing the subject was doing or the writing process in general.

6. *Revisions:* written changes to the text (of handwriting, spelling, or content), usually indicated by erasures or crossing out.

7. *Stop and Think:* pauses without overt language when the subjects appeared to be thinking about their compositions.

8. *Subvocalizing:* rehearsing, sounding out, spelling out, and other subvocalizing (including speech, whispering, or mouth movements of phrases, words, letters, or sounds) during the act of composition.

9. *Teacher involvement:* interactions between the teacher and the student directly related to the child's composition. Teachers' interruptions that appeared not to be directly related to the composition were coded under interruptions.

The frequency of each of these activities in the two years of the study is illustrated in Table 2.1. (All figures are in terms of occurrences per hundred

TABLE 2.1: Activities per 100 Words

	Grade 3	Grade 4	Both Years
Revision	8.3	11.5	10.1
Subvocalization	7.5	9.4	8.6
Interruption	5.7	5.8	5.8
Stop and think	4.4	6.3	5.5
Resource use	3.9	4.3	4.1
Related talk	2.9	3.8	3.4
Rereading	2.8	3.4	3.2
Drawing	0.0	0.3	0.2
Teacher involvement	0.1	0.2	0.2
TOTAL	35.6	45.0	41.1

words and refer to those six students for whom data are available for both years.) These figures represent the activities that the researchers were able to observe and code and can therefore be seen as a systematic but not fully exhaustive reflection of that activity. There was at least this much activity going on, but there may have been more. We developed a rich profile of the ways in which the classroom environment and interactions influenced these young writers and became continually more aware of the *social* nature of writing in the classroom. Wendy Kasten (1984/1985) did an in-depth study of all these activities and their interrelationships and discusses some of her findings in Chapter 4 of this book.

The Creation of Meaning

The creation of meaning by young writers involves complex interactions of intention, content, and form. Looking at writing episodes from four of the children in the study (Gordon, Anna, Vincent, and Elaine) illustrates the variety of processes that go on as writers make decisions about content and form.

Involvement and Belief Systems.   Any writing episode reflects the level of involvement and ownership that the author is experiencing at the time. (See Chapters 7 and 8 for detailed examples of how involvement can range from minimal to intense.) Although involvement is only one factor affecting how a piece of writing eventually turns out and is not always directly reflected in a piece's quality, in the long run a writer who is interested in what he or she is doing will be more successful in creating meaning. Elaine's growth as a writer during third grade, which was characterized by a gradually increasing ownership of the process, makes this point particularly clear. Early in the year her focus tended to be on meeting the teacher's expectations and on surface features such as accurate spelling. When she was not particularly interested in a topic, which was often, she seemed to write just to fill up space and produced uninteresting, disjointed stories. Sometime around February, when Linda Howard's class was doing tall tale and legend units, Elaine began to show greater involvement in her writing, which was reflected in the more coherent nature of her stories. Although this change began when she was working in genres that she found interesting, by the end of the year she was able to take any topic and use it as a jumping-off point for a highly personal narrative; she had come a long way in taking control of an assigned topic.

Another influence on how meaning is created is the writer's belief systems about what the process is all about and how it works. Most of the time, these young writers were not able to articulate very sophisticated notions about how the process works. To Gordon, writing was a fairly simple matter, both in his description of the process and in his composing behavior; he never agonized over what to write about but just plunged right in. Similarly, Anna described what she did but without a conscious sense of how she did it:

> *Anna:* First I look at the pictures on the board and see what I'm going to write about. Then I start writing about that picture.
> *Researcher:* What do you do when you want to end it?
> *Anna:* I just put an ending, like put "The End" or something.

These examples of how the children talked about the writing process suggest that much of their knowledge about that process may have been unexamined: What they could do outstripped what they could articulate. Some development was apparent over time. For instance, Gordon, in the second year of the study, showed that he was beginning to take a slightly broader perspective on his writing. In October, he described the way he began a story as, "Sometimes I always put 'one day'"; to end a story, "I put a period . . . and if I don't feel like writing any more I can just write 'the ending.'" By April he said that the first thing he did was to think of a title, and that the last thing he did was to "read it over and see if it makes sense." These comments don't necessarily reflect a change in his actual behavior, but they do suggest that he may have begun thinking of a story more holistically and less as a linear string.

Topic Choice and Development. Gordon, in an interview, suggested that a writer's themes may be influenced by the scope of his or her world and interests. When asked if he'd write different kinds of stories when he was older (in sixth grade), he said he'd write about buildings and skyscrapers then, and that when he was in first grade he wrote about sheep and plants. When asked what he wrote about currently, he replied "interesting stuff."

The scope of the "interesting stuff" found in these children's writings reflected the scope of their lives and culture. Bird (1985/1986) has looked at such information in these children's compositions in great depth, as we will see in Chapter 3. First of all, the children sometimes wrote about topics that were specifically identifiable as being part of Tohono O'odham culture. A rodeo and carnival are major annual events in the Tohono O'odham community, and many of the children wrote about them.

These stories sometimes described events that the children had experienced directly; in other cases they drew on the oral narrative tradition of Tohono O'odham culture, as when Dana wrote a legend about a wolf and an eagle. Vincent, who usually was uninterested in classroom writing topics and wrote only with reluctance, had one of his best experiences with writing when he had a chance to use it to explore an aspect of his culture that meant a great deal to him. During February of the second year of the study, his class was writing stories about the Southwest for a statewide writing conference. Vincent, proud and aware of his Tohono O'odham culture, found something he cared to write about. For several weeks, his writing became deeply personal and even emotional. It was at this point, in several long dialogues with one of the researchers, that Vincent expressed his deep-felt desire to become a medicine man for his tribe when he grew up. He ended up writing this piece:

> Some day I would like to become a medicine man just like some of my uncles are. I wish I was one right now. But I have to know a lot of stuff before I can become a medicine man. I have to know how to sing in Tohono O'odham and know how to talk to the ghosts and know when they are coming and when they are here. Only if I knew how to become a medicine man. The End.

One might assume that Tohono O'odham children writing about their culture would mean primarily writing about legends, the desert, and other aspects of specifically Native American life. But their culture also included Pac-Man, "Peanuts," Pink Floyd, and all the other elements of a more general North American culture experienced by eight- to ten-year-olds. It is only to the outsider that these two sets of influences are so separate; for the children, their culture was for the most part a seamless whole.

These children therefore also had images and ideas from popular culture in their mental storehouses and wrote pieces reflecting and recombining them. For instance, the children wrote many stories reflecting that a PacMan cartoon television program had begun that year.

Young writers also create meaning out of the classroom culture that surrounds them, a culture that includes not only instruction but children's literature and other materials as well as fellow students. When the students were writing on topics of their own choice, a story idea thought up by one student would often be picked up by others sitting nearby and occasionally by the whole classroom, so there was sometimes a whole series of stories about the desert or E.T.

Another important source of what children decide to write about is their own idiosyncracies and personal interests. Elaine, for instance, often wrote stories of car crashes and hospitals, and Gordon often chose to write about religious themes.

We became aware that personal content in writing emerges spontaneously; if students were asked to do an activity such as journal writing but were not given the opportunity to develop their own purposes for doing it, it became as constraining as any other assignment, as Vincent demonstrated when he was told to write "a journal entry." Journals had not been used in the classroom since the beginning of the year, and Vincent did not understand what the teacher wanted. He was up and down in his seat three or four times getting the right kind of paper, sharpening his pencil, and asking his teacher a question. He finally sat down, commenting, "I don't know what to write about. How do you write in a journal?" and continued to squirm and to change from a seated to a kneeling pose in his chair every few seconds. This incident was full of frustration, off-task behavior, and very little writing, largely because Vincent didn't understand the teacher's expectation, nor did he have his own conceptualization of what a journal was.

Assignments.   In many classrooms, assignments are an important part of determining what children write about. The children in this study wrote both in response to assignments and without them. Although Graves found in a previous study (1975) that unassigned pieces are longer and that "an environment that requires large amounts of assigned writing inhibits the range, content, and amount of writing done by children" (p. 235), we saw a more complex pattern. In Linda Howard's classroom, which included all of our subjects during the first year of the study, most writing was at least partially assigned; the curriculum was structured around thematic units, with students usually choosing topics from an assigned list of ideas, pictures, or story starters. Her classroom therefore provided an extensive picture of how children respond to assignments. An assignment definitely imposes constraints on a young writer, but in a way that is modified by the extent to which the writer accepts the constraints and the teacher insists on them. Over and over again, these children demonstrated how they were the ones who chose (consciously or not) whether an assignment would be the major determiner of what a piece of writing would look like, merely a jumping-off point, or something in between. These choices were determined by the students' proficiency as writers, their interest in pleasing their teacher, and their interest in a particular topic (Bird, 1985/1986).

Some assignments were difficult for all the children, although some children were more successful with them than others. In November, Linda Howard asked the students to write imaginary diaries of young pilgrims on the *Mayflower*. The intent was to produce a collaborative effort, with all the boys writing in a single male persona for different dates and all the girls in a female persona. The final product was to be several diary pages for each character. Linda spent quite a bit of time discussing the assignment with the class. She stressed writing in the first person and writing about things that might really have happened and elicited ideas from the students about what it might have been like on the *Mayflower*. The class chose a boy's name and a girl's name for these characters. The boy's name chosen was Micah Antone, which is a plausible name in the Tohono O'odham community but not, of course, a typical *Mayflower* name. Gordon wrote the following piece: "One day Micah Antone went to have a feast with the Pueblos. But as they went a storm came and Micah

Antone didn't know what to do with the people. Then all the people were mad." Gordon's product was a mixture of his teacher's and his own intentions. Like every child we observed working on this assignment, he wrote about his pilgrim character in the third person rather than the first. He incorporated the fact that the pilgrims had a feast with Native Americans (but Pueblos are, of course, a Southwestern tribe) and that they faced storms at sea. He ended up with the beginning of what could have been an adventure narrative. This assignment was a difficult one for all the children because of the expectation that they would write in the first person as someone other than themselves. (The assignment was also culturally dissonant.) Gordon dealt with this task better than most, in the sense that he was able to produce a piece with some of the elements his teacher had been looking for.

Another child in the class, Diana, writing in the female persona, produced a longer text but one that was far less what Linda had in mind:

> Mary Johnson was nice to her children. They play on the Mayflower.
> She let them do what they wanted to do. Sometimes she was mean to
> her children and didn't let them play because they were nice. So she
> doesn't let them play with their friends. Their friends come to her
> house but Mary said that they couldn't play with her friends but some-
> time they could play on the Mayflower.

In this case, the teacher-intended story of a pilgrim child named Mary Johnson became a story of how mothers treat their children, with the *Mayflower* serving as a giant piece of playground equipment. Mary Johnson became the mother, and the pronoun references show Diana's inconsistency in keeping the characters straight.

A writer who follows an assignment closely is not necessarily more accomplished than one who doesn't. At the beginning of her year in Linda Howard's class, Elaine was very concerned with trying to please her teacher and stayed close to the assigned topics, but later in the year she was writing more for herself. Four of her stories from March through May were written as part of four very different curriculum units, in response to assignments in all cases, but were very similar in that they all dealt with imagined experiences from her own life. In a story about the circus and one about "riding safe" on her bicycle, she had accidents and went to the hospital. In a report about Egypt, the country looked remarkably like Tucson, with motels, zoos, toy stores, and ice cream cones. Saturn, in another piece, was different from home, with red sky and round-headed people, but Elaine stayed there with her friend May and watched cartoons. In all four of these texts the teacher-selected topic made a brief appearance, but then Elaine's desire for self-expression took over. This may be seen as a reflection of her growing independence as a writer. She was able to use a story starter as a jumping-off place but was not particularly constrained by it; she wrote based on what she wanted to say rather than being concerned with the teacher's or the story starter's intentions.

It is important to consider the role of the teacher in this process. The children who were best able to handle the constraints of assignments were those who took control of the process and decided how much they would let themselves be influenced by the assignment. Often a single child exhibited a range of choices over time, from paying only minimal attention to the assignment to trying to produce just what was expected. Linda allowed this to happen. Although she was sometimes disappointed when the stories produced by the children in response to an assignment didn't live up to her expectations, she rarely pressured them to change their work to fit those expectations.

Genre and Style.   Along with deciding what to say, writing involves choices about how to say it; meaning is always created in some form. These young writers explored a variety of genres and stylistic elements as part of their development.

The vast majority of writing done during the two years of the study took the form of stories. These were usually purely imaginative, like Gordon's Pac-Man story; fictionalized personal narrative, like Elaine often wrote; or true personal episodes, like Anna's story of her trip to Tucson. When the children attempted other genres, the impetus usually came from the teacher. Expository writing was more difficult for the students. Linda Howard's unit on the state of Arizona is an example of this. Her goal was for the students to write research papers, and she spent a good deal of time talking with them about how to use reference books and what form their pieces should take. However, this form of expository writing was still too difficult or unfamiliar for some of the children. Marian's piece about the state bird, also seen in Chapter 1, is a classic example: "One day the state bird is going to get a worm. He's going to eat the worm. And he wants to get some more of the same worm. And he's going to eat lots of it, lots of the worm. He likes worms."

Some expository writing, however, was more successful. Susan Caldwell didn't plan a research unit for her class but encouraged this type of writing when a good opportunity for it occurred spontaneously. A period of expository writing came about as the result of one child's request for help in finding something to write about. The teacher suggested that he try factual writing, so he wrote a report on a particular breed of dog he was interested in. When he shared his writing with the class, everyone wanted to do reports. Anna's report on Saturn that Sherry Vaughan describes in Chapter 9 was part of this group of pieces.

Although the children had a long way to go before they could produce polished expository pieces, it seems valuable to let children experiment with the form as well as to read many expository materials. It is important for teachers to help children develop functions for expository writing and to provide many realistic opportunities to write reports and other types of informational texts.

Students also occasionally wrote pieces in a variety of other genres. Letters were of various types, as these three examples show:

Anna's Text

Dear Mr. and Mrs. Turkey, I am sorry that your son died in a dinner. I felt sad for you. I think the next Thanksgiving you should hide. But on Thanksgiving I will not eat you because I think you are nice people. I am sorry your son Bob died.

Dana's Text

Oct. 29, 1981
Dear Ghouls, I liked your program very much and thank you for coming to our school today. It was fun being scared by you. Are you coming next year? I hope you do. Love, Dana.

Anna's Text

Dear Louella, How are you? I am doing fine. How was the operation? Was Phoenix a long ride? How long was the operation? Is the hospital big? I like you very much. From Anna.

Anna's first letter was a fictional one, while Dana's was a real one, written to another class that had put on a Halloween presentation. These were both assigned, but children also occasionally wrote spontaneous letters, like Anna's second one, written to a classroom aide who was in the hospital. In the second year of the study, Darlene Pagett arranged for her class to have pen pals in another part of the state, which provided an opportunity to write real letters, but to someone the students had never met.

Writing that described something originally seen in another medium appeared from time to time. Elaine's favorite piece of writing was one that was based on a picture, as described in Chapter 1.

In Darlene Pagett's class, the children occasionally watched short films in class and then wrote about them; children in all three classrooms also wrote about movies they'd seen outside of school, such as Gordon's retelling of "The Cross and the Switchblade":

One day a man was surrounded by a gang of other men. The men had bats, blades, chains and axes to kill people. Then the man tried to jump over a fence, but the gang just pulled the man down and started to hit him and stick him, and the man died. The man that killed the other man had to go to court.

This kind of writing makes special demands; the writer must communicate the experience of the picture, film, or other content to a reader who is not necessarily familiar with it. When the writer's sense of audience is not well developed, lack of cohesion due to omissions and exophoric (i.e., text-external) references may result. Again, greater proficiency in the genre comes about through experience with it and appropriate teacher guidance.

A genre that emerged only once during the study was poetry; Linda Howard spent most of one week's writing time having her class write haiku, a Japanese verse form often used in elementary school writing because of its apparent simplicity. Elaine's experience with it suggests some of the issues involved when children are asked to write in unfamiliar genres. On March 25, Elaine attempted a haiku, which was a very different kind of writing from any she'd done previously. Two days before, Linda had told the class about what a haiku is and they had written one together. The elements that she stressed in her instruction were the 5-7-5 syllable pattern of the haiku, nature as the usual subject matter for haiku, and poetry as being made up of word pictures that aren't necessarily complete sentences. She also gave the students a handout summarizing these points and others.

On the day that we observed Elaine, the children were asked to write individual haiku. She chose to write about the desert and was quite absorbed in the task and intrigued by the genre, clapping out syllables as she went in order to fit into the haiku form. Her first version read as follows (the numbers at the ends of the lines are the syllable counts that Linda Howard had asked them to include):

Desert is HOTD [hot] and FALL [fun]	5
there is LOSTED [lots] of trees	7
I like the desert	5

She was quite pleased with it. The researcher pointed out that she had miscounted the syllables, in order to see how she'd react. When she realized that she'd actually produced a 6-5-5 pattern, she chose to leave the poem as it was, but did change the numbers to reflect the actual syllable count. She then asked the researcher to edit with her; she liked the content but wanted help with capitalization and spelling. With the researcher's help she capitalized the beginning of each line and corrected the spelling of *hot, fun,* and *lots.*

At this point Linda chose to come over to work with Elaine. She began to suggest changes so that the haiku would be more descriptive and picturesque and have the correct syllable count. She asked questions such as, "What makes the desert hot? What makes it fun?" and wrote parts of Elaine's answers on her paper. She told Elaine that in a poem you write pictures rather than sentences and at some points had Elaine close her eyes to picture the desert better. When they had generated a number of images, Linda worked with Elaine to cut down the number of syllables in each line. Figure 2.2 shows what Elaine's paper looked like at the end of the session. The final version of the haiku, which Elaine was to copy over, read:

> Desert is hot, fun.
> Hot desert, the sun shining.
> Fun, happy, running.

This is a much closer fit to Linda's idea of what a haiku was, but Elaine preferred her original version. Throughout the first year of the study, Elaine had gradually assumed a greater sense of control over her writing, but on this occasion she couldn't retain the ownership she'd clearly felt in relation to her first draft. The piece that resulted was in a sense more Linda Howard's writing than Elaine's. The problems that arose were not because of the unfamiliar genre itself; Elaine was in fact quite captivated by the chance to experiment with this new form. The difficulty came when more emphasis was put on the haiku form itself than on the expression of the child who wrote it. This episode suggests a useful general touchstone for exploring varied genres with children as they write: Even young elementary school children are capable of writing in a wide variety of prosodic and poetic forms, and indeed are likely to enjoy doing so, but they must always be allowed to use the form in a way that is comfortable for them. They can benefit from many opportunities to explore different genres, but the child must always retain both interest and ownership in the piece.

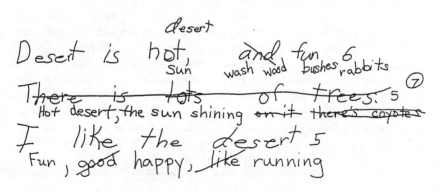

FIGURE 2.2: Elaine's Haiku—Final Version

These young writers also explored a number of stylistic options as they wrote. The choices they made suggested that they were involved in a process of playing with a variety of forms and of gaining increasing knowledge and control of how written language works. Some observations about what we saw in these children's writing suggest the diversity of learning involved.

Children used both reality and fantasy in their writing. A piece of Elaine's is a good illustration of the blend of reality and fantasy that was typical of her stories: "One day I went to the Rodeo. I was in the Rodeo. I was the Rodeo Queen. I went to the carnival. I rode the round-up. When it stopped I went to the Rodeo and rode the horse, and the Rodeo was starting." She almost certainly did go to the rodeo and carnival and ride the round-up (a carnival ride), but was not really the rodeo queen or a rider in the rodeo. In most cases, only knowledge of Elaine's life, not the story itself, lets the reader know how much of the story was true (Bird, 1985/1986). Interestingly, the one story Elaine wrote that was based entirely on her real life, which was about being afraid of going on the round-up, was the most unified of her pieces, perhaps because its scope was defined by the logic of the incident rather than the range of her imagination.

> One day I wanted to ride the round-up. I got scared. After I rode the round-up I was not scared anymore. I got the hang of it. I kept riding it. Then I rode with my cousin. She said, "How come you didn't ride with us on the first time?" I said, "Because I was scared." Me and my brother went home. I missed the carnival.

Elaine also stated in her interview dealing with this group of stories that this one was her favorite because "it's true. . . . It's not fun if they're not true." She mentioned that it was the first factual story she'd written.

Anna wrote realistic stories sometimes and fantasy at other times. When assigned to write an outer-space story in third grade, Anna manipulated the topic to suit herself. She didn't really write a space story but instead wrote about a realistic phenomenon that may have happened to her personally, that of waking up and not knowing where she was. During the next year, Anna wrote many stories growing out of real events such as the Arizona State Fair and trips to Tucson and Rocky Point, Mexico. Anna indicated that she liked to make her readers laugh or show surprise when they read or listened to her pieces, which led her to write more imaginative pieces on occasion. She especially liked a piece about winning a lottery because she felt it was exciting to win money and go to places like Hawaii and Mexico.

Gordon tended to write more fantasy than realism, though his fantasies often began in a realistic situation. In one story, seen in Figure 2.3, he began

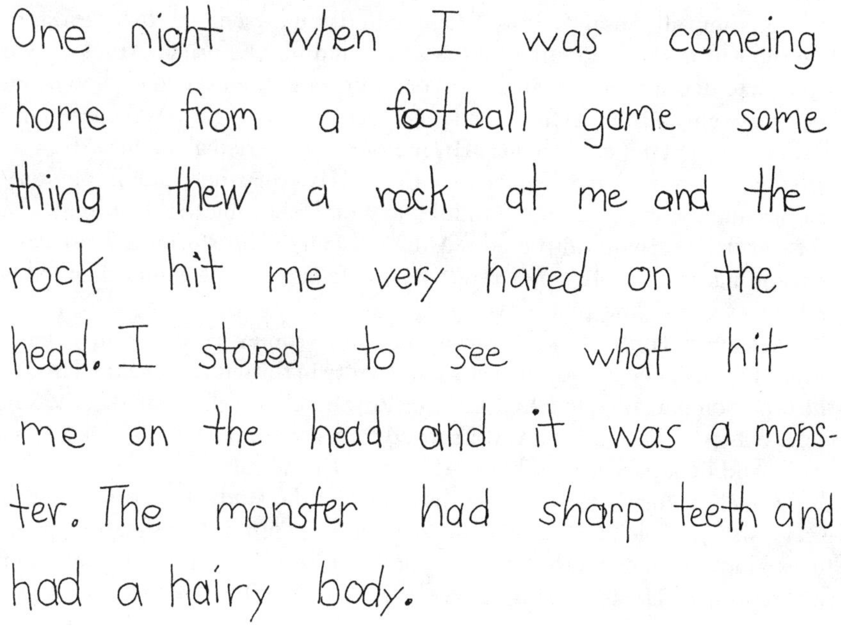

One night when I was comeing
home from a football game some
thing thew a rock at me and the
rock hit me very hared on the
head. I stoped to see what hit
me on the head and it was a monster. The monster had sharp teeth and
had a hairy body.

FIGURE 2.3: Gordon's Football Game Story

with a real incident and extrapolated from it to the supernatural. Gordon described how he got the idea for the story: "When my father took me to a football game I just decided to write about it and the monster." He then added that in real life it wasn't at all scary when he came home from the football game, and he didn't see any monsters. His teacher commented on the way it began with a realistic incident of being hit on the head with a rock and then went in the direction of fantasy. She appreciated the plot twist, the way it "could be taken from [a real] incident and then changed into a creative figure." It was typical of Gordon to start a story in a low-key uneventful way in order to set a scene and provide a context for his imagination to work on. His ideas often came not before he began to write but during the process of writing, so that a beginning drawn from real life may have been the easiest way to set the process in motion.

Children had a good sense of the beginning, middle, and end of stories. Fairly consistently throughout the two years, the children wrote stories with a clear sense of a beginning, middle, and end. Gordon, for instance, was able to write about a large variety of topics and to maintain a strong story sense through them all. Susan Caldwell commented that he seemed "to have a story line right from the beginning [of the year]" and that he usually stuck to one topic: "He doesn't seem to just go to one thing and then skip and then come back like some kids do." This is evident even in one of his earliest pieces: "One day a turkey got out of his home. His mother was worried about him. He was walking in the woods and he got eaten up." This is a very short and simple story but has an obvious beginning, middle, and end, showing that Gordon had a sense of story early in third grade. Although some of his stories didn't have a real ending, this usually appeared to be due to lack of time rather than to his lacking a sense of how plots develop.

Elaine, in contrast, wrote stories that were somewhat less tightly structured. For instance, a snowman story she wrote in third grade changed from a third-person narrative to a first-person story about herself: "One day the sun came out. And he melted. And I started to cry and my mom got back from work. And I got back from school." However, Elaine gained greater control of this aspect of story structure over the course of the study. By April of fourth grade, she was able to use a very simple picture (Figure 2.4) as a starting point to develop a strongly plotted story; her sense of story structure is shown by her final sentence. The text reads:

> One day the sun came up. Me and Monica were going to town.
> Then the sun was up. And it was brighting in our eyes. Then we
> couldn't see and we almost went off the road. Then we started to cry.
> But we crashed. Then the police came. And the ambulance. And we
> got in the hospital. So that's how it all happened.

Her teacher liked this story quite a bit; she felt it was both creative and realistic and liked the use of detail: "If you live out here and you go to town in the morning, that's what happens. The sun gets in your eyes."

Children were aware of and used humor, imagery, and richness of plot. Three incidents illustrate this observation. First of all, Anna said that she liked one of her pieces because of the surprise ending. She called the ending "a joke" and laughed every time she read it. The class praised her highly when she read it aloud to them; they liked the ending too.

Second, when the students were asked to write about what circus act they would like to be, Gordon added a typically vibrant touch, about lions being whipped so they would jump through flaming circles. Although this was a very short story, no more than a vignette really, it created a very effective image.

Finally, Gordon, in an interview, said that good writers are those who write funny stories and stories with "interesting stuff put in." When asked why he liked one of his stories less than some others, he said, "It's just about going in somebody's house! I mean it sounds boring like."

One day the sun came up. Me and Monica were going to twon. Then the sun was up. And it was bring in are eyes. Then we con't see and we almots went of the rode. Then we stered to cry. But we crrsted. Then the plicea cameAnd the ambeleng. And we got in the hapldol so that's hold it all hapend.

The End

FIGURE 2.4: Elaine's Me and Monica Story with Picture

Use of Linguistic Systems

Since writing is a language process, whenever it occurs the writer uses linguistic systems as the framework through which meaning is expressed. An overview of what we learned about these children's use of syntax and of orthography (spelling and punctuation) in their 278 texts suggests that they used their knowledge about language in complex and sophisticated ways. The data we worked from included:

17,026 words
14,578 conventional spellings
2,448 invented spellings
1,415 punctuation marks
2,218 t-units (defined below)
3,142 clauses
9,625 phrases

Syntax.   Through a detailed analysis of these students' syntax (including sentence and clause length, sentence types, and other features), we can make and illustrate several observations about their use of the syntactic system of English.

These students showed English syntactic development comparable to that of other North American children. Length of t-units, as expressed in number of words and number of clauses per t-unit, is an established measure of syntactic development (Hunt, 1966). (A t-unit is defined as an independent clause plus any accompanying dependent clauses.) We used these measures in order to make comparisons with other research studies. Table 2.2 shows clause per t-unit and word per t-unit statistics for the 2,218 t-units our subjects wrote during grades three and four and compares them with statistics from four other studies (Milz, 1983/1984; O'Donnell, Griffin & Norris, 1967; Hunt, 1965; Ward, 1974/1975, reported in Milz, 1983/1984).

For our statistics, we used only the data from the six students who participated in both years of the study, so the comparison represents the same children across time. The average number of clauses per t-unit (a measure of syntactic complexity) for each of our subjects ranged from 1.16 to 1.73 with a mean of 1.40 in third grade. This mean is somewhat higher than that of the third graders studied by O'Donnell and his colleagues (1.18) and slightly higher than the mean of 1.29 for Hunt's fourth-grade subjects. In fourth grade, our subjects' number of clauses per t-unit ranged from 1.28 to 1.58, with a mean of 1.43. This is somewhat higher than Hunt's fourth-grade subjects and similar to his eighth-grade subjects. Clauses per t-unit do not change much statistically across time, as the means for Hunt's fourth and eighth graders show. However,

TABLE 2.2: T-Unit Development: Five Research Studies

	Clauses/ T-unit	Words/ T-unit
Milz, Grade 1		5.46
Ward, Grade 2		6.98
O'Donnell, Grade 3	1.18	7.67
O'odham, Grade 3	1.40	7.14
Hunt, Grade 4	1.29	8.51
O'odham, Grade 4	1.43	7.54
Hunt, Grade 8	1.42	11.34

these results indicate that the six Tohono O'odham children produced sentences of a complexity at least comparable to that of other children their age.

Our third graders had slightly fewer words per t-unit (a measure of sentence length) than did O'Donnell's third graders or Hunt's fourth graders, and slightly more than Ward's second graders. Our subjects produced 0.4 more words per t-unit in fourth grade than in third grade. A comparison of the other studies shows that there is a definite developmental trend statistically from grade to grade, and that our subjects were generally comparable to children from other North American groups.

We tested the significance of the change from third to fourth grade in the number of clauses per t-unit and words per t-unit of our subjects. The growth in clauses per t-unit was significant at the .01 level, and the words per t-unit growth was significant beyond the .0001 level.

These students used primarily declarative, nondialogue sentences, but were capable of using other sentence types as well. Table 2.3 shows a breakdown of t-unit types. Most of the t-units produced by the subjects were declarative statements, but the children also wrote some exclamations, imperatives, and interrogatives (questions). In the first year of the study, 97 percent of all the t-units produced were declaratives; in the second year, 95 percent were, indicating a slightly growing use of other kinds of sentences. Dialogue was also used to a slightly greater extent in the second year than in the first.

These students used a variety of clause types. As shown in Table 2.4, about 72 percent of clauses used by the subjects were main (independent) clauses; the remainder were conjoined, nominal, and adverbial ones (all of these are types of dependent clauses), suggesting that the subjects were able

TABLE 2.3: T-Unit Types: Third and Fourth Grades

| | Grade 3 | | Grade 4 | |
	Number	%	Number	%
Texts	176		102	
Total t-units	1,236		982	
Declarative	1,202	97.2	925	95.2
Interrogative	29	2.3	39	4.0
Exclamatory	1	0.1	2	0.2
Imperative	4	0.3	16	1.6
Dialogue	84	6.8	84	8.6
Nondialogue	1,152	93.2	898	91.5

to create a variety of sentence structures. They were not limited to choppy, single-clause t-units but were able to produce the more complex sentences associated with the use of subordinate clauses.

These students showed few problems in using syntax appropriately. As part of the analysis, we flagged syntactic and cohesion problems of various types.

Cohesion problems in most cases involved pronoun referents. (Cohesion problems are discussed at length in Chapter 5.) Examples include:

- Pronoun referent. "He shot at him and he died." (Not clear who each *he* refers to.)
- Semantic incongruity. "I stayed with my friend May." (In a story about Saturn with no previous introduction of May.)
- Picture referent. "The green field stands for . . . ." (Referent is not within the story but in the picture that the student is writing about.)

Syntactic problems were those involving lack of control of various syntactic constructions. Examples include:

- Lack of subject/verb agreement.
- Inappropriate use of prepositions. For example, "Something came down of the sky."
- Inappropriate pronoun form, such as *he* for *him*.

TABLE 2.4: Clause Types: Third and Fourth Grades

	Grade 3		Grade 4	
	Number	(%)	Number	(%)
Main	1,236	71.4	1,015	71.8
Conjoined	159	9.2	103	7.3
Adverbial	163	9.4	160	11.3
Nominal	174	10.0	136	9.6
TOTAL	1,732	100.0	1,414	100.0

Multiple problems were those involving both syntax and cohesion.

Complexities were coded whenever something sounded unusual to the researchers but did not fit into the other categories. Examples include:

- Oral language forms used here in written language. "Our class was scared, real scared."
- Uncommon usages. "It was 50 or 40 feet tall." (The convention is to place the smaller number before the larger one in a phrase like this one.)

As seen in Table 2.5, none of these problems occurred often, and all (except for a slight increase in cohesion problems) decreased from the first year to the second.

From the analysis of our subjects' syntax, we concluded that the children

TABLE 2.5: Problem Types and Frequency

	Grade 3		Grade 4	
	Number	Number per 100 words	Number	Number per 100 words
Cohesion	21	.23	21	.28
Syntax	116	1.32	73	.98
Multiple	10	.11	1	.01
Complexity	71	.81	33	.44
TOTAL	218	2.47	128	1.71

were competent users of English. They used all the major syntactic structures of English, as well as many patterns that are less frequent, and basically controlled these patterns from the beginning of third grade. Over a two-year period, their sentences tended to become longer and more complex and they used a larger percentage of dependent clauses. These results were cumulative for all stories and for all subjects combined, even though there was wide variation on a story-by-story or child-by-child basis.

Orthography.   The students' use of the orthographic system of English was examined through analysis of spelling, punctuation, capitalization, and letter formation.

Spelling. The children used 17,026 words in 278 stories over the two-year period of the study. Of those words, 14,578, or 85.6 percent, were spelled conventionally, and 2,448, or 14.4 percent, were invented spellings. (We have used "conventional" here as a synonym for "correct," recognizing that correctness in spelling is a matter of social convention; "invented" refers to the "incorrect" spellings the children created out of their knowledge of language.) Comparisons between third and fourth grade have in most cases been made on the basis of the six children who were followed for both years.

Between third and fourth grade, all the children except for Elaine showed an increase in percentage of conventional spelling. (In Elaine's case, this was probably related to a decision on her part to put less emphasis on trying to spell correctly.) For the six children as a whole, conventional spelling represented 84.6 percent of all words in third grade and 87.6 percent in fourth. The increase, though small, is significant beyond the .0001 level.

There were 1,179 different words used over the two-year period. The 26 words of highest frequency made up only 2.2 percent of the different words used, but they were used 9,475 times and thus made up 43.9 percent of running text. These 26 words were spelled conventionally 97.5 percent of the time over the two years, and this level of control was similar during each year. This suggests that these children entered third grade already knowing the spelling of the most common words in their written language. Table 2.6 shows the 26 words that were used 100 or more times during the two years of the study, the number of times each was spelled conventionally or invented, and the percentage of conventional spelling for each.

In contrast, of the 692 words used only once over the two-year period (which made up 58.7 percent of the different words used but only 4.1 percent of the total running text), there were 310 invented spellings, or 44.8 percent. Another way of stating this is that 310 invented spellings (13 percent of the total) occurred on 4 percent of all words written (692 words), but only 185 invented spellings (or 7.6 percent of the total) occurred on words making up 43.9 percent of all text (as seen in Table 2.7). The very low-frequency words were 18 times as likely to have invented spellings as the high-frequency ones.

TABLE 2.6: High-Frequency Words: Third and Fourth Grades

	Frequency	Conven-tional	Invented	Percent Conventional
the	1,227	1,223	4	99.7
and	686	679	7	99.0
I	594	594	0	100.0
to	585	581	2	99.3
a	479	478	1	99.8
was	478	475	3	99.4
he	311	309	2	99.4
went	267	248	19	92.9
we	240	240	0	100.0
it	238	227	11	95.4
in	211	211	0	100.0
one	199	197	2	99.0
then	195	186	9	95.4
day	192	191	1	99.5
they	180	163	17	90.6
is	149	148	1	99.3
said	149	110	39	73.8
got	147	136	11	92.5
my	147	147	0	100.0
when	125	116	9	92.8
his	123	113	10	91.9
of	119	111	8	93.3
on	116	114	2	98.3
she	110	109	1	99.1
there	108	91	17	84.3
but	100	91	9	91.0
TOTAL	7475	7288	185	97.5

TABLE 2.7: Invented Spellings of High- and Low-Frequency Words

	High Frequency	Low Frequency
Number of different words	26	692
Number of running words	9,475	692
Number of invented spellings of these words	185	310
Invented spellings of these words as a percentage of:		
All spellings of these words	2.5%	44.8%
All invented spellings	7.6%	13%

These results are, of course, not unexpected. It makes sense that children are more likely to know how to spell words that they use more often and that they wouldn't know how to spell words they haven't used before. If children continue to grow as writers and to explore new topics using new vocabulary, they will continue to have a certain proportion of invented spellings. A child who always spells perfectly is likely to be a child who is not using new words or taking very many risks.

The 2,448 invented spellings produced by the children during the two years of the study are a rich data base for exploring children's use of linguistic systems in the orthography of English. Wilde (1986/1987) conducted a detailed analysis of all the invented spellings. For the purposes of this chapter, a few patterns of development that emerged from the data (initial letters, reversals, and real-word substitutions) are described and exemplified; other patterns are explored at length in Chapter 6. It should be noted that examples are given to illustrate a particular feature but not to suggest that any single invented spelling had a single cause. Invented spellings are the result of many linguistic systems interacting at once.

Part of learning how to spell involves learning about the relationships between phonological patterns and orthographic patterns; that is, how different sound sequences are spelled. Looking at children's success in spelling the initial sounds of words gives a sense of how much control they have of this aspect of spelling, since the beginning letter of a word is the most likely of all its letters to have a relatively clear-cut relationship to the corresponding phoneme. Out of the 17,026 words written by our subjects, only 153, or 0.8 percent, did not begin with the appropriate initial letter. In the first year there were 97 such cases, or 1.1 percent of all words written that year; in the second year there were only 56, or 0.7 percent of all words. Seventy-eight of these 153 invented spellings (51.0 percent) occurred on words beginning with vowels, although only 24 percent of all words used began with vowels, reflecting the fact that consonant phonemes in English are much more regular in their spelling than vowel phonemes are. These data show that these third and fourth graders controlled initial letter spelling almost perfectly. Looking at a few examples illustrates that even when they didn't spell initial letters conventionally, the children were often making plausible rather than random decisions about what letter to use first.

OLMOST/almost
ROMS/arms
PRING/bring
WHO/how
GEST/just
NIFE/knife
KNOW/no

The beginning vowel sound in *almost* is usually spelled with an *a* before *l*, but is closer in most American dialects to the sound usually represented by *o* in words such as *log* and *loss*. The *r* at the beginning of ROMS may be representing the name of the letter rather than just the consonant phoneme it usually stands for (cf. Read, 1975). *P* (in PRING) is related both phonetically and graphically to *b*. WHO begins with the same phoneme as *how*, contains the same letters, and has a similar grammatical function. When *g* occurs before *e*, as in *gem*, it is pronounced the same as *j* (GEST). In NIFE and KNOW, a silent letter is being dropped or added, each word following the pattern the other one should have. (KNOW is also, of course, a homophone of *no*.)

Our data included quite a few invented spellings in which the order of two or more letters was changed. Indeed, 8 percent of all the invented spellings were permutations in which all the right letters appeared but in the wrong order. (Wilde, 1986/1987):

BAESBALL/baseball
FRINEDS/friends
SIAD/said
UPNO/upon

It seems that in these cases the child had a good sense of the letters in a word but did not fully control their serial order.

Another important pattern of invented spellings that we observed frequently in the children was the substitution of one real word for another. Third and fourth graders have a considerable and increasing vocabulary of words whose spelling they know; when one word is substituted for another it may be either an attempt to have a spelling that looks like a real word or a slip of the pen (intending one word but inadvertently writing another). In the case of homophones, there is, of course, likely to be a phonetic representation involved as well:

HERD/heard
NO/know
MAID/made
PRIES/prize
TO/too (this occurred 35 times)

But even more of these spellings involved words that were similar phonetically but not identical:

BAKE/back
CAKE/chase
POUND/pond
QUITE/quit
TURK/truck

Punctuation. Our subjects had 2,414 punctuation opportunities (i.e., places where they either used punctuation or should have) over the two-year period. In 1,233 of those instances, or 51.1 percent, punctuation was used conventionally. These students thus controlled punctuation to a far lesser extent than they did spelling.

All the writers who were part of the study for two years showed an increase in percentage of conventional punctuation from third to fourth grade. Across all six children, conventional punctuation increased from 42.7 percent in the first year to 57.6 percent in the second year. The significance of the increase was found to be well beyond the .0001 level.

The primary reason that the percentage of conventional punctuation increased from the first year to the second was that omissions decreased dramatically, as shown in Table 2.8. (Wilde [1986/1987] conducted a more complex analysis of these data, using a somewhat different format.) In the first year, punctuation was omitted nearly half the time, but in the second year omissions dropped to a bit more than a third of the total. The table also shows the numbers and percentages of punctuation marks inserted in inappropriate places and those that were substituted inappropriately, such as a period for a question mark. Insertions and substitutions were never numerous to begin with. Although they did diminish, they didn't affect the overall percentages very much.

TABLE 2.8: Punctuation Categories: Third and Fourth Grades

	Grade 3		Grade 4	
	Number	%	Number	%
Conventional	450	42.7	783	57.6
Omitted	520	49.4	479	35.2
Inserted	55	5.2	66	4.8
Substituted	28	2.7	33	2.4
TOTAL	1,053	100.0	1,361	100.0

There were opportunities for use of seven different types of punctuation marks during the two-year period. Their patterns of use are presented in Table 2.9. In both years, periods made up more than two-thirds of all punctuation opportunities, but in fourth grade the children were using an increasing number of text structures that required punctuation other than periods. They also showed increasing control over most types of punctuation, as Table 2.10 indicates.

Four of the five punctuation types used most frequently increased in conventionality of use from third to fourth grade. Since periods accounted for

TABLE 2.9: Punctuation Types: Opportunities in Third and Fourth Grades

	Grade 3		Grade 4	
	Number	% of Total	Number	% of Total
Period	781	72.2	936	67.1
Comma	125	11.6	217	15.6
Quotation mark	137	12.7	184	13.2
Question mark	26	2.4	43	3.1
Exclamation mark	5	0.5	11	0.8
Colon	3	0.3	3	0.2
Semicolon	4	0.4	0	0.0

Note: The totals of all punctuation types add up to more than the totals in Table 2.8 because substitutions were counted twice (e.g., as both a period and a comma opportunity).

TABLE 2.10: Conventional Punctuation: Third and Fourth Grades

	Grade 3 (%)	Grade 4 (%)
Period	52.1	71.4
Comma	16.0	23.5
Quotation mark	9.5	18.5
Question mark	11.5	55.8
Exclamation mark	80.0	54.6
Colon	0	0
Semicolon	0	0

nearly 70 percent of all punctuation opportunities, the overall improvement in punctuation use was due largely to increasing control of periods. The only punctuation type that was used less effectively in fourth grade was the exclamation point, which is more open to interpretation in its use than others.

It should be noted that the increasing control of punctuation indicated here took place largely in the absence of formal instruction in its use. However, all three teachers discussed punctuation as necessary, with individuals in conferences or with the whole class. Punctuation was clearly an important area of growth in the third and fourth grade for these children.

Capitalization. Our six subjects had a total of 600 capitalization problems (omission or overgeneralization), or 10.05 per hundred words, during third grade. This decreased to 455, or 6.08 per hundred words, during fourth grade. The six subjects, therefore, went from having approximately one capitalization problem every 10 words to having only one every 17 words. Although the six subjects varied quite a bit, they all showed a decrease in the number of capitalization problems.

Capitalization problems were often a result of failing to either punctuate or capitalize at sentence boundaries, but also included failure to capitalize story titles and proper nouns, as well as many idiosyncratic capitalizations of nouns and other words.

Letter Formation. Letter formation problems were minimal for all six children. There were 60,624 letters produced, with 200 letter formation problems (0.3 percent of all letters) over the two-year period. All but two of the problems could be categorized as being of two major types: cursive handwriting formation of some letters and reversals of other letters. Fifty-nine of the problems involved reversal of lower-case manuscript *b* and *d*; the letters causing most cursive problems were lower-case *m* and *u*.

Reversal problems were rare. None of the reversal problems occurred consistently over time; that is, no subject reversed all reversible letters nor did any one subject reverse any one letter on all occasions. The proportion of reversals in this data was even smaller than data reported in other literature (Frith, 1971). Most research on reversals has been done on reading and writing or copying of individual forms, letters, or words out of the context of text. The smaller number of reversals produced by our subjects and reported (for reading) in miscue analysis research (K. Goodman & Y. Goodman, 1978) may be due to the context of the letter within a written text, strongly suggesting that context has an influence on the production of reversals: that is, that letter orientation is more predictable in context.

SUMMARY

We hope that this overview has given you a sense of who we were looking at, what we did, and what we found out in a broad sense. Our story continues in the following chapters as each researcher provides a more detailed view of one aspect of the writing process.

NOTES

1. This chapter was produced by Sandra Wilde, largely from material that originally appeared in a different format in Y. Goodman (1984) or Y. Goodman and Wilde (1985). It includes material originally written by all the authors listed.

2. This section was written by Lois Bridges Bird and taken, with some adaptations, from Bird (1985/1986).

CHAPTER 3

Self in the Writings
of Tohono O'odham Children

Lois Bridges Bird

Cleaning a closet, I found a box of my old manuscripts and quotations. Threw a lot away, only glanced at the stories and novel, found some pages good, some bad, all stamped with *me* one way or another. (M. Murray, 1980, p. 81)

SO WRITES MICHELE MURRAY in *The Writer on Her Work*, thus confirming what all professional writers know to be true—that writing is a reflection of self, an outgrowth of personal experience. The "self" or the "I" of the writer is always there. It must be deliberately suppressed in certain kinds of journalistic or technical composition, since special techniques are needed in order to produce reports and expositions that are relatively impersonal. But the stories most of us write express our individuality, like the ones that Michele Murray found in the pages retrieved from her closet.

Moreover, if we agree with Barbara Hardy's (1968) contention that "narrative is a primary act of mind," stories are not simply an aesthetic experience, given form by professional writers, nor merely a treat reserved for special occasions, brought out with the dessert wine and shared sparingly with the other dinner guests once the dishes and important conversation have been cleared from the table. They are much more. As Hardy writes:

We dream in narrative, remember, anticipate, hope, despair, believe, doubt, plan, revise, criticize, construct, gossip, learn, hate and love by narrative. In order really to live, we make up stories about ourselves and others, about the personal as well as the social past and the future. (p. 5)

Stories are a part of the fabric of our lives. Young and old alike come to share, indeed come to know, their experience through narrative.

The essence of our human nature is, perhaps, our need to make sense of our experience. We struggle to know and to understand, and invariably our understanding finds form in stories. As Harold Rosen (1983) writes, "life is an unremitting flow of events." To function, to live, we must assign this flow a beginning and an end and create some semblance of order and cohesion in our living text through "relationships, causes, motives, feelings, consequences, in a word, meanings" (p. 13).

Immersed in a stream of sense experience, we find meaningful respite from that endless flux when we select, interpret, and shape our experience in words. Gordon Wells (1986) describes us as "meaning-makers." We have a propensity to make sense of our experience, and more often than not our meaning is realized through narrative.

All this is vividly apparent in 237 compositions written by 17 third-grade Tohono O'odham schoolchildren over the course of one school year. I followed these 17 young authors (those discussed elsewhere in this book as well as others from the same classroom) for my doctoral research (Bird, 1985/1986). As I watched these children at work on their stories, what struck me most was the reflection of self in each piece, a reflection that was evident even as the children responded to writing assignments about topics that were frequently far removed from the realm of their own life experiences. Their writing inevitably revealed their lives as they used writing to make sense of those lives. As I examined this reflection of self, I was able to delineate five distinct realities that these children lived and brought to their writing: a personal, individual reality; the dual realities of the Tohono O'odham and American mainstream cultures; the reality of a fantasy world influenced by male-female perspectives; and the pragmatic reality of the instructional school setting in which the children wrote.

MULTIPLE REALITIES

Life is at once both a social and a personal experience. As social beings, we share much in common; yet, at the same time, each human responds to each experience in his or her own uniquely personal way. This personal response is inevitably reflected in writing. Like Murray, each child brought an individual stamp to every piece written, a stamp that included information about the child's relationships with family and friends, salient life experiences, favorite pastime activities, and thoughts and feelings about home, school, and other involvements.

Molding the individual persona are cultural influences. As discussed in Chapter 2, today the Tohono O'odham way is shaped by two forces: the ways of the old and the ways of the new. Elements of the traditional culture that persist today and that influenced these children and their writing include the relationship to the natural environment as reflected in, for some of the children, traditional food and housing, traditional religious practice, community feasts and festivals, basketry and pottery making, traditional music and dance, and, of course, the Tohono O'odham language. Newer cultural adaptations include Western religions, particularly Catholicism; elements of Southwestern U.S. culture, such as the cowboy tradition; the influence of Mexico (although the federally defined Tohono O'odham reservation ends at the border, the community itself extends into Mexico); and a formal governmental structure that has increasingly reclaimed much of the decision making over tribal life (including education) that had been administered by the federal government's Bureau of Indian Affairs. Perhaps most important in the lives of children is the traditional and ongoing importance of the extended family in the O'odham culture. The children grow up surrounded by the love and support of not only the nuclear family but grandparents, aunts and uncles, and cousins, all usually living close by. Children are viewed as integral members of the group, and the rigid division among age groups of mainstream North American society is far less common among the O'odham.

The Tohono O'odham children are also influenced by a larger, mainstream experience. (Heath, 1983, defines mainstreamers as those who hold "positions of power" in society.) The Tohono O'odham reservation is surrounded by a largely white, mainstream population; accordingly, many aspects of this culture are part of everyday life on the reservation. For example, the curricular content the O'odham children encountered in their school— the texts they read, the worksheets they completed—could be found in one form or another in most classrooms at the same grade level across the country. Mainstream culture also infiltrates the reservation through such multiple media as books, newspapers, television, video, and film. The Tohono O'odham children we worked with may have seemed to be a culture apart, yet at the same time they were American schoolchildren who shared a common experience with all American schoolchildren in their age group.

James Britton (1970a) reminds us that personal experience includes not only the more commonplace realm of home, but also the world of fantasy. Langer (1942) leaves no question about the origin of fantasy: "Like all symbols, fantasies are derived from specific experiences; even the most elaborately monstrous ones go back to witnessed events" (p. 118). Fantasy draws its life from the imagination, but the imagination grows from and is shaped by the commonplace experiences of day-to-day living.

Finally, the children had to consider the pragmatics of the classroom as they put pen to paper and attempted to meet the instructional demands of the teacher and the assigned topic. In this regard, as writers in a traditional classroom where the writing topics were assigned, the children always carried the burden of a double agenda: (1) an agenda as meaning-makers, who used writing to capture their experience in print; and (2) an agenda as students, who were playing the instructional game of giving the teacher what she wanted.

I was present for much of the writing of the 237 stories discussed here and had the opportunity to observe and interact with the students as each piece evolved. In addition, I interviewed the children at the end of the year, engaging each of them in open-ended discussions about their writing, asking them to explain the underlying story behind each piece. As a result, I learned details of their experience not present in the texts themselves. Which details and events were selected and which remained unshared is a story in itself. What became clear, however, over the course of the year was that all five facets of the children's experiences (personal responses, O'odham culture, mainstream culture, fantasy, and classroom pragmatics) were simultaneously present and interacting in almost every piece. In other words, as children use writing to make meaning, they are always dealing with the totality of their experience.

In the final analysis, they can write only what they know, and what they know is what they live day in and day out. Thus the evolution of their texts cannot be seen apart from the complexity of who they are as writers, working within the context of their multiple communities.

PERSONAL REFLECTIONS

Just as the sensory details of our past experiences filter into the light of our consciousness through writing, so the emotion and feelings surrounding those experiences often emerge as well. Writing as therapy, as an emotional outlet, is well-recognized. Donald Murray (1985), discussing the origins of his ideas, confides, "Writing is my way of achieving moments of sanity or understanding. . . . I was a sickly, only child in a world filled with the threat of disease and death, punishment and retribution, and much of my writing is a psychological necessity" (p. 11).

For many years, educators have noted the therapeutic value of writing for children. In 1936, Holmes suggested that teachers help students experience writing as a means of releasing their innermost thoughts, feelings, desires, and ambitions. Similarly, Rupley (1976) contended that writing provides a way for children to relieve themselves of tension and anxieties. Witty (1941) linked writing to well-rounded development and sound mental health. More recently, Nancie Atwell (1987) has recommended that students "use writing as a way to capture their feelings . . . to give shape to their inner experience" (p. 24). As an eighth-grade English teacher, she found that her students' poetry was her "best window on adolescents' hearts and minds" (p. 26).

Perhaps the most poignant example of writing as an emotional outlet for children is the collection of drawings and poems written from 1942 to 1944 in Terezin concentration camp, compiled in *I Never Saw Another Butterfly* (Volavková, 1978). In their cold, concrete barracks, children poured their pain and suffering into simple poems. In their poems can be found thoughts and feelings about "painful Terezin," about "the little girl who got lost." They wrote of their longing "to go somewhere where there are kinder people," and of "old grandfathers gnawing stale bread and rotten potatoes for lunch." They wrote of their longing for home and they wrote about their fear: "Fear came to them and they could tell of it in their poems" (p. 52).

Children may not share their painful experiences and feelings as openly as did these young prisoners of Terezin. Indeed, in the case of potentially painful feelings, children may deliberately disguise the true story. In this way, they may find some relief through the disguised written release, yet avoid the painful confrontation a full-blown account might involve.

For example, I unknowingly uncovered one such painful true story that

Christine had carefully disguised in a retelling of the popular book, *Annie and the Old One* by Miska Miles (1971), about a Navajo grandmother who weaves one last blanket for her granddaughter before she dies. During an interview with Christine, I asked her why she chose to write about this particular book. She suddenly burst into tears, explaining that her mother's cousin (whom Christine considered her aunt in keeping with O'odham kinship ties) had been killed only the week before in a freak car accident. Christine needed to deal with her aunt's death, but at this point, still so painfully close to the actual experience, she chose to write about it in a disguised and emotionally manageable way.

This phenomenon, first introduced by Bullough (1912) as "psychical distance," is explained by Applebee (1978) as a strategy writers may use to reduce the degree of threat present in the material with which they are dealing. Applebee notes that researchers who are interested in exploring psychical distance must first determine the degree of threat present in the materials they are investigating. This was a task he found difficult, since the stories he examined were written by children in a context he knew little about. To remedy the situation, he compared the stories to a "cultural norm" as a way to determine their "social acceptability" (p. 77).

In contrast, I was well-acquainted with the young authors in this study and, through our lengthy discussions, privy to the experiential material on which they drew to create their written stories. The "degree of threat," then, was evident; so too were the ways in which the children sought to deal with the threat through their writing.

Research by Pitcher and Prelinger (1963), reported in Applebee (1978), suggests that there may be formal devices through which writers distance and protect themselves from potentially painful materials. These include the "use of realistic characters, the use of a consistent past tense, and the inclusion of the narrator in the action of the story" (p. 79).

Gordon used these devices in a piece he wrote in response to an instructional unit on cowboys. Adopting a television Western cowboy theme and style to adhere to the assignment, Gordon dealt simultaneously with the assignment and with his experiences and feelings as one of three children of a young, abjectly poor woman who was faced with continual threats of eviction:

> The boy was going to buy a house but he didn't because the sign said sold. The boy got so mad he robbed the bank, then the police arrested the boy. When the boy got out of jail he never robbed banks again. Then when Thanksgiving came the boy had to go back to jail. When he got to the jailhouse they asked him where he lives. He didn't tell them where he lived because if he told them where he lived, if he did, he would be in trouble.

The true story behind the composition makes Gordon's desire for a house painfully clear. Gordon's parents were divorced. His mother struggled to support the three children. They were forced to leave their house after the divorce and were desperately searching for another place to live. I learned of Gordon's story directly from his mother when I visited his home one morning to request an interview with her. She replied that she did not have time because she was packing to move. And then, standing on the doorstep of the home she was losing, she burst into tears. (Gordon and his sisters went to live with their father shortly thereafter.)

This phenomenon of psychical distancing is also evident in Florence's piece, "My Father, Peter Robinson, in Mars." Like Gordon, Florence also set her story in the past tense, used realistic characters, and included herself in the story. Florence, too, had to mold her story to conform to the pragmatic demands of the assignment to write a space adventure story. The result is a bittersweet tale of a little girl who travels to Mars to visit with her father, who had moved there when she was five years old. When her father caught sight of her, he was "so happy that he jumped up and down." In reality, Florence had not seen her father since he abandoned the family when Florence was five years old. Through this story, Florence appeared to express her desire to be reunited with him.

Although Florence and Gordon may have found some small relief through their disguised writing, the real power of writing as a tool to explore and illuminate experience, such as Don Murray (1985) described, was lost to them. And since their writing masked their pain, their teacher remained unaware of their suffering and was not able to extend her sympathy and support. Children who are unfettered by assignments can begin to use writing as a path to their inner knowledge as well as a bridge to others who might help them.

CULTURAL REFLECTIONS

As the children's lives were shaped by their dual cultural experience, so was their writing. This is evident in Darren's piece, "E.T. the God," which mirrored his experiences as a child of the O'odham and a child of the United States, influenced by the American cultural scene and mass media. As mentioned in Chapter 2, E'etoi (pronounced approximately "Ee-toy"), the god responsible for bringing the O'odham into the world, is said to live in a cave on Baboquivari Mountain, where to this day he watches over his people, "grant[s] children luck, and provide[s] medicine men with the healing power they request" (Nabhan, 1982, p. 14).

In Darren's story, it is not a medicine man who finds his way to E'etoi's cave with a request for power, but E.T., Steven Spielberg's nimble-fingered alien who captured the hearts and imagination of the American public. Here, in the darkness of Baboquivari's sacred cave, the god of the Tohono O'odham meets the media idol of the summer of 1982:

E.T. the God

One day E.T. was walking in the desert. He saw some dark clouds coming so he ran into a cave. He didn't know it was E'etoi's cave. He was sort of scared. He went further into the cave. All of a sudden he saw something glow farther into the cave. He didn't know it was E'etoi. He just knew it was a man that could glow. The man said, "Come closer." So E.T. went closer. He said to E.T., "I can't use my powers any more so I am giving them to you." He got the powers. He knew how to fly. He flew to his home planet. He got married to a Martian and had some baby Martians. He still had the power E'etoi gave him.

One can see, in Darren's piece, the overlap of mainstream and O'odham culture in the two superheroes, E.T. and E'etoi. No culture is without heroes. What makes this piece remarkable is that within the realm of Darren's own dual cultural experience, two heroes from two diverse cultures can come together and interact. One hero is a traditional Native American religious figure who is centuries old; the other, a recent celluloid creation with Hollywood-style mystical nuances. But in Darren's world, they share something in common. One hopes the exchange of power between E.T. and E'etoi is not in some way symbolic of the increasing encroachment of the white mainstream society on the O'odham. The fear is assuaged in Darren's ending. E.T. marries his Martian sweetheart and together they have Martian babies.

Marriage and children are a typical denouement in the stories of the O'odham children. One of the great strengths of the O'odham people is the loving, close-knit ties of family, which was reflected in many of the children's stories. The family theme recurred throughout their writing, across a range of topics and genre. The children repeatedly wrote of their involvement with their immediate and extended families, particularly with their grandparents. Out of 237 stories I collected, some 66 (28 percent of the total number) contained a home or family reference.

A blending of two cultures is apparent in a story Mary wrote in response to the assignment to write a space adventure, which was part of an instructional unit on space and the nine planets. Her story reads:

One day I went to Uranus. We had Easter. We found a rabbit. We cook it. We eat it. It was good. We eat the eggs. There were 41,000 eggs and we boiled it. We had a good time. It was funny. I saw the sky. It was beautiful. I asked them, "what is it called?" They said, "It is called the Roman God of the Sky." I went home to Little Tucson [a village on the reservation]. The end.

To readers unfamiliar with Mary's background and recent experiences, her response to the assignment may seem strange. But once they are aware of the experiential content Mary used to create the story, her piece makes sense, and readers come to understand Mary's double writing agenda. On the one hand, she is a student who must meet the writing requirements for a space adventure; on the other hand, she is a meaning-maker, whose writing helps her understand the events and experiences of her own life.

In adherence to the space adventure assignment, Mary set her piece on Uranus, but it was Easter on Uranus, just as it had been in her town, Little Tucson, a week earlier. The Easter bunny brings eggs to the Tohono O'odham children just as he does to mainstream children, but when visiting Little Tucson (or on "O'odham Uranus") he had better beware, for there he may be shot, skinned, roasted over an open fire, and served as the main course on an O'odham dinner table. Rabbit, which is plentiful in the Sonoran Desert and easily hunted, is a staple food for many O'odham. (I remember Monica, a first grader in my class on the reservation some years ago. She drew a picture of a rabbit etched against a starry sky, its broken body spurting blood. Equally memorable were her words: "At night, we hunt rabbit. There is blood everywhere at dark time.")

Mary ended her piece with an instructional fact about one of the planets, taken from the class bulletin board. Construction paper planets spun across the board; lines of yarn connected each planet to a colorful fact. One such fact, "Saturn is called the Roman God of the Sky," formed the basis of Mary's conversation with the Uranus "natives" in her piece. Writers draw from the whole of their experience for material. Harold Rosen writes:

> We are always in a high state of readiness to transform into story not only what we experience directly but also what we hear and read—a cross on a mountainside, graffiti, "Accident Black Spot," a row of empty whisky bottles, a limp, a scar, a dog howling in the night, a headline, a cryptic note. (1983, p. 12)

The unique experiences of the Tohono O'odham that Mary, like the other children in her classroom, chose to write about may be viewed as a continuum. At one end, some reflected cultural features are almost offhand references to subtleties that distinguish the everyday O'odham experience from that of mainstream culture. Examples include James's one-line reference to operating a C.B. radio out in space to get help after his spaceship crashed, and Dana's remark that he ate beans for lunch. The outside observer unfamiliar with present-day life on the reservation might not recognize these references as identifying features of the contemporary O'odham experience. C.B. radios help to bridge the great distances between isolated villages and are a safety feature as well as a convenience in many O'odham pickup trucks and cars. A variety of beans have been an O'odham staple for centuries.

At the other end of the continuum, Eleanor's description of the basket-making process or Anna's account of her trip into the desert with her mother to harvest the saguaro fruit for later use as syrup served over fried bread signal even the uninformed reader that these students are writing from a perspective unique to the O'odham.

These written cultural artifacts, then, create the richness and color of the children's writing that identify it as having life outside the dominant main-stream North American experience. However, lying somewhat outside main-stream culture does not imply a total divorce. These young O'odham writers lived only an hour or two from the large metropolitan city of Tucson and were daily participants in the mainstream experience through school as well as through the television programs they invited into their homes every night, the books and newspapers they read, and the movies they saw. On occasion they visited Tucson or other Arizona cities such as Casa Grande and Phoenix, gaining further exposure to mainstream life through trips to shopping malls, amusement parks, and rock concerts. Theirs was not an isolated experience, and their exposure to mainstream ways of living and believing was clearly re-flected in their writing.

This involvement in two worlds is exemplified by Michael's fictional hero, Dan Hackman, who, in typical television Western style, put the "bad guys" underground. In this story, however, written from the perspective of a Native American, the bad guys were the cowboys, and the righteous victors the In-dians:

> One day in the desert some cowboys were shooting Indians. A
> man named Dan Hackman heard the shooting. He went to see what
> was going on. He saw some dead Indians. He shot all the cowboys. The
> Indians celebrated. Dan got married and lived happily ever after.

Dan Hackman may have come into being in the instructional setting of a main-stream public school, and he may owe his dramatic flair to the hours of televi-sion Westerns his creator had absorbed over the years, but his allegiances lay with the O'odham.

Although both the Native American and mainstream cultures played ac-tive roles on the reservation, the children experienced them, for the most part, as one culture. They simply lived their lives, seldom if ever stopping to analyze the dual cultural influences on their lives. Wolcott (1991) discusses the term *propriospect* (derived from Goodenough, 1976), meaning any human being's understanding of the numerous cultures and subcultures within which he or she lives; this concept identifies the important idea that, although cultures may be multiple, the individual's cultural knowledge is unitary.

FANTASY, CONFLICT, AND MALE-FEMALE DIFFERENCES

Applebee (1978) contends that "fantasy is not so much the 'fantastical' as it is part of a continuum that begins in the world of immediate experience, passes outward toward distant lands, and outward again into purely imaginative realms" (p. 74). Accordingly, he suggests that the ability to distance oneself from real-life experience is a sign of developmental maturity. As children grow and develop, they are able to explore ideas and situations that are further removed from their own immediate experience. Applebee considers the ability to fantasize a sign of the greatest maturity, since fantasy is the most "distant" from real-life experience.

Graves (1974) further explores the developmental issue through the concept of territoriality. Primary territory includes those things that are of central concern to children: their possessions, their home, and school. Secondary territory is defined as "the metropolitan area beyond the child's school and home" and may include such topics as crime and sports. Expanded territory is the area beyond secondary and includes "current events, history and geography on a national and world scale" (p. 97).

Graves found clear differences between male and female writers' willingness to explore writing across the territorial continuum. Boys wrote more about secondary and expanded territories, and girls wrote more about themes in primary territory.

Differences between the O'odham boys and girls of this study are evident as well. It is not surprising, perhaps, that gender operates as a powerful experiential filter. Born of physiological features, sanctioned by society, male and female experiences differ widely. This is particularly true on the reservation, which to some extent has not participated in mainstream society's efforts to eliminate some of the traditional and arbitrary distinctions between the sexes both in the home and in the workplace.

One of the most striking differences between male and female children in this study occurred in the realm of fantasy and in the resolution of story conflict. Most of the children's stories dealt with some sort of conflict. Following Sutton-Smith's (1975) lead, we may view story conflict as being one of two major types: confrontation with evil or a problem, and deprivation, which is a more subtle and passive type of conflict.

Confrontation with Evil or a Problem

A confrontation with some sort of evil or problem was a common theme across all story assignments and genres; however, it was especially evident in the children's fantasy stories. Shining knights in armor and brave and powerful hunters battled human-eating giants and fire-breathing dragons. Essentially, the children could confront the source of evil or conflict in one of three ways: (1) resort to force or violence; (2) employ peaceful, nonviolent tactics; or (3) ignore the problem or fail to overcome it. What follows are gender-related tendencies that appear to support similar findings by Graves (1973/1974), Paley (1981), and Pitcher and Prelinger (1963).

Resort to Force or Violence. The boys were more likely to resort to violence than were the girls. Out of a total of 237 compositions, 103 were written by boys and 134 by girls. Eleven percent of the boys' writing referred to a violent confrontation, compared to only 4 percent of the girls'. (Because of the small size of the sample, these percentages and the others appearing in this section lack statistical significance; they are, however, suggestive.) In the male compositions, monsters were stabbed to death, dragons' jaws broken, devils burned, and so on; much of the violence was undertaken by a single individual. The solitary warrior who triumphs over one seemingly insurmountable obstacle after another was a popular character in the boys' stories.

One such superhero was George the dragon fighter, a creation of Dana's. In this tale, a king and a prince set out to slay a dragon that is terrorizing the townspeople, but George steps in instead and single-handedly destroys the evil beast:

> One day in a castle in the woods there was a dragon. The people were scared of it. The prince and king were going to fight the dragon but a man was going to kill the dragon first. He was George the dragon fighter. He was a giant. The day came for the fight. The dragon blew fire but George blocked it with his shield. Finally George threw the dragon into the sea. When George got back they had a celebration.

No such conquering heroes appeared in the girls' stories. From the female perspective, even when violence is used, it is a group effort. This is especially apparent in Christine's fairy tale, also about a dragon that causes a king and people untold misery. As in Dana's tale, a single hunter pursues the dragon, but unlike mighty George the dragon fighter, the lowly hunter is quickly devoured by the incensed monster. So the king and his men attack the dragon, but they too are driven back. It is only after the townspeople come together as a united front that the dragon is finally destroyed:

> Once there was a big ugly dragon and it was really, really mean. One time a hunter tried to kill him. The dragon got so mad that he ate the hunter. The king decided to have a war so that king got all his men and they did have a war. The dragon could not be killed by anybody so the dragon was still alive until the king got the whole people to kill the dragon. The townspeople killed the dragon together.

Use Peaceful, Nonviolent Tactics.   Both boys and girls also used peaceful, nonviolent means to overcome conflict; however, the girls were almost twice as likely to rely on peaceful tactics as were the boys (22 percent versus 12 percent). Neither sex was averse to running away from danger, but the girls had other nonviolent options as well, such as negotiation or enlisting the help of a friend or family member. Faith's characters employ several nonviolent tactics in their efforts to conquer the tyranny of a "people-eating" dragon:

> Once upon a time there was a giant. He liked to eat little people. Then one day, one of the little men said, "Will you please stop eating us up?" But the giant did not listen to the little men. For hundreds of years he ate the little people. One day a nice giant who liked the little people came to see the mean giant. The nice giant said, "Stop eating my friends or I will fight you." The mean giant said, "O.K. Let's fight." But he didn't know he [the nice giant] was magic and he made the mean giant disappear.

Note that negotiation is the first tactic used both by the little men and then by the nice giant who comes to their aid. A confrontation ensues between the two giants only when the mean giant refuses all diplomatic requests to end his reign of terror. Even then, the confrontation is nonviolent; the nice giant uses his magic powers to vanquish the evil ogre. Although magic finally saved the day in Faith's fairy tale, the power of prayer drove the devil away in another one of her stories.

Sometimes the source of evil is simply foiled by an unforeseen natural occurrence. One such incident occurs as the robbers in James's piece, "The Sheriff and the Robbers," attempt to escape on horseback. As fate would have it, their stallions encounter a snake. They rear up in fright, throwing the would-be robbers to the ground. This enables the sheriff to easily overpower them and haul them off to jail.

The Problem Is Ignored or the Conflict Is Not Overcome. In a small number of stories, the conflict was not overcome. It may be significant that these compositions were written by children who had much unresolved conflict in their own lives. Their fictional characters' inability to resolve conflict may simply reflect the powerlessness these young authors felt in overcoming their own real-life personal problems. The most pessimistic writer was Rachel, who failed to overcome conflict in four of her twelve compositions. Both her parents were disabled, leaving Rachel largely responsible for running and maintaining the household. Furthermore, her younger brother (who died during the time of our research) was severely handicapped, both physically and mentally.

Deprivation

The second major source of conflict in the children's writing stemmed from some sort of deprivation, although it was not nearly as common as plots with a more overt conflict. Moreover, only two of the boys' compositions dealt with deprivation, whereas fifteen of the girls' were based on a theme of overcoming some want, generally a lack of food or money (2 percent of the boys' compositions versus 13 percent of the girls'). Although the girls insisted on alliance and group effort in their stories that involved a direct confrontation, in deprivation stories they were as likely to depend on their own individual efforts as on help from others.

In the one case in which a specific deprivation was not overcome, the story nonetheless had a happy ending. Joyce wrote a piece about a cowboy who was not allowed to participate in a rodeo because he was too small. Consequently, he never succeeded in riding in the rodeo, but he did marry, have children, and become a happy family man.

In sum, conflict and the overcoming of conflict were common features of these children's writing. Many of their compositions can be viewed as conflict-driven dyads: attack-defend, chase-escape, threat-withdraw. How conflict was dealt with was a major theme, and one that revealed definite differences between young male and female writers. Boys were quick to resort to violence, and in their battle scenes they almost invariably stressed the exploits of the individual hero. Girls were much less likely to use violence; when they did so, it was often the action of a group. In addition, girls preferred peaceful, nonviolent solutions to problems. Moreover, they were more likely than the boys to write of conflict as some sort of deprivation that must be overcome.

These findings corroborate those of Pitcher and Prelinger (1963). They examined the writings of 137 intellectually advanced children from economically advantaged families. Regarding the use of violence in the children's writing, Pitcher and Prelinger noted:

With the boys, aggression tends to be much more violent; one almost hears and feels the reverberation of crashing, shooting and pounding as general catastrophe reigns. (p. 72)

Vivian Paley, a teacher who collected and analyzed the stories of her five-year-old kindergarteners, made a similar observation about differences between her male and female students:

Many family and magical themes are used by both girls and boys, but the most obvious differences lie in the boys' overt use of physical force, contrasted with the girls' emphasis on family serenity. Boys exult in superhuman strength, girls seek gentle relationships. Boys talk of blood and mayhem, girls avoid the subject; a character in a girl's story simply dies, no details given. Boys fly, leap, crash, and dive. Girls have picnics and brush their teeth; the meanest, ugliest character in a girl's story goes on picnics and keeps his teeth clean. (1981, p. 203)

In considering the territorial realms written about by young authors, Graves (1975) identified a male-female difference in distancing; Applebee (1978), however, points out that it is a difference that may be strongly influenced by cultural patterns. Home and family are the primary focus in the traditional pattern of female socialization, a pattern that appears frequently in the Tohono O'odham girls' compositions. They write about marriage and relationships, having and caring for children, housework and the like, all of which are at the heart of the traditional female experience.

Chodorow (1974) attributes personality differences between the sexes to "the fact that women, universally, are largely responsible for early child care." The early social environment is different for and is experienced differently by male and female children, since girls are able to identify with the caretaking female parent while boys must at least somewhat define themselves in opposition to her. Thus, "in any given society, feminine personality comes to define itself in relation and connection to other people more than masculine personality does" (pp. 43–44). My study clearly demonstrates that children wrote about their personal concerns and involvements. Although both young girls and young boys experience home life and family relationships, the girls appear to be socialized to pay more attention to them and thus write about them more extensively.

Young girls' involvement with home and family may also explain why they wrote fewer "true fantasies" than did the boys. Fantasy, of course, is the genre furthest removed from everyday experience. The girls did write fantasies in response to the fairy tale assignment, but they wove in details from their own daily activities to a much greater extent than did the boys. Thus, the queen in Anna's tale cooked breakfast for her family, and the king and queen in Joyce's piece were pleasantly surprised when they had twins, a boy for the king and a girl for the queen. Again, it is around such activities and events that these young girls' lives revolved. It is no wonder such details appeared in their stories, realistic and fantastic alike.

Findings from Other Research

Even within the often rigid framework of assigned writing topics, children find room for material from their own lives, their daily activities, their relationships with friends and family, their hopes and concerns. This should come as no surprise. Real-life experiences often lie at the heart of professional fiction. Maya Angelou, Mark Twain, Eudora Welty, Thomas Wolfe—the list is endless—weave the factual and the imaginary into brilliant narrative, and biographers of famous novelists devote much time and effort to tracing the threads of personal experience that run through published works.

The composition strategies of these Tohono O'odham children do not accord precisely with the findings of Applebee (1978) and Graves (1973/1974), which suggest a link between developmental maturity and distancing. Applebee and Graves suggest that the ability to distance oneself from one's primary experience and write about an abstract world of fantasy is a mark of a sophisticated, mature writer. As meaning-makers structuring and representing the totality of their experience through narrative, these children moved back and forth along the territorial continuum in virtually every piece they wrote, interlacing elements of their own real-life experiences with imaginary characters, events, and settings. Just as professional writers do, the children wove concrete experiences with dreams, real events, places, and people into their fantasies. It was not unusual for a piece to contain elements of both fact and fiction and to span primary, secondary, and expanded territory. In Britton's (1970b) opinion, personal experience includes fantasy. When these children wrote, all their experiences, real and imagined alike, came to life on paper.

PRAGMATIC REFLECTIONS

Language is invariably shaped by the situational context in which it occurs. How language is used and the form it takes are always dependent on who is using it, where they are using it, and why. This pragmatic reality was reflected in every piece the children wrote. In their efforts to play the instructional game and produce the answers they knew the teacher wanted, they often wrote compositions that blended personal experience with textbook facts, sometimes with bizarre results.

Edelsky, Altwerger, and Flores (1990) maintain that when authors are engaged in "authentic" writing they use the four interacting, interrelated subsystems of written language (graphophonics, syntax, semantics, and pragmatics) to create a meaningful text. If even one of these subsystems is missing or distorted, the entire language system breaks down and the end result is something less than real language. Edelsky and her colleagues contrast authentic *writing* with the "practice writing" they contend dominates school curriculum. Because the critical "connections between genre, purpose, audience, syntax, and semantics" (p. 20) become distorted in practice writing, students do not learn control over the medium as they would if they were engaged in real *writing*. An example of a typical school writing experience cited by the authors is a teacher requiring all 30 children in her classroom to write an invitation to the school principal inviting him to a class event. The children are not really *writing* because all the critical information that an authentic inviter would normally need to provide (time, day, and place of the event) is being provided redundantly by every child. Clearly, the purpose is not to invite the principal, but to practice writing invitations. The teacher, guided by behavioral learning theory, believes that when the children do need to write invitations, the knowledge they acquired from this readiness activity will transfer and enable them to do so.

Again and again, these young O'odham writers showed us through their limited and stilted texts what happened when their own authentic purpose for writing to make sense of their experience was short-circuited by their need to comply with the teacher's assignments. Consider the writing assignment connected with an instructional unit on ancient Egypt. The students were given a choice of three topics:

1. Your friend the Pharaoh died.
2. Invite friends to an Egyptian feast.
3. You are an Egyptian slave.

These were third-grade Native American schoolchildren with only a smattering of information about ancient Egypt that they had acquired from their teacher's lectures and from reference materials on the subject. Accordingly, constrained by their lack of knowledge, and with no authentic purpose for writing other than compliance with the assignment, they turned to that which they knew, their own experiences. Elaine's response was typical:

> One day we went to Egypt with Miss Kasten. And it was fun. Me and Miss Kasten rode in a train. We went to a motel. The next morning we went to the zoo. We got an ice cream cone and we went to the toy store and we got a gorilla and an alligator. And Miss Kasten got scared

and I started to laugh. Then we went back to Sells and she took me home.

The reader does not need an intimate knowledge of Elaine's personal experiences to recognize that beyond the opening line, this piece bears no relation to ancient Egypt, but is rather a description of her own possible adventures in a local city.

There were times when children chose to ignore the parameters of the assignment altogether and follow their personal pragmatics instead. Alex wrote a fast-paced action adventure in which he envisioned himself as a famous race-car driver who won a glorious race in Dallas. His mention of the city was the only connection to an assignment that required him to write a series of expository reports on the Texas state flag, seal, bird, and flower.

Similarly, Dana, assigned to write a report on Arizona, wrote about himself as a writer dealing with an assigned topic in the classroom context:

> We talked about the state seal and state bird. We had to read the paper. Then we wrote a story until the bell rang. The state bird's name is the cactus wren. Yesterday we did the state flag with Miss Howard. We had to find out what the yellow and red stripes mean. What the copper star stands for. Same with the state bird and seal. For the state bird we had to find out where it lives and what it eats and its name. Then the bell rang. We had to change. Tomorrow I have to finish the state seal, bird, and flag. Today I am supposed to finish the state. But I didn't have a chance.

In the view of Edelsky and her colleagues, these children were not *writing*, but simply participating in a traditional school literacy event in which they were practicing writing for their teacher. Although they all, in a way, took some ownership of these pieces, they were not operating out of strong, authentic personal goals but were rather making the best of constrained, artificial writing episodes.

INSTRUCTIONAL IMPLICATIONS

The stories of these Tohono O'odham children reveal more than just the experiences of the young authors. They speak to teachers of children everywhere and have much to say about the teaching of writing, in particular the instructional practice of assigning writing topics.

Teachers who assign topics generally do so with the good intentions of giving their students something to write about. But this "help" can be a hindrance. Research (Graves, 1983; Y. Goodman, 1984) shows that topic assignments narrow what children write about; children make the most significant gains as writers when they are dealing with meaningful topics of their own choosing. And children have much to write about: the drama of their own lives, their thoughts, feelings, and concerns. Many an educator (e.g., Britton, 1970a, 1970b; Britton, Burgess, Martin, McLeod & Rosen, 1975; Y. Goodman, 1984; Graves, 1983; Rosen, 1983) has noted that the most meaningful stories are usually created from concrete personal experiences. Children do not need assigned writing topics in order to write. What they do need is a warm, supportive classroom environment and a teacher who will respect them as individuals with a wealth of experiences and insights to write about and share with others (Atwell, 1987; Calkins, 1986, 1991). Through our acceptance of and appreciation for the material of our students' worlds—Alex's obsession with race cars, Florence's longings to see her father, Anna's knowledge of the saguaro harvest—we empower our students as writers, as persons with something unique and valuable to share. Graves (1983) assures us that the most important job of the teacher of writing is to help his or her students realize that they do have stories to tell.

Celebrating students' personal lives as the source of rich writing material in no way precludes critical discussions about the themes that appear in the writing. For example, teachers would do well to discuss with students some of the gender differences in their writing and ask why the topics that boys and girls write about seem to differ. If some writing seems excessively violent, teachers could engage students in a discussion about violence, exploring why they felt the need to include violence in their stories and how violence affects society in general. Is violence *ever* appropriate? If so, when? What are other ways to handle conflict? In this way, teachers can begin to achieve what many view as the true dual role of education: to develop individual potential and to create a sense of social responsibility.

Writing to Learn About the World

If writing must be assigned—for instance, as part of an instructional unit—teachers and students may negotiate the topics they will explore further through writing. Theme cycles (Altwerger & Flores, 1991) are a particularly effective framework for immersing children in authentic research writing. Understanding that learning often begins with the "big questions" that children have about the world, teachers can help children identify their questions and narrow the focus of their study topic. Then, following a three-part cycle, they encourage their students to (1) list everything they know about the chosen topic, (2) identify what they don't know and what questions they have, and (3) brainstorm the resources they can use to find their answers. Students then read a wide variety of both fiction and nonfiction material, interview experts on the topic, conduct surveys, and collect and organize data in much the same way that a physical or social scientist conducts research.

Once the analysis of their data is complete, students design ways in which to share their findings with others. These student experts understand that the learning cycle is complete when they can share what they have learned with others through slide shows, videos, poster sessions, panel discussions, and so on. Knowing that form follows function, teachers can read aloud particularly powerful examples of expository writing, highlighting variations in form, style, and voice that the author may utilize to showcase his or her information. Teachers then encourage their students to experiment and play with similar variations.

At Sunnyslope School in Phoenix, Arizona (Clark, 1991), a master list of resident student experts is posted in the school auditorium. Classrooms may contact an expert and request a presentation. As the requests come in, student experts travel from classroom to classroom with their research portfolios, which may contain maps, flowcharts, slides, and physical specimens, sharing with their schoolmates the findings of their research. Atwell (1990); Calkins (1986, 1991); Gamberg, Kwak, Hutchings, and Altheim (1988); and Mayher, Lester, and Pradl (1983) have written extensively about the benefits of projects that engage students in writing to learn, using writing to explore new information and to share with others what they have learned.

Teachers must recognize that students bring their own purposes to every writing task, including assigned writing. What seems like an inappropriate response from the teacher's perspective may, when viewed through the child's eyes, be a completely understandable, even insightful response. As part of a teacher-student conference, interviewing children about their compositions is an effective way to discover what they learned. I often discovered a second story behind the written one. By asking the children where they got their ideas, why they chose to write about each particular topic, how they felt about the assignment, and what they really knew about the assignment and topic, I discovered a rich source of information about their personal thoughts and feelings as well as their understanding of the academic material and their perceptions of teacher expectations.

For example, during a retrospective interview, Dana shared with me the following thoughts and feelings about the assignment, "If I lived in Switzerland":

Researcher: What do you know about Switzerland?
Dana: The capital is Bonn [*sic*], they have lots of Alps, and lots of snow. . . . That's all I remember.
Researcher: Did you like writing about Switzerland?

Dana: Not really.

Researcher: Not really? How come?

Dana: It was hard.

Researcher: Why do you think it's hard, Dana?

Dana: Because I had to find some of it in a book.

Researcher: What book was that?

Dana: Oh, a book in the classroom. There are lots of books and we had to
find "S" . . . for "Switzerland."

Researcher: Oh, and what were you supposed to do once you found it?

Dana: Try to get something out of it. . . .

Researcher: Try to get something out of it, like what?

Dana: Try to get like . . . like . . . like . . . go get something out of it
and write something.

Researcher: Like information and stuff you were supposed to find about
Switzerland and write down? Did you find this [referring to Dana's
report on Switzerland] in the book?

Dana: Yes

Researcher: Why do you think Ms. Howard gave you this assignment?

Dana: Umm . . . so we could learn about it . . . about Switzerland.

Researcher: Did you learn, Dana?

Dana: Not really . . . ummm . . . I don't really know where Switzerland is.

From Dana's perspective, the assignment was hard and not particularly
interesting because he "had to find . . . it in a book." And, what is more, he
didn't "know where Switzerland [was]." As Dana's comments indicate, he had
not received sufficient guidance. A topic like "Life in Switzerland" is difficult
at best. Careful guidance in the use of reference books and research strategies
is indispensable. Better yet, the teacher could have developed a social studies
unit that was closer to the daily experience of these Tohono O'odham third
graders. When students are engaged in projects that are personally meaningful, they write to learn, they write to inquire, they write to share their newly
discovered knowledge. In short, genuine writing is the result of authentic reasons to write.

Writing to Learn About Oneself

These O'odham children also spoke to us, through their stories, of what
they knew about themselves, of the self-discoveries they were making.
Whether they were retelling the events of an exciting day at the motocross
race or describing the way a close friend braided her long dark hair, writing
brought their thoughts and feelings to the surface. Writing is discovery, and

because of its intensely personal nature it may lead the writer to self-discovery in ways that almost nothing else can (Calkins, 1991; Little, 1987). And through a developing awareness of self, writers often experience enhanced feelings of positive self-regard, as with the O'odham child who said that the thing she liked best about herself was that she told "good, true stories."

Telling good, true stories is the birthright of every healthy child. Storytelling, as demonstrated by these young authors, is a cognitive tool, a powerful meaning-making strategy. Through narration and the corresponding processes of selection and organization, experiences take shape and lead the writer to new levels of awareness and understanding. Several children wrote repeatedly about one topic in particular: Anna wrote again and again about her grandfather's death; Elaine, of her broken leg; Doreen, of her estranged father. It seems that the children, probably without conscious awareness, were exploring these salient experiences from different angles and in different guises in an effort to come to grips with them.

When reading the stories their students have composed, teachers would do well to ask themselves, what meanings are the children creating? What elements of their experiences are they grappling with? Teachers who recognize children's writing as an outgrowth of their rich and varied experiences will appreciate writing as a powerful learning tool for teacher and student alike. Children's writing reveals a wealth of information about them, information that sensitive and perceptive teachers can use to develop a sound educational program, one that meets the needs and interests of their students. Good teaching begins with knowing one's students. Particularly when a teacher is working with students of a different cultural background than his or her own, the students' writings offer the teacher access into their personal worlds. The guiding question for teachers should be, "What is the storyteller doing and why?" (Rosen, 1983, p. 32). In this way, the teacher forms a partnership with his or her students, a partnership in the exploration of meaning that can ultimately bridge the gap between home and school.

CONCLUSION

The children of the Tohono O'odham who shared their stories with us are young adults now and living new stories. But the stories they told us as nine-year-olds live on in their lives and in the lives of all who stood close enough to hear and see the unfolding of their understandings. Langer (1942) reminds us of the complex interweaving of language and meaning:

> Between the facts run the threads of unrecorded reality, momentarily recognized, whenever they come to the surface, in our tacit adaption to

signs; and the bright, twisted thread of symbolic envisagement, imagination, thought-memory, and reconstructed memory, belief beyond experience, dream, make-believe, hypothesis, philosophy—the whole creative process of ideation, metaphor, and abstraction that makes human life an adventure in understanding. (p. 228)

It is an adventure that begins with birth, one we live and come to know through our stories, for we are all storytellers, spinning our tales from the multiple threads of our experience, creating a richly patterned tapestry of infinite complexity, of infinite meaning.

CHAPTER 4

Speaking, Searching, and Sharing in the Community of Writers

Wendy C. Kasten

IF ONE WALKS THROUGH EDITORIAL OFFICES or a newspaper city room, one will undoubtedly see lips moving and hear expert professional writers muttering to themselves as they write (D. Murray, 1982, p. 34). In the elementary classrooms we studied, we saw student writers engaged in a variety of activities and behaviors that included talking to one another, talking to themselves, and seeking help and information from people, books, and other print. Not unlike the professional writers Murray portrays, the children were also muttering to themselves, whispering, and reading aloud. As my colleagues have proposed in the first three chapters, the writing process as observed in the classrooms we studied was dynamic and complex. This chapter explores some of the observable actions that occur when elementary-age writers are at work and examines the role of these activities, which, like those in the bustling newsroom, promote and nurture the making of meaning. As we visited these classrooms and continued to analyze the data, we began to understand these complexities and also see their parallels to the process of our own and other adult writing.

One way to make these complexities visible is by looking in depth at one episode; the following one, which focuses on Anna and her interaction with her classmates on one day in third grade, is as unique yet typical as any. The reconstruction of this episode is based on the detailed observational notes taken by one researcher; it demonstrates our notion of student writers as a community in the classroom as well as the desirability and function of speaking, searching, and sharing during writing.

ANNA'S FAIRY TALE

First I will present Anna's completed story before I show the complex process of how the text evolved. Anna was an average student with an outgoing personality. Her story was on a topic she had chosen herself (an opportunity that was rare in her third-grade classroom). She opted to write a fairy tale, similar in genre to recent required assignments. Her text, shown in Figure 4.1, reads, "One day there was a girl. Her name was Maxine. She was a nice girl. One day her mother said, 'Go and give your grandmother some food.' She said ok, so she went on the way. On the way she met a wolf. The wolf said Hi."

This is the process by which this very brief story evolved. Anna was seated at the writing center. She began by writing the word "One." Anna sat and looked around the room, watching classmates over at the math center doing their work on the chalkboard, and continued writing "day there" on her paper. She paused to erase the *e* at the end of *there* and rewrote it to make it neater (a cosmetic revision). She listened again to the children at the math center, then wrote "was," and paused to play with her paper, fidgeting with

a

One   day   there   was
a   girl. Her   name   was
Maxine.   She   was   a
nice   girl.   One   day
her   mother   said   go
and   give   youe
grandmother   some
food.   She   sad   ok.
So   she   went   on
the   way. On   the   way
she   meat   a   wolf
the   wolf   said   he

FIGURE 4.1: Anna's Fairy Tale

the corners while she was (apparently) thinking. Anna assisted a nearby classmate with something he was writing, and then, back in her own story, wrote "a girl. Her name was." Anna said aloud, to no one in particular, that she would name the girl in her story Tiffany. She read over a classmate's shoulder (Elaine) to see what she had written. Anna then talked again, musing, "What should I name her?" She finally wrote "Maxine [another classmate]. She was a nice girl. One day her."

Anna asked a nearby researcher if the word *mother* needed a capital letter, but received no response. (As participant observers, the researchers often chose not to respond to student questions in order to avoid an intrusive conversation. Students were accustomed to this, but would often ask questions anyway.) Anna then listened to a conversation between two other classmates about their writing. She resumed writing ("mother said go"), then went back into her text and revised the second *one*, changing the *o* to a capital letter. She looked around the room momentarily and wrote "and give your."

Anna watched some classmates again, and then grabbed Walter's pencil (Walter was sitting nearby). Walter retaliated by grabbing her paper and reading aloud her emerging story. While Walter was reading her story, Anna sat with her pencil in her mouth, tried to grab her paper back, and corrected his miscues as he read. Anna then talked briefly with other classmates, read the last few words of her own story aloud, and tried to figure out how to spell the word *grandmother*. She then wrote "grandmother some food." She informed the researcher that she wrote *food* but that it looked like *lood*. (As the study progressed, it was not uncommon for the children to take a moment to inform us about what they were doing, which they would usually do without any serious interruption to their writing process.) Anna talked again to Walter and wrote "She said ok. So."

Anna paused here to write some capital *J*'s on her writing folder. She helped Walter spell a word, and announced that she was going to the dictionary to look for the word *exaggerate*. Walter responded that he didn't need the word *exaggerate*, but Anna insisted she was going to look it up anyway. She continued writing "she went on the way. On the way she meet [met] a."

Anna began to use the dictionary, but changed her mind. She wrote "wolf the wolf." She went back to make a revision on both *wolf*s. She had written both of them beginning with capital letters and revised by erasing both words in order to start each one with a lower-case letter. She concluded "said Hi." Writing center time was over, so Anna put her name on her paper and cleaned up.

ANNA AND HER COMMUNITY OF WRITERS

Anna's writing episode reveals that when children are executing their writing assignments in a typical elementary classroom, whether at their seats or in a writing center, a great deal of oral language, sharing, and use of physical and human resources accompanies the writing process. Anna talked to herself, talked to other classmates, listened to other students, worked with a dictionary, assisted nearby students in solving their writing problems, read a friend's writing, and heard her own story read aloud by another child.

Throughout Anna's writing center experience, she attempted to find what she needed to know from a nearby adult, from a classmate, and from a dictionary. She also used language heuristically by thinking aloud about the naming of her character. In addition, she asked questions, offered suggestions to classmates, and talked or thought quietly to herself. She searched for information and ideas she needed, such as what letters needed to be capitalized and how to spell the word *exaggerate* (for Walter's benefit). She made changes as she went along, trying to improve her work in ways such as rewriting a letter to make it look neater or rewriting entire words even if she only needed to change the first letter from upper to lower case. She shared her story with Walter, who read it aloud, and at one point she read over her classmate Elaine's shoulder.

While Anna was talking, listening, reading, and writing, so were the other children in her class. Some students may have had either more or less to say than Anna did. Some students used resources around the room more or less than Anna did. And some students muttered to themselves either more or less than Anna did. But we observed that all the children did all these things at least some of the time when they were in the process of writing. The variations in the amount and the extent of these activities surrounding the writing experience depended both on the personality and style of the individual writer and on the purpose and context of the writing assignment.

For example, children might talk less during journal writing, since it often has only the writer as its audience and so may not require as much interaction as other kinds of writing (Kasten & Clarke, 1987). Other genres, such as expository writing, might lend themselves to more talk; when children are engaged in difficult or unfamiliar assignments, such as a report from an encyclopedia, interaction and talk might be a more necessary part of the writing process. Children use one another and their classroom as their community to solve problems along the way. In third grade, these students were asked to write about the Arizona state bird, seal, tree, and flower. This assignment was fairly difficult for most of the children, and while observing the writing center that day, we witnessed more talk and interaction than usual. Most of the talk and interaction were related to the children's attempts to try to understand their teacher's expectations and to figure out how to use encyclopedias, which are often difficult for third graders to read.

ORAL LANGUAGE DURING WRITING

When Donald Murray (1989) talks about the writing process, he reveals how writers rehearse: This process includes ordering, forming, structuring, seeing a need in the self or in the reader, and most especially *hearing*. He says that writers hear what they will write, and that they hear these things from inside their heads by talking to themselves, listening to themselves, talking out loud to themselves, and talking to others and listening to themselves as they do so (p. 54).

The process of hearing and listening as a part of the writing process is important not only for adult writers but for children writing in classroom settings; oral language plays an important role in the writing process. All the children we studied talked at some time or another while writing; some children talked more than others, and there were occasional writing episodes in which no oral language was observed. Often the form of oral language that we observed was subvocalizing, which was extensive in some writers and infrequent in others.

The field notes accompanying the 278 texts that were collected over the course of two years were examined for the nature and function of the oral language that occurred during the writing process. All incidences of language, whether directed to a classmate, to a researcher, or to no one in particular, were included in this analysis. These incidents were examined first by looking at what part of the writing process they related to: the prewriting or consideration stage of writing, the actual text generation or drafting, or the revision and reconsideration aspect.

Language related to the parts of the process dealing with prewriting (coded "A") included incidents like Anna's trying to decide what to name her character before actually writing the character's name. This category might also include talking with a classmate about an idea for a story, asking how to spell or capitalize a word before attempting to write it, or subvocalizing a word or phrase before writing it down.

Language that was uttered as the child's text was being produced (coded "B") included obvious subvocalizations of what was being written or comments during drafting, such as "This is hard," or "I'm almost done." Utterances judged to be related to the process of revising or reconsidering the text (coded "C") included, for example, a child's asking about a spelling after having written the word down or checking on whether a capital letter or a punctuation mark needed to be added to an already written part of the text. (Although the episode of Anna's described here did not include any of these, they were not uncommon.)

In addition to language that was directly linked to the emerging text, we often noted statements related to writing but in a more general way (coded "D" and defined as "related talk"). For example, Anna informed the researcher that she had written the word *food* but that it looked like *lood*. Anna also discussed looking up the word *exaggerate* in the dictionary, although it wasn't related to her own writing. Other examples of related talk might be interactions between classmates asking to borrow erasers, checking on assignment expectations ("How much are we supposed to write?" "Is there supposed to be a title?"), or expressing other writer concerns ("I need more paper.").

TABLE 4.1: Language Utilization in the Writing Process: Third and Fourth Grades

Code	Description	Percentage of Talk
A	Language during prewriting	46
B	Language during text generation	10
C	Language during revision/reconsideration	18
D	Other language related to writing	<u>16</u>
	All language related to writing	90
E	Language unrelated to writing	10

Sometimes language that was observed during writing was judged as unrelated to writing (coded "E"); it could sometimes be considered as "off-task" language, in the sense of being focused on concerns other than writing. Utterances of this type might be children's asking one another what time lunch would begin or what time they needed to leave for a special class (such as music or art) or commenting about a television program.

I analyzed a sample of the oral language that accompanied the 278 texts collected in this study in order to determine the percentage of utterances fitting into each of the codes described above, as summarized in Table 4.1 (Kasten, 1984/1985). Oral language related to prewriting was observed most frequently (46 percent of all utterances), with another 44 percent of utterances being related to text generation, revision, and other aspects of the writing process. In other words, 90 percent of the children's talk while writing was related to the writing itself. Later I analyzed all the texts written in third grade and found that the categories relating directly to writing added up to 98 percent of all observable utterances (Kasten & Clarke, 1987) (see Table 4.2). In the highly engaging process of writing, there is clearly little room for that which is unrelated to writing, especially unrelated talk. A subsequent study of third and fifth graders produced comparable findings (Kasten & Clarke, 1987).

TABLE 4.2: Language Utilization in the Writing Process: Third Grade

Code	Description	Percentage of Talk
A	Language during prewriting	31
B	Language during text generation	27
C	Language during revision/reconsideration	18
D	Other language related to writing	<u>22</u>
	All language related to writing	98
E	Language unrelated to writing	2

The most important conclusion of this analysis is that when these children had the opportunity to talk during writing episodes, their talk was related to their work at hand. Although they may have talked about some unrelated events as well, such talk was at most only 10 percent of their oral language.

Another way of looking at the oral language spoken by writers in this study is from the perspective of Halliday's functions of language (1977). Halliday's categories provide additional understanding about the language use of Anna and her classmates. All oral language in the third-grade portion of the two-year study was analyzed using Halliday's seven functions of language:

1. *Instrumental.* Language used to obtain something for the speaker, such as "Can I use your eraser?"
2. *Regulatory.* Language used to control the behavior of others, such as "Give me my paper back."
3. *Interactional.* The "me and you" function of language, such as "Can I read your story?"
4. *Personal.* Language used to express the child's uniqueness or awareness of self, such as "This is hard," or "I think I'll name her Tiffany."
5. *Heuristic.* Language used to explore the environment, ask questions, or find things out, such as "Does *mother* need a capital letter?"
6. *Imaginative.* Language through which the child creates an environment of his or her own, such as "Let's pretend."
7. *Informative.* Language with the "I've got something to tell you" function, such as "I wrote *food* but it looks like *lood*." (Halliday, 1977, pp. 18–24)

There was a consistency across all the children concerning the kinds of functions that were used during writing. Language episodes that were interactional, informative, or heuristic were the most frequent, with interactional language making up 31 percent of all episodes. Personal and instrumental language were used on occasion, but regulatory and imaginative language were rarely observed.

Table 4.3 summarizes the percentage of utterances that were judged to serve each function. The percentages are based on total codings rather than total utterances, since many utterances were assigned to two or even three categories. For example, if a student asked a classmate how to spell a word, the utterance was both heuristic and interactional. Once Anna, referring to why she had two drafts of the same story of her paper, said, "I keep messing them up." This utterance was personal, interactional (she said it to the researcher), and informative.

The findings in this study are consistent with those of two other studies (Goldstone, 1983; Kasten & Clarke, 1987), which also found only rare occur-

TABLE 4.3: Halliday's Functions of Oral Language During Writing: Third Grade

Function	Frequency (%)
Interactional	31.3
Informative	17.0
Heuristic	18.6
Personal	6.9
Instrumental	3.2
Regulatory	0.5
Imaginative	0.5
Undetermined*	22.2

*Field notes insufficient to determine function.

rences of language that could be described as imaginative but noted frequent incidences of interactional, informative, and heuristic language accompanying elementary classroom writing and other academic tasks. Further research may examine whether the nature of the assignment, the focus of the writing process, or other factors influence the functions of talk during writing.

Two types of oral language that I observed during the process of writing in elementary classrooms are not included in Halliday's functional categories, since his studies did not involve a relationship between oral language and writing: subvocalizing and reading aloud.

It is not unusual for writing researchers to observe students subvocalizing. Certain student writers subvocalize extensively and consistently, but other young writers subvocalize only occasionally. Anna subvocalized almost constantly, and other writers we studied subvocalized often when they were reading their emerging text or while revising (Kasten, 1984/1985, 1990).

Subvocalizing and reading aloud in concert with writing seem to fit into Vygotsky's description (1978, p. 2) of an intrapersonal function of language. This is language that we direct toward ourselves to assist in the cognitive, problem-solving roles of everyday life, as when revising a text (Kasten, 1984/1985, 1990). This function is not unlike what adults do when they choose to read a difficult passage aloud from a textbook or computer manual or to review aloud while studying for a difficult exam.

Subvocalizing seems to be both normal and helpful within the process of writing. In contrast, guidelines for teaching reading have often suggested that subvocalizing is a possible crutch or handicap that should be extinguished. Subvocalizing during reading was thought to "reduce speed, and for that reason [to be] a stumbling block in the attainment of mastery of silent reading" (Durkin, 1976, p. 195).

The evidence presented here seems to suggest that within the writing process, subvocalizing is a varied and individual activity that at times seems to assist the writer in solving writing-related problems. In some circumstances, even adult writers (and readers) subvocalize, as Murray described in the busy newsroom (1982) and in his comments about the importance of a writer "hearing" his or her words (1989) as a part of rehearsing. Adult and developing writers subvocalize for similar reasons.

Throughout our observations, students were also observed reading stories aloud regularly and in different contexts. Sometimes they read aloud to themselves; sometimes they read to share with their classmates or teachers; sometimes they read aloud over another student's shoulder to see what the latter was writing, or were asked to read aloud the writing of another student. We heard comments like "Can I hear your story?" or "Now you listen to mine."

Reading aloud served different purposes; sometimes, for instance, it seemed to have Halliday's interactional function, because the sharing of the writing was deliberate and was being enjoyed by two or more classmates. At other times, the student writer appeared to use reading aloud as a strategy to solve a writing problem, such as making a decision about revision or how to continue a story. In these cases, the occurrences were related to Halliday's heuristic function of language. Other occurrences of reading aloud seemed to represent an intrapersonal function of language; the reader/writer seemed to be rehearsing the writing with self as audience in order to consider it more consciously, to see if it "sounded right." In these cases, the reading aloud had both an intrapersonal function and a heuristic one; the act of hearing the words had a powerful influence on the writer's decision making. As mentioned earlier, Murray (1989) talks about the importance of rehearsal and the act of reading aloud. "Hearing is a way of knowing for the writer" (p. 55). Again, we as researchers observed aspects of these children's writing processes that were not unlike our own.

Observations of Anna illustrate the heuristic and intrapersonal functions of reading aloud and of subvocalizing. One of Anna's stories from third grade, in its final version, read:

> One day I went to space to see how it looks. I did not know where I was going because I did not make plans. I fell asleep and when I woke up I was on Mars. I said, "What I was [was I] doing here?" Every time I looked out I said "hi" but no one said anything. So I went and returned to Earth.

Watch Anna's use of reading aloud and subvocalizing as I describe how her text emerged. Anna wrote "One day I went into space," at the same time subvocalizing each word or syllable before writing it down. She continued to write "to see," audibly pronouncing it as she wrote. She reread aloud what she had written so far, and then added "how it looks." She whispered *looks* as she worked. As she continued writing, she audibly rehearsed each word of her next line: "I did not NOW [know] where I was going DECAUSE [because] I did not make plans."

Anna continued to subvocalize as she resumed: "I fell A SLEEP [asleep] and WHAN [when] I WINE [woke] up I was on Mars I said what I was [was I] doing HER [here]." Still subvocalizing, she continued to write "EVAR [every] time I looked out," her pronunciation of *out* clearly audible. At this point she stopped writing and reread her last phrase. She reread the phrase a second time and then softly rehearsed her next selections.

Next she wrote "I said and said WHARE [where] am" (writing *am* by first writing the *m* and then adding the *a* as if she'd originally planned to write a different word). She wrote "I," subvocalizing consistently, then audibly reread much of what she had written, this time pointing to each word as she read it. She returned to the line above and scratched out *and*, using *it* as a replacement. Then she scratched out "said WHARE [where] am I," and reread what was left.

There was a long pause, and the researcher asked, "What are you thinking about?" Anna replied, "What to say next." She continued writing "but NOONE [no one] said ANTHINE [anything]." The researcher requested that she read aloud her last few words (to verify what the words were). At this point Anna was still subvocalizing every word she wrote. She resumed, "So I went. And ROND [returned] to Earth." Anna reread part of her text again, this time silently and with no observable mouth movements, and in the process placed a period after "I looked out" in an earlier line. Anna's story was complete.

As a relatively inexperienced writer, Anna's speech may have been more vital to the creation of a story than for a more experienced writer, for whom the process might be much more subtle. Vygotsky (1978) explains that "just as a mold gives shape to a substance, words can shape an activity into a structure" (p. 28). Anna utilized her own speech to spawn her emerging text carefully, step by step, using oral and written language in a vital, interrelated fashion.

Vygotsky goes on to explain that the structure may be changed or reshaped when children learn to use language in ways that allow them to go "beyond previous experience when planning future action" (1978, p. 28). Anna would likely, with experience, use her speech more internally and more effectively for planning instead of relying on it to structure and guide her entire writing episode, as well as learn to read more silently, without mouth movements. Vygotsky similarly suggests that the result of a developing child's using internal speech as a planning function is that the child will "acquire the ability to engage in complex operations extending over time" (1978, p. 28). Field notes on Anna a year after this particular episode showed far fewer incidences of observable subvocalizing.

USING CLASSROOM RESOURCES

Children are very resourceful in a classroom environment when they need information such as how to spell a word or what to name a character in a story. The resources that children use to fill their needs as they write can be either human or inanimate. The inanimate resources we observed included dictionaries, pictures, cursive penmanship charts, trade books, bulletin boards, and other print sources in the classroom. Children used their classmates, teachers, teacher aides, and other people they encountered in the classroom or school community as human resources.

I examined the field notes taken during all the writing episodes we observed in order to categorize resources used by the students and found that they used resources of some kind a total of 575 times. Nearly all the resource use was related to questions about how to spell words or to confirm the spelling of words already written. A small amount of resource use, about 5 percent, pertained to issues concerning the use of punctuation, capitalization, handwriting, or story content. Although the most frequently used inanimate resources were dictionaries, trade books, chalkboards, and bulletin boards, children also used more unusual things such as wall charts, classroom mailboxes, calendars, book bags, posters, previous pieces of their own writing, and accessible pieces of writing from their classmates. Two interesting examples of resource use included an instance in which a child found the spelling for the word *off* on the classroom light switch, and another instance in which a child found the spelling for the name of Baboquivari Mountain (namesake of one of the schools) on a school bus parked outside the classroom window. In the course of the two-year study, there was only one incident of a student attempting to use a spelling book to find the spelling of a word; it proved unsuccessful and the child abandoned the attempt.

The students in this study used human resources more often than inanimate ones. Most often, they used (or attempted to use) researchers who were sitting next to them, despite the fact that they would almost never get a specific answer to their questions. (Typically a child would ask the researchers how to spell a word, and the researcher's response would be "Do the best you can" or "What do you think?")

Classmates were the next most frequently used resource, with both teachers and aides being asked for help occasionally. Students used human resources most because they found them readily available and accessible. They were typically successful in finding help whenever they asked for it (with the exception of the researchers, because of their special role). Someone nearby often knew how to spell the word that the writer was asking about, and student writers did not hesitate to help one another when interaction was permitted. Students made use of the knowledge that was available in their community of writers. They often seemed to know who would be most useful to help them solve their problems or answer their questions.

Students using print resources that were readily available and accessible such as trade books, bulletin boards, classroom posters, and other print were also frequently successful in their attempts to find out how to spell the words they wanted. They were not always quite as productive in their use of dictionaries and encyclopedias. The students sometimes initiated the use of such reference materials themselves and were sometimes referred to them by their teacher. Vincent used or attempted to use a dictionary more often than some of the other students; the following anecdote is representative.

It was February 18, and Vincent was writing a "tall tale," the writing assignment for the day. He chose to write about Pecos Bill, the American folk hero. When he reached the third line of his story, he was unsure of how to spell *cyclone*. He began by asking the nearby researcher, "How do you spell cyclone?" Remembering that the researcher would not be likely to answer his question, he said immediately, "Oh, never mind." He got out a dictionary and looked through it while classmate Chris was talking to him.

Vincent said aloud that it would probably be under "C-I." Off on the wrong track, Vincent had little hope of finding *cyclone* on his own. The researcher decided to subtly steer him toward the correct page and column. Vincent, successfully locating the word, asked, "Does there have to be a little dot in the middle?" (noticing the dot used to divide into syllables). Two words later in his emerging text, Vincent needed to know how to spell *mad*. He again began to use the dictionary but became discouraged, abandoned his attempt, and was content to spell the word in his own way.

Two lines later, Vincent needed to spell *saddle* and looked in the dictionary. He started at the beginning of the *s* section and looked at every entry, finally locating *saddle* on the second page of the section. He seemed to be enjoying playing with the dictionary. Two words later, he was back in the *s* section looking for the word *stiff*; unable to find it, he wrote STIF.

At this point, the researcher asked him if it would be a good idea to check his spelling in the dictionary. "It's too hard," he replied. The researcher offered to help him, and with minimal assistance, he located *stiff*, returned to his story, and added the second *f*.

Two words later, Vincent could not remember how to spell *does*. He wanted to look it up but expressed confusion about how to begin. The researcher again encouraged him. When he finally saw *does* in print, he didn't quite believe that D-O-E-S could spell the word *does*.

The writing center where Vincent had been working on his story typically lasted half an hour. Vincent had devoted a considerable amount of his allotted time to using the dictionary. It was evident that his skill at using the dictionary was not sufficient for him to be successful when working entirely alone. With minimal help from the researcher, Vincent became somewhat more successful in finding what he needed to spell.

Throughout the study, when researchers observed students being successful at using the dictionary, they were often using the reference books in pairs or small groups. This seemed to be a useful strategy, both for the social benefits and for a more successful use of these more difficult resources. Collaboration promoted the more successful use of reference books throughout our observations.

In Sr. Susan Caldwell's pre-fourth-grade class, the children's use of resources increased in comparison to resource use in the previous year's third-grade class. Darlene Pagett's regular fourth-grade class, however, used resources and reference books less than the third graders. The two fourth-grade classrooms had very different environments in general. Darlene used primarily whole-group instruction; student movement around the class was restricted, as were talking and opportunities for collaboration. Resources and reference books were stored in assigned places where they were expected to remain when not being used.

In contrast, Sr. Susan's classroom was organized so that students could move around freely. Collaborations and small-group or even individual projects were strongly encouraged. Reference books were on a handy cart, and students were encouraged to take them to their tables. The children in this class not only used reference books more, but they also revised their texts more than the other fourth graders did. The use of reference books often led directly to changes in the text (Kasten, 1984/1985).

It was in this environment that the students' ability to judge easy and hard dictionaries came to light. Sr. Susan not only encouraged flexible use of reference materials, she also made available a variety of different dictionaries that represented a range of difficulties, sizes, shapes, and formats. On one occasion, Gordon wrote "One day a man was," then went to a standard elementary school dictionary and said, "I know how to spell [the word I want]: 'S-R-round,' then 'E-D.'" When he couldn't find it, he said, "I'll write it that way anyway, but then looked in a picture dictionary to confirm the spelling of *round*. He then wrote "SRROUNDED by a g" and returned to the elementary school dictionary for *gang*. He wasn't very systematic in his search strategy, but eventually found *gang* and copied it out. His comments indicated that he was sensitive to which dictionaries had harder and easier words and was therefore selective in dictionary use. At moments such as these, a lesson on dictionary use can support a child's interests and needs. Opportunities to use a variety of resource materials for a variety of purposes support young writers in learning new and useful ways to take advantage of such materials.

Most resource use in this study was tied to students' desire to spell conventionally, which can be related to students' conceptualizations about spelling. The children considered spelling to be a very important part of writing. Whether or not the teachers intended to convey this attitude, it was clearly prevalent. Vincent's comments reflected this pressure for correctness in one of our concepts of writing interviews. In Vincent's interview on October 27 of third grade, he was asked, "Who's a good writer that you know?"

> *Vincent:* Mike. He's helpful. He can spell.
> *Researcher:* What does a good writer need to know to write well?
> *Vincent:* Spell. Practice writing.
> *Researcher:* How can you tell when someone is a bad writer?
> *Vincent:* They misspell words.
> *Researcher:* How do you decide that what you wrote is good?
> *Vincent:* [The] spelling's okay.

It is not surprising then that Vincent and his classmates put a great deal of effort during writing time into the issue of correct spelling. Teachers need to be aware of the messages they give to their students through what they have implicitly or explicitly praised or valued. As Vincent and his classmates learned more about the writing process, it is hoped that they learned to value their meaning and intent and see spelling as an editing function. An overemphasis on spelling, especially during first-draft writing, can hamper the making of meaning in a community of writers.

LEARNING IN COLLABORATION

Recently, teachers and other educators have started to promote the value of learning in collaboration. This notion was developed by Vygotsky (1978) in his discussion of the "zone of proximal development" (p. 84) as a region within learning that represents the difference between what a learner can do all alone in problem solving and what he or she can do with others.

Throughout our study, there were many examples of children's helping one another solve issues during writing, whether it involved deciding what to write about, spelling or punctuation, or clarifying expectations for an assignment. It is through the medium of oral language that this rich, purposeful interaction occurs. When oral language is prohibited in the classroom, these avenues of learning are not available. This was evident in the contrast between the two fourth grades. In one, which was structured and restricted children's talk and movement to prescribed times, we observed collaboration only rarely. In the other fourth-grade classroom, where children were encouraged to help one another and move around the room purposefully and responsibly, there were many rich incidents of effective collaboration.

Elementary school children struggle with dictionaries, encyclopedias, unfamiliar punctuation, and spelling. The opportunity for collaboration is not only an appropriate learning strategy when using such resources but a vital one. Teachers who cling to notions about children's needing to "do their own work" may actually be hampering valuable learning.

SUMMARY

Oral language, using resources in the classroom, and collaborating during writing all help to form the community of writers in elementary school classrooms. The language and interaction that accompany writing play an important role as children learn more about the making of meaning in written language.

In summary, my analysis of oral language experiences and resource use provides evidence that this community of writers:

1. Was mostly "on task," as revealed by the examination of children's utterances during writing;
2. Used oral language as part of prewriting to discuss topics, name characters, use various resources, help one another spell words, and explore punctuation, capitalization, or grammatical questions;
3. Used oral language to reconsider or confirm writing, as they checked spellings, punctuations, and capitalizations, or read aloud their stories to interested listeners in the classroom;
4. Used their peers, teachers, paraprofessionals, and researchers as audiences for their writing; and
5. Collaborated with their peers and others in the classroom to use resources and to solve writing issues.

In the classroom milieu, where there are no walls between students, a community of writers at work will use all the available resources, human and otherwise, to help them solve their writing problems. Reading, writing, listening, and speaking, which are all dynamically present and functioning, are the media through which this community works. Students are in control of their own emerging written text, using oral and written language as well as external resources to assist them in accomplishing their task. Accordingly, the classroom milieu with its community of writers becomes a "whole language" environment, since the processes of reading, writing, listening, and speaking are occurring naturally and for real, authentic purposes.

Classroom management styles, availability and accessibility of resources, and teacher encouragement are all factors in how students solve their writing problems within their community. In this context, control over writing grows, and the confidence to become a writer is established.

CHAPTER 5

Pronoun Use in the Work of Young Writers

"HE GOT HOME BEFORE HE COULD GET HIM"

Suzanne Gespass

A NUMBER OF YEARS AGO when the Miami Dolphins were in the Super Bowl, my three-year-old nephew Gregory wandered into the room where his father was watching the game. As part of the conversation, Greg's father said to him, "Miami is winning." Gregory found some blocks and began to play. Five minutes into his playing, he looked up at his father and asked, "Is your ami still winning?"

This language story points out how easily we, as language users, manipulate the seemingly complicated pronoun system of English. That a three-year-old has no difficulty shifting perspective and using the appropriate possessive pronoun is remarkable here only because of the obvious misunderstanding. If the conversation had been, "My team is winning," and Greg had later asked, "Is your team still winning?" the whole dialogue would have gone unnoticed because we expect even three-year-olds to control, for the most part, the pronoun system. And although the focus of this chapter is pronouns, any other feature of the grammar could be used to demonstrate the powerful control children have of language.

PRONOUNS IN READING AND IN WRITING

In this chapter I discuss the control and use of pronouns in the writing of the six third and fourth graders who are the subject of this book. I focus on the extent of pronoun use, strategies for establishing reference, identification of pronoun ambiguity, and the conditions that influence choice of pronouns. I believe that some background information related to this will help clarify what prompted me to investigate how these young Tohono O'odham writers used pronouns. The story of this part of the research begins with my own theoretical orientation to reading and writing.

The strongest influence I had in arriving at this orientation is the work of Kenneth Goodman (e.g., K. & Y. Goodman, 1978; K. Goodman, 1984), which states that reading is a sociopsycholinguistic process whereby the reader is engaged in transactions with texts that are always embedded in a situational context. This view has been supported by extensive research in miscue analysis. (See Marek and Goodman, 1985, for an annotated bibliography of studies using miscue analysis.) Miscue analysis looks at the process of comprehending text through an analysis of how the observed response in a person's oral reading differs from the expected response. Each miscue is coded by asking a set of hierarchically arranged questions that determine the degree to which that miscue is acceptable in relation to the cuing systems of language: the semantic, the syntactic, the graphophonic, and the pragmatic.

Miscue analysis has three main purposes: to provide insight into the reading process, to understand the strengths and strategies of a specific reader, and to analyze texts (Y. Goodman, Watson & Burke, 1987). I was involved in a study conducted by Kenneth Goodman (K. Goodman & Gespass, 1983a, 1983b) that used miscue analysis for the third purpose, to analyze text. We used a large preexisting miscue data base that provided the necessary information to look at text from the point of view of the reader. In that study we could look at how real readers read real texts. If the readers were making the same kinds of miscues in the same places of a particular text, if there were predictable patterns of miscues in certain texts, if certain text features consistently generated more or less miscue activity, certainly this could add to our knowledge of texts. It made sense that the types of miscues these readers made could shed light on how texts hold together and how meaning is constructed. What resulted was a research project that looked at text structures as they related to patterns of miscues.

One of these patterns was directly related to an aspect of text cohesion, the elements in connected discourse that hold it together (Halliday & Hasan, 1976); this feature is known as reference. Reference is a necessary element in text cohesion. Referring expressions such as personal pronouns and determiners are what carry a text along and eliminate redundancy. Each time a writer uses an available linguistic device to point to information that is available elsewhere in the text or context, that writer is demonstrating the ability to effectively and efficiently use the language. As an example we can look at the way Dana accomplished this. He began a piece, "Once there lived a warrior. His name was Running Bear. He liked to shoot birds for his dinner." Dana used the possessive pronoun *his* in the second sentence to indicate that it was the warrior's name and the personal pronoun *he* in the third sentence to refer to Running Bear.

This investigation of reference in text cohesion led to a new research project that concentrated on examining the miscues on pronouns (K. Goodman & Gespass, 1983a, 1983b). There is a body of literature in the field of reading comprehension that has looked at how pronouns are processed in reading. Most of these studies have looked at anaphoric relationships, which have to do with the way pronouns are linked to nouns. Some of these reading studies suggest that (1) children have trouble comprehending anaphora, defined as the use of a grammatical substitute to refer to a preceding word, such as a pronoun's referring back to a noun (e.g., Bormuth, Carr, Manning & Pearson, 1970; Richek, 1976–77); (2) the comprehension of anaphora is developmental (e.g., Barnitz, 1979; Chapman, 1981); and (3) direct instruction of anaphoric relationships will lead to improved reading comprehension (e.g., Bauman & Stevenson, 1986).

The conclusions of many of these studies carry instructional implications that lead to the direct teaching of pronoun referents as a discrete and identifiable skill. Thus many of the skills pages in reading workbooks ask students to trace pronoun referents, identify antecedents, find the word or phrase that stands for a particular pronoun, and so on.

Our study of reading (K. Goodman & Gespass, 1983a, 1983b) that looked at readers' responses to texts through their miscues challenged these views (at least in terms of pronominal anaphora), suggesting rather that (1) the percentage of miscues on pronouns is quite small; (2) the comprehension of anaphora is as much situation-dependent as it is developmental; (3) readers expect pronouns to occur in text and immediately assign reference; and (4) direct instruction of anaphoric relationships is unnecessary and can even be confusing. Pollock (1985/1986) and Freeman (1986, 1988) confirmed and extended these conclusions by using the same miscue data to analyze how pronoun reference is assigned.

At the same time as this reading research was taking place I was also involved in the research project conducted by Yetta Goodman that is the focus of this book. In looking at data from this project, it became obvious to me that there were certain patterns in these young writers' use of pronouns that were similar to the miscues on pronouns that we had explored in the reading study. All the writers were using many pronouns, and all seemed to be in control of the knowledge that the use of pronouns is necessary to the meaningful production of text. The kinds of questions I began to ask were: How and when does a writer decide to use a pronoun instead of a noun? How does a writer decide how much shared information the reader possesses? What pronouns are used by developing writers under different circumstances and in varying contexts?

The earlier study of readers' responses to pronouns demonstrated that all real texts must include reference and that all readers, no matter how young or inexperienced, must and do find ways of assigning reference in their reading. Tasks that involve readers transacting with relatively natural texts, as in the miscue analysis study, provide rich examples to explore readers' responses to pronouns.

The data supplied by the writing project research met similar criteria for richness, including the relatively unconstrained production of written pieces and a large enough corpus to provide opportunities for a wide range of pronouns to occur. In addition, the data were collected in such a way as to provide detailed observations of the context in which the writing took place. The children's writing was done over a period of time and in a variety of contexts. The texts produced, although constrained by the general "school" context, were not produced for the sole purpose of looking at pronoun use.

In order to answer my questions about children's use of pronouns, I worked with 210 texts from the children we studied. I coded each pronoun for person, number, gender, and case and identified how pronouns were linked to noun phrases so that I could account for distance. I traced the chain of reference for each character or object referred to through the text it was part of and flagged pronoun ambiguities.

The following text was written by Dana when he was in third grade:

> One day in the wild west a cowboy went to the bank and got some money. He got lots of money that a robber and his horse wanted to get him. But he got home before he could get him. But he shot him instead and missed him. So he went to the bank and robbed it with his horse and broke the window and ran away with his money. The police were going to get him before he got away but the sheriff came out of the jail and got him and put him in jail. Before they could put him in jail they knew that they got the wrong one. So they had to look again for the real robber. Then they found him and put him in jail and that was the end of the robber.

What can we say about Dana's piece? That it rambles, that it is incoherent, and that the cause of all this is because he doesn't use pronoun referents appropriately? One thing is certain. Dana himself had no trouble differentiating the characters in the story. For him, the pronouns were not at all ambiguous. It would have been impossible for him to continue writing for as long as he did if he were confused about the referents or sensed confusion on the part of the reader.

This text does, however, have more pronoun ambiguities than any of the other 209 texts analyzed. There are several factors that contribute to the relatively large amount of pronoun ambiguity in this story. First, there are at least two male characters, a cowboy and a robber. Second, there is a series of events that include a number of actions that take place over a stretch of time. Third, there is a semantic complexity that compounds the ambiguity, a mistaken identity: The police thought it was the cowboy who robbed the bank, not the robber.

Dana's text had more ambiguity than any other text we looked at, yet what makes this especially interesting is that Dana was identified by both his teachers and the team of researchers as the most proficient writer of the six students in the study.

Dana's next text, written only one week later, had no pronoun ambiguity:

> One day Sam took his horse for a walk in the woods. Sam was going hunting for deers. He saw a lost horse. So he took it with him to his barn and gave him some food. He named him Todd. Then he put Todd in the barn.

In this text, Dana utilized what I found to be the most common strategy for establishing reference: that of naming. We know that Sam is the main character in this text. When Dana wanted to introduce another male character, this time a horse, he reduced the chances of ambiguity by naming the horse Todd and then referring to him by name in the next sentence instead of using a pronoun.

In written language, appropriate use of pronouns is governed by the amount and type of information the writer believes the reader has. In order for the writer to know whether a pronoun can be used or whether the noun phrase should be repeated instead, the writer must be able to adopt the viewpoint of the reader. In the analysis that follows, I look at various aspects of the children's control, use, and choice of pronouns.

FREQUENCY AND DISTRIBUTION OF PRONOUNS

Prompted by my interest in the reading miscue research on pronouns, I first wanted to investigate the nature and extent of pronouns used in the children's writing. To do this I looked at the frequency and distribution of pronouns in the children's writing. I found what I expected; these beginning writers did employ the full range of pronouns.

I expected this because of a general language principle of economy developed by Grice (1975) and elaborated by Goodman (K. Goodman & Gespass, 1983a, 1983b). This rule states that in order for language to function efficiently, one must be able to distinguish introductory (new) information from repeated (given) information. We expect that pronouns will be used in place of nouns whenever possible. For example, Anna wrote, "One day there was *a girl. Her* name was *Flower. She* was a nice girl. *Her* mother was nice to *her.* One day *they* went to get syrup from the cactus." After Anna introduced "a girl," she subsequently referred to her with the pronouns *she* and *her.* This signals the reader that the girl has already been introduced. (See Miller, Bartlett & Hirst, 1982, for a detailed account of how this works.) Pronouns exist in the language as part of a pervasive tendency to avoid redundancy and to say as much as (but no more than) needs to be said. The system works because listeners and readers are able, usually, to make inferences, assign appropriate referents and co-referents where needed, and build a meaningful text within an appropriate context. The fact that this system works and is so pervasive demonstrates how little is explicit in language and how much depends on inference.

Pronouns made up 15.6 percent of the 13,666 words the children wrote that were analyzed in this project. The pronoun frequency in these students' texts was higher than that in the basal reader texts we examined in our study of reading (K. Goodman & Gespass, 1983a, 1983b), where pronouns made up 10.1 percent of the words in three stories. This led me to question why the Tohono O'odham children used pronouns more than the professional authors of basal readers.

As my analysis continued, the answer to this question emerged. Nearly half the texts the children produced over the two years were personal narratives, compared to only one of the three stories from the basal readers. In their personal narratives, the children often used the first-person pronouns *I* and *we*. The other reason these young writers used so many pronouns was an overgeneralization of the rule of economy. This happened because of the children's tendency to merge the text and the context (such as a picture they were writing about). They sometimes erroneously (and perhaps unconsciously) believed that the audience had the same amount of information the author did, so they often used a pronoun rather than an introductory noun phrase to refer to something. An example occurred when the third-grade students were asked to write a report about one of the United States. Since they were using resources such as encyclopedias as they wrote, many of the students used pronouns to refer to pictures, without an introductory noun phrase. Looking at a picture, they assumed that anyone who read the piece of writing would also have the picture available.

The distribution of pronoun use in the children's writing depended on the genre, the stance of the narrator, and the amount of dialogue used. The young writers used pronouns in all persons, numbers, genders, and cases. Some of my more specific findings include:

1. Pronouns were used most often as nominatives (e.g., *I* or *she*) and least often as objects (e.g., *me* or *them*).
2. First-person pronouns like *I* and third-person pronouns like *it* were used in approximately the same proportion; the second-person pronoun forms of *you* were used less often.
3. Personal pronouns were used about eight times more often than proper names.

A fuller discussion of these findings appears in Gespass, 1989/1990.

ESTABLISHING REFERENCE

One of the most useful strategies the young writers employed to establish what a pronoun referred to and to disambiguate what could be potentially ambiguous was to name. In order to understand how the children used pronouns as co-referents (alternative names for a character or object), it was necessary to discover how they established reference in the first place. As it turned out, these young writers were much more likely to use a proper name than to differentiate noun phrases through various kinds of modification (e.g., they would refer to "Bob" rather than "the dying man"). Once they established the reference with the insertion of a name, they were then likely to use pronouns as co-referents in the rest of the piece.

Proper names have very clear reference. There is a brief period in very early oral language development when children who are learning to talk use more names than pronouns. This is presumably because the names of people stay the same but pronouns change depending on who is speaking and who is being referred to. It is interesting to examine the relationship between proper names and pronouns in the children's writing. (The proportion of proper names used by individual children remained fairly consistent across the two years. Gordon used the most names, a total of 107; Elaine used the least, a total of 28.)

The following examples from the children's texts demonstrate individual differences in decisions to use names or pronouns. In third grade, Anna produced a series of texts in which an introductory noun phrase was subsequently made more explicit by a proper name.

February 4

One day *a girl* was named *Sally*. *She* was a pretty girl. One day *she* was taking a nap. A mad pirate got *her*. He went . . . and got *Sally*. *She* [thought] *she* was at home. But when *she* woke up *she* was scared. At home, the father tried to call for *her*. But they kill the queen.

February 9

One day *a bear* did not know if it was winter so *he* kept saying "is it winter?" *His* name was *Jo*. *He* was going to sleep.

February 23

One day there was *a girl*. *Her* name was *Flower*. *She* was a nice girl. *Her* mother wasn't nice to *her*. One day they went to get syrup from the cactus. In the morning, they had syrup and bread. The End.

February 25

One day there was *a boy* named *Warrior*. *He* liked to walk in the desert. One day *he* got a jumping sticker. A coyote helped *him*. *He* said, "Thank you."

March 2

Once upon a time there was *a girl. Her* name was *Elaine. She* was a nice girl. *She* lived in a house in Kansas with *her* brother Micah. One day there was a terrible . . .

March 4

One day there was *a girl. Her* name was *Maxine. She* was a nice girl. One day *her* mother said, "Go give your grandmother some food." *She* said, "OK." So *she* went on the way. On the way *she* met a wolf. The wolf said, "Hi."

The above examples were written as part of an assigned unit on fairy tales. They illustrate that Anna had seized upon a comfortable pattern to begin her pieces. She used a conventional story beginning, usually of the type "One day," and then introduced a noun phrase followed by a proper name. Most of the texts were about girls, but she also used a boy (Warrior) and a bear (Jo). The first example of this series is the only one in which Anna reintroduced the proper name (Sally). It was also the most ambitious and the most ambiguous of the series. The main character in the text is Sally, who is introduced in the first sentence and is the subject of the second and third sentences, where she is referred to as "she." In the fourth sentence a new character is introduced (a mad pirate), and Sally becomes the object, referred to as "her." The pirate ("he") is the subject of the fifth sentence, of which Sally is the object, referred to by name. In the next two sentences, Sally remains the subject and is referred to as "she." It is at this point that the piece becomes ambiguous. A definite noun phrase is used in the eighth sentence without a previous introduction ("the father"), and the last sentence contains two references that have not been previously introduced ("they" and "the queen"). It seems as if Anna knew to whom "the father" and "they" and "the queen" referred but did not choose to include this information in the written text.

Referring to a new, unknown character by using a definite article or a pronoun is one kind of anomaly that existed in the students' writing. Usually one would use an expression like "the father" or "they" only to refer to a previously introduced character unless more explanation were provided, but the children sometimes did not follow this principle. I was interested in finding out whether I could identify when this happened most frequently. Some of my findings are addressed in the section related to influences of genre and assignment.

The remaining texts in Anna's series followed much the same pattern. There is an introduction of the main character, the naming of the main character, the introduction of a second character, and the beginning of some event that may or may not include dialogue. This series of Anna's writings serves to illustrate an important feature found in the writing of all six children. There is a proclivity for naming even when, given the constraints of the specific texts, a proper name would not be necessary. Although it seemed important for these young writers to name, they did not unnecessarily repeat the proper name but instead used pronouns very efficiently and appropriately. There is an additional point to be made about this series of Anna's texts. Only one (February 25) used a conjoined subject to introduce a character ("One day there was *a boy named Warrior*"). In most of the other texts, Anna used two separate sentences to accomplish the naming of the character. The clause embedding that created the double subject in the Warrior story is a more sophisticated construction and may also explain why, as clause embeddings become more prevalent in writing, the use of some pronouns can be reduced. This is another example, from a slightly different perspective, of how the principle of economy in language is always functioning.

The following example from Dana illustrates how naming works to clarify previous text that may be considered ambiguous:

> Nov. 18, 1620. Micah Antone was very nice to his crew. He was their captain. He told them what to do. One day one of his men was going to die. The women got *Bob*; *that was his name*. They were taking care of Bob. Micah was there too with Bob.

In this example, Dana had a problem in the fifth sentence, where he used a definite noun phrase, "the women," that had not been previously introduced. He then used the proper name "Bob" but apparently recognized immediately that this reference had to be clarified, so he inserted a little addendum: "that was his name." This is presumably a device that Dana carried over from oral language. From that point on, Dana referred to both male characters by their proper names. It is obvious that Dana knew how to use pronouns but chose not to in this circumstance. It may be presumed that he knew that something in his text needed clarification, and that this was a deliberate strategy to specify. The problem in reference, however, lies neither with "Micah" nor with "Bob," but rather with "the women," never clarified within this text.

Of the six children, four used this or a similar strategy, supplying information by insertion of a name when they sensed that a referent might have been ambiguous to readers of the text. Only one child seemed to repeat proper names for reasons other than clarification or stylistic emphasis. (See *More More More Said the Baby* [Williams, 1990] for an example of a children's book that repeats proper names as a stylistic device.) Gordon tended to use an increased proportion of proper names when he was writing about historical or legendary characters. He did this for Jesus and Santa (both in stories written in fourth grade) and in the following example from February of fourth grade:

> One day when *Paul Bunyan* was going to play baseball, *he* forgot to comb *his* hair. Then *Paul Bunyan* went back and combed *his* hair.

> Then *Paul Bunyan* went back to play baseball. But when *Paul Bunyan*
> was walking to the baseball field, *he* saw a mouse and *Paul Bunyan's*
> hair flew up in the air. And *Paul Bunyan* ran home and *he* never
> combed *his* hair.

In this piece, Gordon's use of the proper name, Paul Bunyan, always occurred
at the beginning of sentences. He did use the pronoun *he* to refer to Paul Bunyan, but only if the proper name had already been used at least once in the
same sentence.

The relationship of proper names to pronouns in the children's writing
may be summarized by the following points:

1. All the students used pronouns to replace proper names in subsequent text, except where ambiguity would result or where the proper name
was repeated as a stylistic variation or for emphasis.

2. The students had a proclivity for naming. The insertion or addition of a
proper name appeared to be a useful strategy for clarification when (a) a second or third character was about to be introduced; (b) a second or third character had already been introduced and there was a need to differentiate them;
(c) the writer sensed confusion due to a totally unrelated ambiguity; or (d) the
writer wished to personalize the narrative in order to engage the intended audience.

3. There were no strong differences in the proportionate use of names
and pronouns among the six children or across the two years, with the exception of Gordon's extensive use of proper names for legendary characters (in
contexts where a pronoun would have been sufficient).

GENRE INFLUENCES

The extent of genre-related pronoun ambiguities had less to do with different text types than with specific assignments within a particular genre. I
expected that genre would influence the amount and kind of pronoun ambiguity. More specifically, I expected that genres with which the writers were most
familiar and most experienced would yield fewer pronoun ambiguities than
those genres that were new to them.

I found that pronoun ambiguities in the children's writing could not be
simply correlated with text type or genre. Pronoun ambiguities tended to
cluster in the children's writing when the writer was uncomfortable with a particular assignment, when the writer was swept up in the momentum of a piece
and did no revision, or when the writer was trying to do something new or
syntactically more complex than usual. Although the relative frequency of

pronoun ambiguity in the children's expository texts was greater than that in their narratives, this cannot be attributed solely to inexperience in expository writing.

The following sections examine different types of texts and describe where and when the clustering of pronoun ambiguity tended to occur.

Letters

These developing writers had no difficulty with the use of the specific pronouns needed to write a letter. They were familiar with the conventional form for letter writing and used *I* and *you* appropriately in their sender/receiver functions.

Of the 210 texts I looked at, 16 (about 8 percent) were letters, categorized as follows:

Self-initiated letters	3
Pen pal letters (assigned)	9
Thank-you letters (assigned)	2
Imaginary letters (assigned)	2

There were no reference ambiguities in the self-initiated letters or the letters written to pen pals. When they were in third grade, two children wrote thank-you notes to a group of older students who had performed for the class around Halloween. These thank-you notes were assigned:

Dear Ghouls,
    I liked *your program* very much and thank you for coming to our school today. It was fun being scared by you. Are you coming next year? I hope you do.
Love, Dana

Dear Ghouls,
    I really like *it*. Our class was scared, real scared. *It* [It's] good. *It* was fun but when you came in, *it* really was scary. I think *it* was scary. I liked *the program*.
From, Anna

Dana's letter is a straightforward thank-you note. In the first sentence he used the possessive "your" (referring to ghouls), which is a strong cohesive tie since it serves both as a determiner for "program" and as a co-referent to the ghouls in the salutation of the letter.

In contrast, Anna's letter began with an ambiguous use of "it" as the object of the verb "like." "It's" becomes the subject of the third sentence, but the reference is still not established. The "it" of "It was fun" may refer to the program or it may (more likely) refer to the general experience of seeing the program. This use of "it" is maintained for the rest of the text until the last sentence. Remarkably, in the final line Anna did make the reference explicit and used the noun phrase "the program," presumably the reference for the preceding pronouns. As the text developed and meaning was built, this writer was ultimately able to clarify any ambiguity that might have existed.

There is one more point to address in this example. Even though Anna's use of "it" at the beginning of the letter could be considered ambiguous, it really wasn't in the context of the communication event. She was writing a letter to the ghouls, who would know exactly what she meant since they had been the performers.

There was another set of letters written by the students that contained ambiguities of a different nature. The ambiguities that arise in the following texts seemed to arise from confusion about the specific assignment. The students were asked to write a condolence letter to Mr. and Mrs. Turkey telling them that their son had been killed for a Thanksgiving dinner. In these instances, the students tended to view the assignment as part of the text in the sense of assuming that the reader would be familiar with it. As a result, the texts standing alone appear to have some ambiguities. The following are examples:

Anna

Dear Mr. and Mrs. Turkey,

I am sorry that your son died in a dinner. I feel sad for you. I think the next Thanksgiving you should hide. But on Thanksgiving I will not eat you because I think you are nice people. I am sorry that your son Bob died.

Vincent

November 17, 1981

I am sorry that your son can't go to the dinner. I never thought that your son had to be the turkey at the Thanksgiving dinner. I felt sorry that day.

In these instances, ambiguities resulted not because of inappropriate use of pronouns within the body of the text, but because of the lack of a closing in Anna's letter and both a heading and a closing in Vincent's letter. Headings and closings constitute the form of a letter and serve to establish the context from which the sender and receiver operate. We know that these students understood the conventional form of writing letters because of previous letters they had written. Because this particular assignment was highly contrived, the students saw no need to make the texts cohesive in terms of designating sender and/or receiver. There was no need because the recipient wasn't real. The only person who would read the letters was the teacher, and since she had given the assignment in the first place, the students saw no need to repeat information that was already present in the wording of the assignment.

In summary, the students generally used pronouns appropriately when they wrote letters. They had no trouble controlling the I-sender, you-receiver aspects of letter writing when the letters were written to real people, asking real questions, and recounting real information. When the assignments asked the students to write letters for which the sole receiver was the teacher rather than a real addressee, pronoun references tended to lie outside the text. Thus the "I" of both Anna's and Vincent's turkey letters was unspecified (since there was no signature), as was the "you" of Vincent's letter (with no salutation).

Two language principles are evident in these examples of the children's writing. The principle of economy is at work because the young writers chose to include in the written text no more than was necessary. They saw no need to repeat information in the written text when that information was available to everyone in the context of the situation. The second principle is that form follows function. When the writing of a letter served an authentic purpose such as communicating with a pen pal or a friend, these young writers either moved toward or attained the conventional form.

Reports

Expositions, especially reports, were among the least successful texts the children produced (Y. Goodman & Wilde, 1985). Writing a report requires obtaining information from one or more sources, selecting what information is to be reported, and then writing it from the writer's own frame of reference. As Bird shows in Chapter 3, it was not always immediately evident which texts were reports, since the students had a tendency to turn a report into a first-person narrative in order to make the assignment more meaningful to them. For instance, students sometimes interjected self-reference into a supposedly expository text, as Rachel did here:

The Saguaro Cactus

I know it grows 50 or 40 feet tall.
It will only grow in May or June.

There were 13 texts that were reports, as shown in Table 5.1. These reports were very short texts, largely between two and four sentences long. Eight of the 13 reports had no pronouns; the assignment itself served as the

TABLE 5.1: Student Reports

	Grade 3		Grade 4	
	Number of Reports*	Average Number of Sentences	Number of Reports	Average Number of Sentences
Anna	2	4	2	7.5
Dana	3	2.7	0	—
Elaine	0	—	0	—
Gordon	1	4	1	2
Rachel	4	3.5	0	—
Vincent	0	—	0	—

*The greater number of reports in third grade was due to assignments.

referent for definite noun phrases within the text, as seen in three examples, all from January of third grade:

Anna   Behind *the seal* is . . .
Gordon   *The green field* stands for . . .
Rachel   *The blue* shows . . .

The definite article in these examples pointed to something in the context of the situation, in this instance the resource materials that the children were using.

Two interesting reports were written by Anna in fourth grade, revealing a strategy of listing as a way of writing a report.

Hawaii

How many islands are there? Oahu, The Aloha Island. Hawaii, The Big Island. Maui, the Valley Island. Kauai, the Garden Island. *They* have a mountain that's called Diamond Head. On the mountain there is a national guard.

In this text, the Hawaiian islands are listed followed by a description. "They" is used as a generalized referent not specified in the text.

In another piece, Anna used the listing strategy again in responding to an assignment that asked for three facts from three different sources.

1. *Saturn* is the second largest planet.
2. *Saturn* is the sixth planet from the sun.
3. *Saturn* is almost bigger than Jupiter.
4. *Saturn* has nine moons.
5. *It's* not a heavy planet.
6. *It* has at least ten moons.
7. *The rings* make *Saturn* look very beautiful.
8. *The rings* are made of icy pieces of rock.
9. *It* also has 15 moons.

Saturn is the subject of the first four sentences. In the fifth and sixth sentences the subject is "it" and refers to Saturn. In the seventh sentence the subject changes to "the rings."

Anna did not have a problem with pronoun reference in this piece. There were, however, some semantic ambiguities related to the number of moons Saturn has. Vaughan (Chapter 7) uses this piece of Anna's to explain how we can learn about writing by looking at the process itself. The conflicting information Anna had to deal with from various reference books regarding the number of Saturn's moons reveals much about her as a writer.

But we can also learn something about the development of writing by looking at this piece from the perspective of pronoun use. What is interesting about this text is that it is numbered like a list, possibly because of the way the assignment was structured. In a list structure, the proper noun "Saturn" is likely to begin each new sentence. And the text appears to start out this way, with the repetition of "Saturn" at the beginning of the first four lines. In the fifth sentence, however, the language rule of economy begins to take hold and the pronoun "it" starts to take the place of the name "Saturn," even in a situation in which the structure of the form presupposes the repetition of the proper name. There appears to be a driving need on the part of the writer to be more efficient; to stop using the noun and to replace it with the appropriate pronoun. The listing strategy allowed Anna to move toward a form for writing a report that was both more cohesive and more conventional.

Retellings

Retellings of texts originating in another medium are distinctive, at least in their usual classroom use, because when a retelling is assigned it is assumed that there is some amount of shared knowledge between writer and audience. It is likely that the audience (the teacher and sometimes classmates) has participated in the same experience.

I expected that a retelling of shared information would produce either more ambiguous referents or referents that could be found in the context of the situation or the assignment rather than in the text. I expected this because of the nature of the shared frame of reference and also because of the principle of economy. Interestingly, my expectations were not borne out in the students' retellings of movies and books. In fact, the assignments that asked students to retell a film that had been shown to the class were among the more successful assignments in terms of the students' involvement and the pieces' length (Y. Goodman & Wilde, 1985).

For pronoun use specifically, the proportion of pronoun ambiguity in these retellings was related to the number of characters introduced in the text and the kinds of interactions the characters had. As Bartlett and Scribner (1981) identified in work with other children, young writers' organization of reference may be influenced by the presence of same-age, same-sex characters.

As an example, I examine pronoun use in the retellings of one movie by two different Tohono O'odham students in fourth grade. (The stories have been presented as numbered sentences so that I can refer to specific sentences.)

The Daisy (Dana)

1. One day *a man* was cutting some weeds.
2. After *the man* got finished cutting the weeds, *a daisy* grew.
3. *The man* tried to pull *the daisy* out.
4. Then *he* tried to cut *the daisy* with his scissors.
5. But the scissors got caught.
6. *The man* tried to pull his scissors out.
7. When *he* pulled them out they were bent.
8. Then *he* tried to saw *the flower* down.
9. But *the edge* got soft.
10. When *he* tried to flatten *the daisy* with a big tractor like thing.
11. But that didn't work.
12. Then *he* tried to pull *the roots* out.
13. But *the root* was too long.
14. Then *he* tried to blow *the daisy* up.
15. But *he* blew *himself* up.
16. Then *a little girl* got *it* and pulled *it* very gently and *it* came off.

In this text, "a man" is introduced in (1) and is referred to as "the man" in (2). The noun phrase "the man" is repeated in (3) because "a daisy" became the subject in (2). From that point on the pronoun "he" is always used and is always in the subject position except in (6), where the noun phrase is repeated because of the new subject in (5).

"A daisy" is introduced in (2). All other instances repeat the noun phrase "the daisy" or a lexical variation that belongs to the daisy ("the roots," "the flower"), and it is always in the object position until (16), where the pronoun "it" is used. This comes just after the introduction of "a girl," whose presence precipitates the resolution of the story.

Rachel's retelling of the same movie follows:

1. There was once *a man*.
2. *He* was cutting plants down and there was *a daisy* growing.
3. *The man* wanted to cut *the daisy* down but *it* didn't fall down.
4. *The man* got mad.
5. *He* wanted to smash *the daisy*.
6. But *the daisy* was alive.
7. And *the man* dug a hole and found *the root*.
8. *It* was long.
9 *The man* got tired.
10. *He* got a rope and a barrel and some matches and lit one.
11. *It* went boom.
12. *The man* was in the hospital and *a nice girl* came and got *the daisy* and *the girl* went.

Rachel used pronouns regularly when the noun phrases to which they referred were immediately preceding. When the referent was more than one clause back, she repeated the noun phrase.

Co-reference for "the man" in both Dana's and Rachel's retellings shows the linkages between use of the noun phrase and the pronoun.

Dana		*Rachel*	
Identity	*Sentence*	*Identity*	*Sentence*
a man	1	a man	1
the man	2	he	2
the man	3	the man	3
he	4	the man	4
the man	6	he	5
he	7	the man	7
he	8	the man	9
he	10	he	10
he	12	the man	12
he	14		
he	15		

In summary, the use of visual stimuli such as pictures and movies to encourage children to write had varying effects. The use of pictures tended to increase the number of times referents were located only outside the text (i.e., within the picture itself). This occurred mainly when the picture was used as a resource to report or describe. Retellings, on the other hand, did not cause problems with reference and seemed to encourage the young writers to establish clear text structures and to write longer and more descriptive texts. Retellings of movies and books seemed to allow the young writers to experiment with other features important in written language, such as the use of descriptive modification and dialogue.

CONCLUSIONS AND IMPLICATIONS

My purpose in this study was to investigate children's use, control, and choice of pronouns in their writing. I found that these children did use the full range of pronouns in their writing and that they controlled and manipulated the pronoun system quite effectively. In addition, I found that these young writers did not have difficulty expressing co-reference through the use of pronouns. Although this finding was not a surprise, given my underlying assumptions about the way children learn language, I think that the implication of this finding for classroom teachers is that the direct teaching of pronouns through tracing referents in isolation is unnecessary and can even be confusing to students.

English teachers often comment that their students use pronouns ambiguously in writing, that they don't distinguish between referents. I wanted to find out about the nature and extent of this ambiguity. I found that less than 2 percent of the pronouns used by writers in this study were ambiguous. Pronoun ambiguity was found most often when the purpose of the writing was not clear to the author, as in the case of imaginary letters, or when the author was caught up in the piece and did not consider the reader's perspective, as in Dana's piece about the cowboy and the robber.

I had assumed when I began this study that an unsophisticated sense of audience would account for many of the pronoun ambiguities in the children's writing. I found that this was both true and untrue. On the one hand, the writers had a very developed sense of audience. They knew that the primary audience was the teacher. Through application of the rule of economy, the children sometimes used pronouns that referred to noun phrases that could not be found in the text itself. To find the referent, the reader had to go to the context of the writing situation or the assignment the children were writing in response to. On the other hand, most of the writing that I examined was first-draft writing, and there was little evidence of the kind of self-monitoring or peer conferencing that leads to revisions that consider the reader's perspective. It was in this way that sense of audience was underdeveloped.

The strategies the writers used to govern their choice of pronouns depended on what they were trying to do. Two factors had a pronounced influence on this choice: (1) the nature and type of assignment, and (2) the amount of experience the writer had in the particular genre or kind of writing.

How the context of the writing situation affected the writers' choice of pronouns turned out to be one of the most interesting things I investigated. Although I knew all along that the context would affect the choice of pronouns, I was surprised to discover how a specific assignment entered into the writers' choice of pronouns. I didn't expect to look directly at assignments nor did I expect to differentiate genres in my original data analysis. But when I began to investigate the question of how the context of the writing situation affected the writers' use and choice of pronouns, I was struck immediately by what seemed to be the writers' stance toward both genre in general and specific assignments. This led to the finding of a complex relationship between assignment and genre. It was not that any particular genre or any particular assignment gave the writers more or fewer problems; rather, problems were related to the way the individual writer chose to approach the writing in conjunction with the purposes for writing established by the classroom context.

These findings reinforce Bird's implications (Chapter 3, this volume) that classroom teachers ought to ensure that assignments are meaningful to students. If we ask students to write reports, then they need to know what a report is and what it does, and they also need to be personally engaged in the information to be reported. To do this, teachers must expose students to many different kinds of writing. The practice of reading aloud to students in elementary classrooms has increased in recent years, but from what I have seen, the choice of reading material remains mostly fiction with a smattering of poetry. By expanding the genres that we read to children we open up new frames of reference. Another way to broaden children's understanding of genre is to contrast various genres by welcoming and encouraging unconventional use. One teacher, Jack Wilde, explains how he accomplished this. In his article "The Written Report: Old Wine in New Bottles" (1988), he explains that before giving his fifth graders the assignment to write reports about animals, he did a great deal of preparation by reading to the students many accounts of animals by many authors in many styles and many forms. When it came time for them to write their own reports, they had the necessary background to be able to consciously choose the way they wished to express information about the animal of their choice. Many chose to write first-person narratives from the animal's point of view.

Implications regarding retellings suggest that retellings can be used in the classroom not simply as a way to assess students' learning but also as an instructional strategy. Brown and Cambourne (1989) provide practical guidelines for using retellings in this way and give detailed examples of how to design a series of lessons on a particular genre. The lessons begin with immersion in the genre through hearing and reading many examples and then proceed through many variations of both oral and written retellings.

In addition, classroom teachers need to provide time for students to share their writing with their peers and with the teacher and other adults in both informal and formal settings. These exchanges give young writers opportunities to monitor and to make conscious their own purposes for writing.

Finally, why look at pronouns anyway? In the years since I did the original research for this study I have worked mainly with pre-service and in-service teachers who, frankly, are not very interested in pronouns. That is, they are not interested in pronouns until I ask them what their greatest concerns are. Often these concerns involve establishing priorities in the classroom and finding the time to do everything they want to do. They are also concerned about students learning "skills." When faced with a piece of writing that contains pronoun ambiguity, their reaction is often that the student needs to learn about pronouns. Their solution is to bring out the page in the language arts textbook that asks the student to substitute a pronoun for a noun phrase or trace the referent to a pronoun. But once these same teachers realize how students actually use pronouns in their writing, that they do control the pronoun system, and that pronoun ambiguities occur for complex reasons related to the context and the purpose of the writing, they are less likely to employ the textbook solution. (For instance, do third-grade students who use pronouns as well as these Tohono O'odham children did really need to complete exercises in which they rewrite "The crow flew away" using a pronoun, or choose the correct pronoun for "We/Us will go later"?) And if teachers know something about the role of the specific features of language in the writing process, they can be more confident about letting those four students in the back of the room talk for an extra few minutes about what sounds better and what makes more sense in their own pieces of writing.

The implications for teacher educators are that we must find ways of highlighting current research about the way language is learned, the way language works, and the way in which language cueing systems must function together. We need to heed Halliday's warning that we look at language too solemnly but don't take it seriously enough. By looking at pronouns or any other feature of the language such as conjunctions, verb tense, time adverbials, and so on, we add a dimension to our exploration of the writing process. The patterns of pronoun ambiguity that I saw in children's writing confirm and support the other ways of looking at children's writing that are explained in this book.

CHAPTER 6

Spelling in Third and Fourth Grade

FOCUS ON GROWTH

Sandra Wilde

A THIRD GRADER NAMED GORDON WROTE THE FOLLOWING STORY:

One day a turkey got out of his home his mother was WEDA [worried] ABBITE [about] HEM [him]. He was walking in the woods and he got EATAIN [eaten] up.

The next year, he wrote the following piece:

The Cross and the SWICH BLADE [Switchblade]

One day a man was SROUNDED [surrounded] by a gang of other MAN [men]. The MANS had BAT [bats] blades chains AXS [axes] to kill people. Then the man TRYED [tried] to jump over a fence but the gang just pulled the man down and STARED [started] to hit him and stick him and the man died. The MANS that killed the OUTHER [other] man had to go to CORT [court].

Children in third and fourth grade are, of course, still learning to spell, but the spellings that they invent show different patterns from those of younger children. I looked at the invented spellings of six students in our study of Tohono O'odham children. In this chapter, I explore four areas of their spelling that showed growth during those years. Invented spellings involving these four features appear in both of the above stories. The features are:

1. Rounded vowels other than long and short *o* and *u* (i.e., the vowels of f*oo*d, g*oo*d, h*ou*se, b*oy*, and d*aw*n). Examples from Gordon are AB-BITE/about and CORT/court.
2. Unstressed vowels, specifically, schwa vowels (ə) in unstressed syllables, like the first vowel of *about*. Examples from Gordon are EAT-AIN/eat*e*n and SROUNDED/s*u*rrounded).
3. Double consonants, seen in ABBITE/about and SROUNDED/ surrounded.
4. The inflectional suffixes -*ed* and -*ing*, as in WEDA/worried and TRYED/tried.

Before I examine the children's spelling of these features, I'd like to place the discussion into two larger contexts: the nature of the English spelling system and the paths that children's development as spellers typically follows.

THE NATURE OF THE ENGLISH SPELLING SYSTEM

English spelling includes different kinds of information from several levels of language: phoneme-grapheme patterns (including rounded and unstressed vowels), orthographic and graphemic patterns (including double consonants), bound morpheme patterns (such as *-ed* and *-ing*), and lexical/semantic patterns.

The most obvious kind of information contained in English spelling, since it's an alphabetic system, is phoneme-grapheme correspondences: the relationship between sounds and the letters used to represent them. Since English contains about 40 phonemes (depending on dialect) but only 26 letters, these correspondences can't be one-to-one but must be more complex. For instance, the letter *a* is commonly used to represent both the short *a* sound of *cat* and the long *a* sound of *apron*. Because of this lack of one-to-one correspondence and other factors such as etymology (the history of word origins), any single phoneme can be spelled in a variety of ways. Horn (1957) pointed out that for many sounds, the most common spelling occurs less than 90 percent of the time. For instance, /t/ (phonemes are enclosed between slashes) is spelled *t* only 82 percent of the time, since it is sometimes doubled and sometimes accompanied by a silent letter as in *debt*.

The most significant piece of work establishing the nature and regularity of phoneme-grapheme correspondences in English, which also takes constraints beyond the phoneme into account, is the research commonly known as the "Stanford studies" (Hanna, Hanna, Hodges & Rudorf, 1966), which developed an algorithm (formula) for translating sound sequences into letter sequences. It was an attempt to discover the extent to which such a formula could come up with the actual, correct spellings of words. The algorithm was based not only on the phonemes themselves but on their position in the syllable, whether the syllable was accented or not, and the environment, defined as the influence of neighboring phonemes. (For instance, when long *i* occurs in the middle of an accented syllable before *t*, it's often spelled *igh* as in *light*. The 203 rules in the algorithm, when applied to 17,009 words, produced correct spellings 49.9 percent of the time and spellings with no more than one error 86.3 percent of the time. These results illustrate both the power and the limitations of sound-letter correspondences in determining English spelling. It is clearly possible to come up with rules relating sound to spelling in our alphabetic system, but the number of rules needed is quite high and they are far from perfect in their application. Because of these limitations, one of the authors of the Stanford report (Hodges, 1982) later commented that its authors overlooked the possibility that the word rather than the phoneme is the most appropriate level of analysis for spelling. At any rate, this work clearly demonstrates that it would be impractical to teach children to spell by giving them a list of rules relating sounds and letters.

Orthographic features of spelling can be defined as those that work beyond the level of single sound-letter relationships and include the positional and environmental factors taken into account in the Stanford studies, as well as other influences. Venezky (1970) has pointed out that many variations and seeming irregularities at the phoneme-grapheme level can be explained through orthographic rules that are actually quite regular.

Orthographic features of the English spelling system include:

1. *Positional constraints.* For instance, the phoneme /ĵ/ found at the end of *fudge* is usually spelled *ge* or *dge* at the ends of words but never *j*, even though *j* is one of its most common spellings at the beginning of words (Hanna et al., 1966).

2. *Environmental constraints.* For instance, the phoneme /k/, when it occurs at the beginning of a word, is usually spelled *k* before the vowel sounds occurring in *key*, *kept*, *kite*, and *kit*, *q* before /w/ (as in *quick*), and *c* in all other cases (Hanna et al., 1966).

3. *Stress influences.* For instance, when the phoneme /sh/ occurs at the beginning of a syllable, it is usually spelled *sh* in accented syllables and *t* or *ti* in unaccented ones (as in *nation*) (Hanna et al., 1966).

4. *Markers* (Venezky, 1970). These are patterns in which letters do not represent phonemes directly but provide information about the phonemes represented by other graphemes, such as the silent final *e* that indicates a preceding long vowel (as in *like*) and the double consonant that marks a preceding short vowel (as in *supper*).

Graphemic (or visual) patterns in spelling are those that occur for relatively arbitrary reasons. A sign that a pattern is graphemic rather than orthographic is that failure to follow it wouldn't change the word's pronunciation. Examples include a doubling of final *f* or *z* (as in *stiff* or *buzz*) (P. Smith, 1980), or the *e* added after final *u* or *v* (as in *glue* or *have*). These rules developed historically and were often established by printers concerned with the visual aesthetics of words. I use the term *bound morpheme spelling patterns* here to describe cases in which an underlying meaning unit (often a suffix) that can't stand on its own as a word is spelled consistently despite its pronunciation varying in patterned ways (Chao, 1968). For instance, the past-tense ending is pronounced differently but spelled the same in *walked*, *weighed*, and *wanted*.

A final level of spelling pattern is a lexical or semantic one, referring to the ability of spelling to represent meaning. Bolinger (1946) has described "visual morphemes," such as those found in homophones, in which spelling distinguishes not pronunciation but meaning. (For instance, in oral language, *sail* and *sale* differ only in their meaning; when they are spoken, only the context can distinguish them. When they are written, however, the spelling disambiguates them.) The most elaborate view of the semantic component of spelling has been presented by Chomsky and Halle (1968). (See also N. Chomsky, 1970, and C. Chomsky, 1970; of the three, the last is the most readable for teachers.) According to this view, conventional spelling is very close to being an "underlying lexical representation" of any given word, which is then converted into its final spoken form by phonological rules that are known implicitly by native speakers of the language. Thus, for instance, the words *medical* and *medicinal*, which differ in stress, vowel pronunciation, and pronunciation of the consonant letter *c*, are spelled in parallel ways because they share the same underlying root form. (The different pronunciations are due to phonological rules that are applied to *medicinal* after the suffix is added. For instance, the accent remains three syllables from the end of the word and therefore falls on a different vowel than in *medical*.) Chomsky and Halle also hypothesize that the underlying representations of words depicted in their spellings include features such as the double *f* and final *e* in *giraffe*, which aren't heard when the word is spoken but help predict its stress pattern. Chomsky and Halle believe that a more phonetic spelling system (i.e., one representing surface-level phonemes) would be unnecessarily redundant for native speakers of the language. (For instance, we don't need to replace the *c* in *medical* with a *k*, since we know that *c* before *a* is pronounced /k/.)

Why is English spelling so complicated? Largely because of the complex history of the English language. Scragg (1974) shows how the complexity of English spelling can be traced through its history, which has been influenced by linguistic, dialectal, cultural, and technological factors. Spelling tends to change more slowly than oral language does, so that spellings that began as phonetic ones have not remained so. For instance, the initial silent letters in words such as *gnarled* and *knife* were once pronounced. "We represent in the spelling of many words their sound as it was five or six centuries ago. It is for this reason that English spelling is sometimes said to be not phonetic but etymological. . . . Modern spelling is 'historically phonemic'" (Vallins, 1965, pp. 11–12).

HOW CHILDREN LEARN TO SPELL

Any discussion of how children learn one aspect of language is grounded in notions about how language learning and indeed all learning take place in a general sense.

Cognitive Processes

First of all, it is useful to think of intellectual development as the generation of increasingly varied and sophisticated schemata, which can be described as mental processes that organize and structure experience (Neisser, 1976). Any learner's conceptualization of his or her language's spelling system, which has both conscious and unconscious elements, is an example of a sche-ma. As children learn and grow, we can describe their thinking as operating at increasingly higher levels of organization; it's not primarily a process of ac-cumulating information but one of elaborating schemata. For example, chil-dren learn the names of more and more animals over time; these names be-come categories for classifying the new animals they see. To a young child, any four-legged animal might be a "doggie" or a "horsie," but an older child has a far more sophisticated animal classification system. Knowledge begins globally and develops through both greater differentiation and greater ab-straction or integration (Gibson & Levin, 1975). For instance, a speller must learn to abstract out the category of past-tense words that end in -ed even when that morpheme's pronunciation differs, yet also differentiate those words from others ending in the same sounds in order to avoid overgeneraliza-tion. Thus *walked*, *played*, and *wanted* all end with the same letters despite their different pronunciations, and *played*, *braid*, and *fade* all end in /ād/ but are spelled differently.

The concept-development process involved in learning a complex body of knowledge like a spelling system entails learning that is often tacit and dis-continuous and takes place in a social context. Much of our knowledge and learning apparently are tacit, below the level of consciousness (Polanyi, 1966). Lashley (1951), for instance, has demonstrated that many integrated motor and conceptual processes, from playing arpeggios to touch-typing to speech, take place far too rapidly for each step to be consciously directed; these ac-tivities must therefore be under the control of higher-level patterns, which are all that the person involved is aware of. Similar conclusions about tacit knowl-edge and oral language learning can be inferred from research on children's vocabulary size; children are estimated to learn anywhere from two to ten words a day, 365 days a year (Lindfors, 1987). This is obviously far beyond what instruction or other explicit acquisition could account for, and must therefore reflect a good deal of tacit and incidental learning. In the case of spelling, sim-ilarly, we all know how to spell many, many words that we were never formally taught.

It is also important to realize that tacit learning does not mean passive or only gradual learning. It occurs actively and sometimes by leaps and bounds rather than smoothly. Ferreiro and Teberosky (1982), taking a Piagetian per-spective, suggest that language and other cognitive development take place through an active process of assimilation and accommodation; learners oper-ate out of one conceptual schema as long as the available data can be made to fit it, but eventually reach a point of cognitive dissonance at which the schema itself must change. Thus periods of gradual growth are punctuated by discon-tinuous leaps.

One further point about conceptual development is that it cannot be separated from the social context in which it occurs; indeed, it is grounded in that context. Bissex (1980) talks about language development as moving from the universal to the culture specific, and the Soviet psychologist Vygotsky (1978, p. 88) spoke of culture as providing the framework that enables humans to learn in a way that animals cannot: "human learning presupposes a specific social nature and a process by which children grow into the intellectual life of those around them." Another way of stating this is that children's inventions, in most if not all areas of learning, are tempered by the conventions of their community and society (Y. Goodman & K. Goodman, 1990).

Forester (1980) summarizes how the basic principles of cognitive development apply to spelling in particular:

> The learner internalizes patterns and structures rather than discrete elements. The rules generated for dealing with spoken or written language are based upon the internalization of these patterns at a subconscious level. Development is gradual, moving from gross processing to fine discrimination. It is not simply a matter of assembling the parts of spelling or grammar into a mosaic of language. Instead, it constitutes the gradual development of an inner program or code that becomes the tool for receiving and creating language. (p. 190)

Children's Growth as Spellers

Studies of children learning to spell are extensive. Knowledge about spelling begins somewhat globally and eventually becomes more specific. The child's first task in learning about spelling is to discover some basic principles about how spelling systems work and about the particular system his or her culture uses, such as the Roman alphabet (Clay, 1975; Ferreiro & Teberosky, 1982). The child's early written representations of language evolve from scribbling to recognizable alphabetic characters (Heald-Taylor, 1984; Hildreth, 1936). Writing intended to represent a message globally is soon supplanted by phonetic spellings that often represent sounds more precisely than the standard spelling system does (Read, 1975, 1986). With more experience, young spellers move beyond the merely phonetic and begin more and more to represent orthographic and other patterns (Beers & Henderson, 1977; Gentry, 1978) and to remember the spellings of the words they use most frequently (Milz, 1983/1984; Wilde, 1986/1987).

If children begin learning to spell by discovering general principles and characteristics of written language and continue by exploring how to represent phonology, they eventually, and gradually, mature as writers by moving beyond phonology to use and integrate the other kinds of information contained in the spelling system (Marino, 1979; Marsh, Friedman, Welch & Desberg, 1980; Nolen & McCartin, 1984; Schwartz & Doehring, 1977; Templeton,

1979). In looking at how six children in third and fourth grade dealt with some of the more intricate aspects of the English spelling system, I hope to shed light on this process of increasing maturity in spelling.

SIX CHILDREN SPELLING

As mentioned earlier, the subjects of this study were six children of the Tohono O'odham tribe during their third- and fourth-grade years of school. In analyzing the children's invented spellings (Wilde, 1986/1987), I looked at 1,896 invented spellings (out of 13,793 words written in 215 stories), focusing primarily on features such as different kinds of vowels, consonant spelling patterns, and so on. The findings of that study are the basis for the discussion of the four spelling features in this chapter. (A more general discussion of the children's spelling appears in Chapter 2.)

There were two special features about these children and their classrooms that relate to their spelling. First, all the children spoke English as their first language, but most of them also understood and spoke limited amounts of the Tohono O'odham language, although none was fluent in it. A phonetic analysis of one of the children was conducted to determine whether there were features of the local dialect that were likely to influence spelling. Although there were slight variations from other dialects of American English, they were primarily subphonemic,[1] such as vowel length and the insertion of glottal stops. There was therefore no attempt to systematically seek out dialect influence on spelling, although it was considered in the few cases in which it might have influenced a particular spelling. It should also be remembered that *all* spellers (e.g., Read's 1975 Boston-area subjects) speak a dialect variant of English.

Second, there was virtually no formal instruction about spelling in the children's classrooms. The teachers did not use spelling textbooks or conduct class or group spelling instruction, although they did discuss spelling informally from time to time, with the entire class or in individual conferences.

FOUR SPELLING FEATURES AND HOW THEY GREW

The four spelling features discussed in this chapter (the rounded vowels heard in *food, good, house, boy,* and *dawn;* unstressed vowels; double consonants; and the inflectional suffixes *-ed* and *-ing*) are features that children spell increasingly proficiently during the middle grades of elementary school. This has been shown both in previous research (described below) and for these particular children. These children showed more improvement from third to fourth grade in the spelling of most of these features than in the spelling of any of the other eight features I examined (lax vowels, tense vowels, rhotacized or controlled vowels, hard and soft *g* and *c*, digraphs containing *h*, within-word apostrophes, homophones, and initial letters; see Wilde, 1986/1987). The one exception was the spelling of the -*ing* suffix, which was the only feature that the children actually spelled less successfully in fourth grade than in third. These changes are shown in Table 6.1, arranged in order of relative change, with the final column showing proportional change from third to fourth grade. (For comparison purposes, other features, such as long and short vowels, changed an average of 3.3 percent.)

Rounded Vowels

It is obvious that vowels are harder to spell in English than consonants are. But some vowels are harder to spell than others. The short vowels found in the words *cat*, *bed*, *hit*, *pop*, and *cut* are often spelled with just a single letter, so children learn how to spell them fairly quickly. These six children wrote 717 different words containing short vowels during two years of writing, and the vowels in 84.2 percent of those words are spelled with a single letter. It's therefore not surprising that the children were very successful at spelling these short vowel sounds; they got them right 94.4 percent of the time. The rounded vowels were a different matter, however, since they are far less predictable. Five rounded vowel sounds were examined; each of them had one

TABLE 6.1: Conventional Spelling of Selected Features: Third and Fourth Grades

Feature	Percentage Conventional (Correct) Spelling			
	Both Years	Grade 3	Grade 4	Change
-*ed* suffix	62.0 (of 254)	50.8	71.7	41.4*
Unstressed vowels	79.8 (of 1,478)	74.0	83.3	12.6*
Rounded vowels	88.9 (of 1,495)	83.5	92.5	10.8*
Double consonants	79.9 (of 564)	75.3	83.3	10.6**
-*ing* suffix	80.4 (of 230)	82.8	78.5	-5.2

This table includes only the relationship between correct spellings and *under*generalizations, such as failing to double a consonant. *Over*generalizations (such as inappropriately doubling a consonant) are, however, included in some of the tables and discussions later in this chapter.
 *Statistically significant beyond the .001 level.
**Statistically significant beyond the .01 level.

most common spelling in the words that the children chose to write, but those most common spellings made up only 39.7 percent of all spellings of the words. This pattern is shown in Table 6.2.

Many of these rounded vowel spellings are influenced by the environment in which they occur. There is often a "default" spelling, which is not necessarily the most common one but the one that occurs if no special conditions hold. For instance, *o* is the default spelling for /ô/ (e.g., d*o*g), but *a* occurs before *ll* (t*a*ll) or after *w* (w*a*tch), *al* occurs before *k* (t*al*k), and *aw* occurs at the end of a word or morpheme (s*aw*). Other spellings reflect historical changes, such as the *augh* and *ough* in *daughter* and *bought*. But still other spellings cannot be explained very simply at all. Why do we write *June* instead of *Joon*, or *two* as well as *too* and *to*? Obviously it takes time for children to learn all these variations.

When children spelled these vowels with letters other than the expected ones, their spellings were logical ones a good deal of the time. Read (1975) found that preschoolers tended to spell rounded vowels with *o*, *u*, or some combination thereof, suggesting that his subjects recognized a similarity between all the rounded sounds, which implied a single spelling category for them. The vast majority of these Tohono O'odham third and fourth graders' invented spellings of the rounded vowels followed similar patterns: either *o* in place of another spelling, a spelling not otherwise categorizable that contained *o* or *u*, or another common spelling of the sound. This was even more true in

TABLE 6.2: Spellings of Rounded Vowels

Sound	Most Common Spelling*		Other Spellings* (in order of frequency)	Total Words
/ô/	t*a*ll	29.4% (of all ô words)	l*o*st, t*a*lk, c*augh*t, s*aw*, s*au*cer, b*ou*ght, c*au*se, g*o*ne, br*oa*d	68
/u/ (long oo)	f*oo*d	32.8%	bl*ew*, s*u*per, t*o*, s*ou*p, J*u*ne, tw*o*, bl*ue*, m*o*ve, thr*ough*, sh*oe*s, Si*ou*x	58
/au/	cl*ou*d	46.9%	c*ow*, h*ou*se, Top*a*wa, M*au*i	49
/U/ (short oo)	b*oo*k	55.9%	p*u*t, w*o*man, w*ou*ld	34
/oi/	b*oy*	53.3%	p*oi*nt, n*oi*se, ch*o*lla	15

*These are the spellings found in the words themselves, not children's invented spellings of them.

TABLE 6.3: Invented Spellings for Rounded Vowels

	Grade 3		Grade 4	
	No.	%	No.	%
o for another spelling	51	44.4	37	50.0
Spelling with *o* or *u*	30	26.1	22	29.7
Other spellings (i.e., less logical ones)	25	21.7	10	13.5
Common spelling of sound	9	7.8	5	6.8
TOTAL	115	100.0	74	100.0

fourth grade than in third. The figures are shown in Table 6.3. What did these spellings look like? Table 6.4 shows examples of each pattern for each vowel, when they existed.

Therefore, even when the children did not spell these rounded vowels correctly, they tended to spell them in ways that reflected their knowledge that rounded vowels are usually spelled with certain letters rather than others. (Of course, in some cases, they lacked the sophistication to realize that certain spellings of a phoneme usually occur only in particular environments. For instance, the spelling *a* for /ô/ is usually restricted to after a *w* or before *ll*, making LAST for *lost* unlikely.) In fourth grade the children not only spelled rounded vowels correctly more often than in third grade, but had fewer unlikely or unreasonable spellings for them.

TABLE 6.4: Examples of Invented Spellings for Rounded Vowels

	/ô/	/u/	/U/	/au/	/oi/
o for another spelling	COLD/ called	TO/ too	COLD/ could	CLOD/ clouds	PONT/ point
Spelling with *o* or *u*	LOUST/ lost	TRAO/ threw	TOKE/ took	MOUAITAN/ mountain	PUNCT/ poison
Other spellings	WICTH/ watch	FILL/ flew	SIND/ should	ABBITE/ about	—
Common spelling of sound	LAST/ lost	THEW/ through	WOOD/ would	OUL/ owl	—

Unstressed Vowels

It is easy to see why unstressed vowels, defined here as those taking the form of schwa (ə) in unstressed syllables, are considered to be the most difficult vowels to remember how to spell. An unstressed vowel is "reduced" to a sound that does not retain the phonetic identity of the comparable vowel in a related word. For instance, the short *a* in the first syllable of *adaptation* is not preserved in *adapt*. (Some schwa sounds, however, start out as unstressed and can't be related to an accented vowel in a comparable word, such as the *i* in *pencil*.) Since the schwa sound can be spelled with any vowel letter (e.g., *a*bout, it*e*m, rig*i*d, parr*o*t, circ*u*s), or with more than one vowel letter (e.g., por*ous*), the only way one can be sure of spelling it correctly is through knowing either the word itself or a related word. Phonics is of no help here. One of the children we studied, Gordon, illustrated this in practice while trying to spell the word *ago*: He asked aloud if it began with *o* or *u* and, unable to settle on an answer through the sound of the word, moved to a visual strategy, writing various possible spellings of the word.

For the purposes of this study, unstressed vowels were defined as also including instances of syllabic /r/, /l/, /m/, and /n/. These are the sounds found in the unstressed final syllables of *father*, *wiggle*, *bottom*, and *ribbon*, respectively, which are called "syllabic" because the consonant can be pronounced on its own, without an intervening vowel. These have been included in the unstressed vowel category because, depending on pronunciation, they can frequently be described as schwa plus consonant and indeed are often shown that way in dictionary pronunciation guides. Also, their spelling almost always includes a vowel and presents many of the same difficulties in choosing the correct vowel letter as does the spelling of the schwa vowel. It is also important to remember that the vowels in many words, particularly short function words such as *a*, *of*, and *the*, are frequently reduced to schwa in connected speech. For the purposes of this analysis, unstressed vowels were defined as only those that always appear as schwa, but there may have been other cases in which the children were attempting to represent reduced vowels.

As seen in Table 6.1, the subjects spelled unstressed vowels correctly 79.8 percent of the time. The 299 cases (out of 1,478) in which there were invented spellings for these vowels can be classified into three types. If there was a substitution, another letter (or letters) was substituted for the appropriate vowel; in the case of omission, no vowel letter was used; and some spellings were defined as indeterminate when it was not possible to determine which, if any, letters were intended to represent the unstressed vowel. Table 6.5 indicates how many spellings fell into each category.

Substitution of other letters for the appropriate spelling of an unstressed

TABLE 6.5: Invented Spelling Categories for Unstressed Vowels

	Substitution		Omission		Indeterminate		
	No.	%	No.	%	No.	%	TOTAL
Schwa	(OPON/upon)		(FINSH/finish)		GOTSL/gorilla)		
Grade 3	23	41.1	14	25.0	19	33.9	56
Grade 4	20	36.4	29	52.7	6	10.9	55
Both	43	38.7	43	38.7	25	22.5	111
Syllabic	(DALLER/dollar)		(CEREL/cereal)		(PUNCT/poison)		
Grade 3	31	34.1	29	31.9	31	37.1	91
Grade 4	65	67.1	20	20.6	12	12.4	97
Both	96	51.1	49	26.1	43	22.9	188
All unstressed							
Grade 3	54	36.7	43	29.3	50	34.0	147
Grade 4	85	55.9	49	32.2	18	11.8	152
Both	139	46.5	92	30.8	68	22.7	299

vowel was the most common strategy, although omission was also common, particularly in the case of schwa on its own. By contrast, with younger children, omission has been found to be the most common spelling of /ə/, occurring in 35 percent of *all* spellings of it (Read, 1975). Similarly, younger children tend to spell unstressed syllabic consonants with only a consonant letter, omitting the vowel (Beers & Henderson, 1977; Read, 1975). The invented spellings of unstressed vowels by the children in this study did not follow any clearly defined patterns within or across the categories of substitution and omission. This is partly because many of the children's inventions were unusual spellings that were not necessarily attempts at accurate representation of sound sequences. Of 299 words with invented spellings of unstressed vowels, only 66 (23 in third grade and 43 in fourth), or 22 percent, were simple vowel substitutions or omissions in words that were otherwise spelled conventionally. The remaining spellings included some possible rough phonemic approximations, such as ARSDA/arrested, as well as more anomalous examples such as PELANP/people. The only general pattern seen in the substitution category was a tendency to represent unstressed vowels with a single letter, particularly *e* or *a*; this was more true in fourth grade than in third. Some of the invented spellings of unstressed vowels were the result of failing to make generalizations about common orthographic patterns: the past tense -*ed* and -*en* suffixes, the agentive and comparative affix -*er* (as in walk*er* and cold*er*, respectively), and the common word ending -*le*. However, these were involved in only 38 invented spellings (13 percent), 28 in third grade and 10 in fourth. It would appear that unstressed vowels are likely to be spelled conventionally when the writer either is familiar with the word or can draw on an orthographic or lexical generalization (e.g., knowing that *le* is found at the end of many words but that *al* is common if the word is an adjective such as *topical*). If neither of these strategies is successful, a phonological strategy is less likely to produce conventional spelling of unstressed than of stressed vowels, since the former are all phonetically neutralized to /ə/, making it impossible to "hear" what the spelling is. As Read (1975) has commented, children's spelling of unstressed vowels gives their writing much of its distinctive character; these spellings reveal the writers' relative lack of orthographic sophistication by failing to preserve morphophonemic and lexical relationships. Perhaps what is most remarkable is that these third and fourth graders did successfully spell unstressed vowels about 80 percent of the time.

Double Consonants

A writer who knew the alphabet but had never seen words in print would never use a double consonant (i.e., two of the same consonant letter appearing together) in spelling English words. Double consonants are used not to represent two sounds but to provide other information, often about vowel pronunciation. Smith (1980) describes cases in which a double consonant following a short vowel is obligatory: in environments where a single consonant would signal a long vowel (*tapping* versus *taping*); for word-final /f/, /z/, or /k/, which do not occur as single letters in English (*stiff*, *jazz*, and the special double consonant *ck*, as in *back*); to signal stress patterns (*umbrella* versus *cinema*); to avoid suggesting a plural (*brass* versus *bras*); to avoid two-letter content words, which do not usually occur in English (*inn* versus *in*); and to distinguish homophones (*hall* versus *haul*). There are some exceptions to these rules, however (Venezky, 1970): Some consonants do not usually double (*fixed*, *river*), and consonants do not double after short vowels spelled with a digraph (*heading* versus *bedding*).

Until a writer either knows these rules, whether consciously or not, or knows the spellings of a number of words, there is no reason to use a double consonant. There is also a period of time in a writer's development when he or she may be aware that double consonants exist without having a well-defined schema for their use. The young speller who never uses double consonants turns into one who sometimes uses them, but not always in the right places. Beers and Henderson (1977) and Lancaster, Nelson, and Morris (1982) have described the emergence of double consonants, sometimes appropriate and sometimes not, in primary school children. Similarly, Zutell (1979) looked at the use of double consonants by children from first through fourth grade and found increasing conventionality as age increased. He observed both inappropriate doubling and failure to double and, except for fourth graders, found far more of the latter.

The Tohono O'odham children failed to use double consonants when they should have in 142 cases (out of 646) and used double consonants inappropriately 58 times. Within each of these categories, most cases were simple substitutions of one consonant for two (e.g., HAMER for *hammer*) or two for one (e.g., SHINNING for *shining*), as shown in Table 6.6, but other patterns also occurred.

The cases in which children used one consonant for two or vice versa can be explained in a variety of ways:

1. The substitution was a real word: OF/off, HISS/his.
2. The child's spelling was reasonable phonetically: COLD/called, AGENN/again (a final double consonant often indicates final-syllable stress).
3. The writer didn't double before a suffix, or overgeneralized the doubling rule: BIGER/bigger, SHINNING/shining. There was also one case (HELLED/held) that assumed an *-ed* past tense marker for an irregular verb.
4. There were only two cases (HAMER/hammer, MISED/missed) in which a double consonant was needed to indicate a short vowel, but not because of a suffix, and the child did not double the consonant.

TABLE 6.6: Invented Spelling Categories for Double Consonants

	One for Two/ Two for One		Other		
	No.	%	No.	%	TOTAL
Failure to double					
Grade 3	48	64.0	27	36.0	75
Grade 4	54	80.6	13	19.4	67
Both	102	71.8	40	28.2	142
Inappropriate doubling					
Grade 3	20	69.0	9	31.0	19
Grade 4	19	65.5	10	34.5	29
Both	39	67.2	19	32.8	58

5. Many of the spellings appeared to be attempts to represent the relevant sound without a full knowledge of orthographic rules such as those concerning final *f* (OF/off) or *ck* (TRUK/truck) or stress rules (AROW/arrow).

About a third of the invented spellings involving double consonants were not simple cases of substituting one letter for two or the reverse; these tended to be spellings in which the consonant was not the only problem. They included cases in which one consonant of two was changed (PRICTLY/prickly), a vowel was inserted between the two consonants (HAPEPAED/happened), or another consonant altogether was used (TLLKEK/took, DEZERT/dessert). (If these spellings were of a word that should have had a double consonant, they were classified under "failure to double"; a spelling like TLLKEK was classified as "inappropriate doubling.")

When spelling instruction deals with consonant doubling, it usually focuses on learning when to double a consonant before adding a suffix and perhaps on comparing short and long vowel pairs (*supper* versus *super*). However, only a few of the invented spellings involving double consonants produced by these children would have been amenable to correction by such instruction. Of the 142 cases in which the children should have used a double consonant but didn't, only 11 (all in fourth grade) were simple cases of failing to double a consonant before adding a suffix (e.g., CLAPING/clapping). (There were also only 20 spellings in which the subjects followed that rule; words involving it were simply not all that common in their writing.) Similarly, of the 58 inappropriate doublings, only one involved the suffixing rule (SHINNING/shining) and one produced an inappropriate short vowel (TEPPES/tepees). Improvement of most of the remaining spellings would not come through greater knowledge of doubling rules but through more knowledge of words in general.

There were two major areas of improvement from third to fourth grade in these students' spelling of double consonants. First, as mentioned above, in fourth grade the children had 11 spellings in which the only error was in failing to double a consonant before adding a suffix; in third grade all 10 invented spellings to which this rule would have applied had other problems as well (e.g., WERT/winner). If teaching the appropriate rule is of some value, it would presumably be of most use at a point when students are creating inflected forms through correct spelling of both root and suffix rather than at an earlier stage when they are less aware of the separate morphemes. Second, most of the improvement in spelling double consonants from third to fourth grade was due to the increased correctness of the double consonants that were most common in the subjects' writing (*ck* and *ll*). The unusual double consonant *ck* accounted for 19 percent of all double consonants; by fourth grade the subjects were aware enough of it to spell it correctly 95 percent of the time (as opposed to 65 percent in third grade). The double consonant *ll* was by far the most common (representing 37 percent of the total) and also showed improvement, from 86 percent to 94 percent correct. The other double consonants occurred less frequently, so changes in their use from third to fourth grade did not have much effect on the overall picture.

Suffixes: *-ed* and *-ing*

The past-tense suffix *-ed* has three different pronunciations, which can be predicted from the phonological environment, as seen in *walked*, *dragged*, and *flooded*. (This is comparable to the three pronunciations of *-s* in *walks*, *drags*, and *wishes*.) The young writer must therefore learn to abstract out this category of past-tense words across different pronunciations as well as differentiating those words from others ending in the same sounds, so that the *-ed* ending is not overgeneralized to words such as *fact* and *hand*. Spellers must also learn to make changes in root words when adding either the *-ed* or the *-ing* suffix (e.g., *tried*, *coming*, and *batting/batted*).

Several studies have looked at young spellers' use of suffixes. Berko (1958) showed how generalization of suffix pronunciation is learned only gradually in oral language, and that some forms are more difficult to learn than others. When first graders were asked to add suffixes to nonsense words, their ability to do so appropriately ranged from 25 percent on some words to 99 percent on others, with /ə plus z/ and /ə plus d/ forms being the most difficult ones for plurals and verbs, respectively. Preschool children tend to spell the *-ed* suffix phonetically (Gentry, 1978; Read, 1975). Read discovered that they first move away from the three-way distinction that this involves "by using *d* to represent both /t/ and /d/. . . . The first abstraction is from the voicing contrast" (pp. 65–66). (To expand on this explanation, the phonemes /t/ and /d/ differ only in that the former is an unvoiced sound and the latter a voiced one; children learn fairly early to collapse this distinction in past-tense endings in order to produce a more abstract spelling, but the addition of the vowel letter heard only in the words ending in /əd/ to all past-tense words is more abstract still and is done consistently only later on.)

A few studies have described how children become more conventional in their spelling of suffixes as they grow older. Schwartz and Doehring (1977) found an increase in abstraction of suffixation patterns from grades two through five. Zutell (1979) found increasing conventionality as children progressed through grades one through four: Earlier strategies included phonetic spelling, the use of *-d* (with no *e*) for all words, and use of a vowel other than *e* before the -d. Thomas (1982) found that Australian children spelled the past-tense suffix appropriately 44 percent of the time in second grade, 76 percent in third, and 87 percent in fourth. Words with the /əd/ pronunciation were easiest to spell, since the spelling reflects their pronunciations most closely, and /d/ forms were the most difficult. Unconventional spellings tended to reflect pronunciation. With irregularly spelled past-tense words (i.e., those that don't use -ed, such as *slept*), low-frequency ones were spelled more correctly (i.e., phonetically); about 10 percent of spellings of the high-frequency ones involved an overgeneralization of the -ed phoneme, particularly in third graders. In French, the plural forms of both nouns and third-person verbs are marked in orthography but usually unmarked in oral language. For instance, *livre* (book) and *livres* (books) are usually pronounced identically (with no /s/). Gill (1980) found that French first graders rarely included those plural markers in their spellings, but third and fourth graders, capable of greater abstraction and presumably more familiar with plural forms from reading, usually did.

Uniform spelling of suffixes that vary in pronunciation appears to be a useful feature of English orthography. When asked to "reform" word spellings (Baker, 1980), subjects maintained the -s suffix spelling 75 percent of the time and the -ed suffix 50 percent of the time (it was also changed to -d 40 percent of the time). This uniform spelling has evolved gradually over time; Bradley (1919, p. 13) pointed out that *missed* used to be spelled *mist* (which is, of course, reminiscent of children's spelling) but that the "pressure of ideographic need" (to differentiate homophones) caused the change to a spelling that reflected meaning as well as (if not even more than) pronunciation.

The Tohono O'odham children spelled the -ed ending appropriately in 254 words but under-, mis-, or overgeneralized it in 194. The -ing ending was spelled appropriately in 230 words and under-, mis-, or overgeneralized in 65. The children's spelling of -ing was actually slightly worse in fourth grade than in third, although not to a statistically significant extent. The types of invented spellings involved varied quite a bit, as seen in Table 6.7.

The past-tense -ed suffix produced both the greater number and the greater variety of invented spellings. The most common types of spelling in which -ed was not included appropriately were invented spellings that ended either with a *d* not preceded by an *e* or with a *t*. These endings usually but not always reflected pronunciation (e.g., WACHT/watched, but also HOLPD/helped). Many of these spellings also had invented features other than the suffix.

The next most common category involved total omission of the suffix. This could be due to factors such as a lack of awareness of the past-tense morpheme or, in some cases, consonant cluster reduction. These were all cases in which the students used the past-tense form when reading their texts aloud,

TABLE 6.7: Invented Spellings for Suffixes

Category	Example	Grade 3		Grade 4	
		No.	%	No.	%
-ed: Under- or misgeneralization					
d or *t* only	CALLD/called	34	36.2	19	30.64
Suffix omitted	KISS/kissed	20	21.2	23	37.10
-de for *-ed*	WALKDE/walked	6	6.4	5	8.06
Doubling	POPED/popped	2	2.1	5	8.06
y to *i* problems	TRYED/tried	5	5.3	2	3.23
Other	WEDA/worried KILLS/killed	27	28.7	8	12.90
TOTAL		94	100.0	62	100.0
-ed: Overgeneralization					
Verbs	HELLED/held	4	22.2	13	65.0
Nouns	ROED/road	12	66.7	4	20.0
Other	HARED/hard, ASFED/after	2	11.1	3	15.0
TOTAL		18	100.0	20	100.0
-ing: Under- or misgeneralization					
Final *e* problem	COMEING/coming	5	22.7	15	44.1
Doubling	CLAPING/clapping	1	4.6	9	26.5
Other	RAN/running, TRING/trying	16	72.7	10	29.4
TOTAL		22	100.0	34	100.0
-ing: Overgeneralization					
Other tense	MELTING/melted	1	16.7	1	33.3
Other	AING/again	5	83.3	2	66.7
TOTAL		6	100.0	3	100.0

so their inventions represented a spelling issue rather than a syntactic one. Next, there were spellings in which -*ed* was reversed to -*de* and some invented spellings caused by either not doubling a consonant or not changing a *y* to *i* before the suffix. The "other" category included unusual spellings (WEDA/worried), using another ending (STARID/started), and so on. There were few changes from third to fourth grade.

There were also cases in which the subjects used an -*ed* ending on a word that did not need one. Many of these were in irregularly spelled past-tense verbs (SIED/said), but nearly as many were in nouns and a few in other parts of speech. The verb forms, which were more common in fourth grade, probably represented overgeneralization of the morpheme in cases in which it was reasonable semantically; the other cases may have involved its use in words that were similar only phonetically to -*ed* verb forms or as a generalized end marker. At any rate, -*ed* overgeneralization was relatively rare.

In cases of invented spelling involving the -*ing* suffix, the suffix itself was usually spelled appropriately (unless it was omitted). Problems in using it often involved rules related to how it combines with root words. The two most common types of invented spelling for this suffix involved not dropping a final *e* or not doubling a final consonant before adding the suffix. These accounted for just over half of the -*ing* invented spellings; the remainder either had some other problem (adding, deleting, or changing a letter) at the juncture of root and suffix or involved a larger change such as an unusual spelling, use of another tense, or deletion of the suffix altogether. The greatest change from third to fourth grade was a decrease in unusual spellings and an increase in spellings in which an obligatory change in the root word was not made. There were only a few spellings in which -*ing* appeared unexpectedly. Two of these were other tenses of verbs; the remainder involved either a change in letter order (ANGING/again) or phonetic similarity (THING/think).

In summary, invented spellings involving the -*ed* suffix were primarily a result of limited knowledge of the suffix itself, including knowledge about whether the suffix is present at all and knowledge about how it is spelled, with the phonetic spellings -*d* and -*t* used fairly often. With -*ing*, the suffix itself tended to be present and correctly spelled, but the root morphemes were not always appropriately altered. This was, in fact, more of a problem in fourth grade than in third; the rule about dropping final *e* was followed 74 percent of the time in third grade but only 29 percent in fourth. This may be a case of overgeneralization of a regular form, a phenomenon that often occurs in oral language development; a word like *making* may first be spelled as a whole (correctly or not), but the word will later be analyzed and spelled as root plus suffix, or MAKEING. Presumably a similar process takes place as children abstract out the more difficult -*ed* suffix.

CONCLUSIONS AND IMPLICATIONS

The analysis I performed on these four spelling features in the writing of six third- and fourth-grade children demonstrates (similar to the findings of other research on spelling growth) that invented spelling is not just a strategy of beginning writers. When a writer of any age needs to spell an unknown word, he or she often creates a spelling based on his or her knowledge of written language and the spelling system. For younger writers, that knowledge is largely phonetic in nature; for more mature ones, increasing information about orthographic and graphemic patterns is incorporated into spelling. In addition, the spellings of more and more words are learned over time and are available to influence those that are not yet known; this type of spelling by analogy to or by substitution of a familiar word is particularly common in the invented spelling of adults, such as teachers who refer to "basil" readers in their first-draft writing.

In addition to this general awareness that invented spellings are still growing and changing in children around the ages of eight and nine, what specific conclusions can be drawn from my findings? First of all, the focus on invented spelling patterns should not blind us to the fact that the features that I looked at were spelled appropriately by these six children the majority of the time, ranging from 50 percent to 83 percent in third grade and from 72 percent to 92 percent in fourth (see Table 6.1). It would be incorrect to say that the students did not know how to spell these features, did not understand them, did not have "-ing skills," and so on. Indeed, their spelling of these features had progressed beyond what could be called "emergent" or even "developing" into something more like "high-level" or "refined." *Any* interpretation of children's invented spellings must always be seen in the context of the larger picture that includes the extent to which knowledge of dictionary spellings has replaced invention.

Second, the logicality of the invented spellings examined here (as of most invented spellings) is impressive. Although a certain proportion of invented spellings will always seem anomalous, given students' frequent choice to sacrifice accuracy for speed as they write (an appropriate decision when expression of thought is the goal), one cannot fail to be impressed by the reasonableness of spellings like OUL for *owl*, OPON for *upon*, DEZERT for *dessert*, and CALLD for *called*. Although a spelling like COLD for *called* or FINSH for *finish* is less obviously logical, sophisticated observers of invented spelling know that these two were produced for good and specific reasons and that the omitted letters are not random.

A third, and related, conclusion is that even in the small sample of words that was available for each feature from these children, there is evidence that a decrease in the frequency of invented spellings was often also accompanied by improvement in the quality of those that remained. Some of the examples discussed earlier include a decrease in indeterminate (i.e., less logical) spellings of unstressed vowels from third to fourth grade; a decrease in the proportion of double consonants whose invented spelling took a form other than using just a single letter (e.g., spellings like HAMER for *hammer* became more common than those like HAPEPAED for *happened*); and the increasing emergence of final *e* and doubling problems as a replacement for less mature invented spellings of *-ing* words.

What are the implications of these findings for theory, research, and practice? I hope that they will be seen as a contribution to the continuing examination of invented spelling at a variety of age levels, and that their basis in natural writing samples will help us continue to think about and examine how knowledge about spelling emerges in the real world of writing as an expression of meaning, in a variety of settings where both children themselves and their classroom communities take diverse forms. Features such as schwa vowels and double consonants also lead to invented spellings in adults; further research on how this knowledge develops in elementary school learners may illuminate ways to further its continued growth in older writers.

This leads to implications for practice. First of all, teachers need to look at both quantity and quality of invented spellings in evaluating children's knowledge and growth (see Wilde, 1989). These young writers showed us that even when looked at in a fair amount of detail, their spelling revealed both quantitative and qualitative change. Second, the more that teachers are able to learn about the underlying logic behind children's invented spellings, the more they will be able to appreciate and build on the strengths that that logic represents. Teachers' perceptions of invented spelling have changed, as the research has evolved, from seeing such spellings as wrong to seeing them as intelligent expressions of linguistic knowledge. With a deeper understanding of the particular forms that children's invented spellings take, teachers have begun to realize that not only do children sound out words as they write, they also think about related words and about various kinds of spelling patterns to help them spell a new word. Teachers can support and encourage further growth through mini-lessons that might, for instance, ask children to think of as many words as they can with the same vowel sound as *found*, and then examine all the possible ways the sound is spelled and which ones are most likely to be good choices when spelling an unknown word. (See Wilde, 1992, for detailed suggestions for such lessons.)

Teachers working to help children develop as spellers do not need to conduct the kind of detailed analysis I have done here. But I hope that reading such an analysis will encourage teachers to look at their own students' invented spellings with a more educated, appreciative eye and to build on what children's spellings reveal about their underlying knowledge Although the research I've described here focuses on particular features in the spellings of six children from a narrow grade-level span in a single community, the probing approach to invented spelling that it represents, the looking below the surface in a attempt to understand the learner's intellectual processes, is much broader. It represents, I hope, an inquiring-mind approach to invented spelling that all teachers can adopt in looking at their students' writing.

NOTES

1. Subphonemic features of pronunciation are those that do not change one word into another. For instance, one speaker may pronounce vowels more nasally than another, but they are still clearly saying the same word. An example of a phoneme-level dialect difference is a speaker who pronounces *cot* and *caught* identically. This speaker's pronunciation creates a potentially ambiguous meaning.

CHAPTER 7

Bringing It All Together

ANNA WRITING IN A COMMUNITY OF WRITERS

Sherry Vaughan

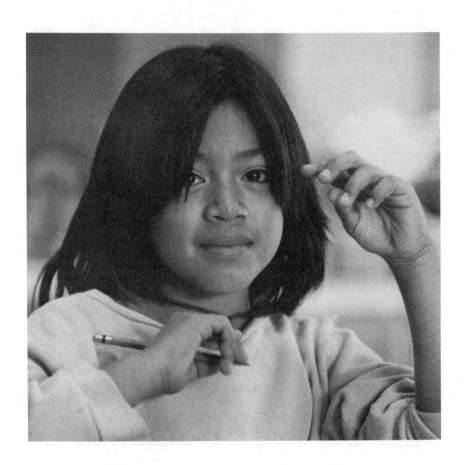

THE AUTHORS OF THE PRECEDING FOUR CHAPTERS have looked at separate aspects of the writing process and of written text, in each case across a variety of children. In this chapter, I look at writing in a different way, by examining how the many facets of the process worked for a single child over a two-year period. I look at the social context in which Anna's writing took place and highlight the kind of writer she was and how that changed over time, gathering this information both from field notes and from her texts themselves.

SOCIAL CONTEXT

As Yetta Goodman and others have already pointed out in this volume, written text results from the interaction of multiple contexts, all of them social. Although it may not be possible for researchers and teachers to discover all the factors that influence any single act of composing, surely they include the writer, the text, and the physical and interpersonal context, including in this case the teacher, the classroom aides, the researchers, and classmates. These immediate influences always share the spotlight with the more long-term influences of the writer's home life and culture. Sharing the story of a writer's development over time requires weaving together the interaction of those influences. Before I present the story of Anna's writing development over the two years of our study, I separate each major influence and describe its salient features as it applied to Anna.

The Writer: Anna

The Anna referred to here is the same dark-eyed, dark-haired child described earlier in Chapter 2. Perhaps some of the characteristics mentioned there are important to mention again here. Anna lived with her father, mother, two brothers, and a sister in a village just outside the largest town on the reservation. Even though both parents spoke both English and Tohono O'odham at home and Anna understood both languages, she spoke English almost exclusively. Anna's parents were strong supporters of writing and reading, creating opportunities for her to engage in both at home. They listened to the stories she wrote, and though Anna admitted that reading was not her favorite activity, they encouraged her to read widely.

The Teachers: Linda Howard and Sr. Susan Caldwell

The two teachers Anna worked with in grades three and four were different in many ways. Although both valued writing as a learning tool and provided time for students to write, Linda Howard's writing assignments were usually specific and detailed, relating to topics being studied in the content areas; writing in Sr. Susan Caldwell's classroom was more likely to be directed by students' choice. Linda tended to focus more on editing students' final products herself before students rewrote them, but Sr. Susan was more likely to discuss the final product within a group context and leave the major responsibility for revising and editing with the children themselves. Although she valued and provided time for social interaction during writing time, Linda's major emphasis was usually content first, then form. Sr. Susan emphasized the social interaction aspect, focusing first on positive attitude about self and respect for others, then on content and skill. In spite of those differences, however, Anna worked well in Linda's third-grade class and then quickly made the adjustment to meet Sr. Susan's somewhat different requirements.

The following episodes serve as representative examples of each teacher's expectations and Anna's typical interactions with the teachers in meeting them. One day, Linda Howard went over to Anna, who was working in the writing center; Linda asked Anna why she was rewriting a letter that hadn't been edited yet and offered to help. They read the piece together. Linda helped correct spelling errors by reminding Anna of the long *i* rule and pointing out that even though Anna intended to write the word *sad* she had actually written SAID. When they came to the word *Thanksgiving*, Linda asked her to say the word aloud and listen for the sound of a missing letter. Anna recognized *k* and added it. Linda pointed out needed capitals and the long vowel rule, referred her to the dictionary for a word, pointed out an earlier instance of the word in her own text, and then asked her about how a formal letter is supposed to end. Anna added the appropriate ending as Linda moved on to another student.

In October of fourth grade, Anna wrote a report on Hawaii during a draw/write/share activity. Earlier, Sr. Susan Caldwell had introduced a new form of writing to the group, writing to provide information rather than to tell stories. Working from informative materials Sr. Susan and the students had chosen together, each student wrote a few sentences about a topic of choice. Anna's topic was Hawaii.

This new informative function and discourse form turned out to be difficult for Anna. She ran into trouble immediately with strange vocabulary words and large amounts of information that she didn't know how to condense. Sr. Susan pulled up a chair and began to help Anna decide what to write. Drawing Anna's attention away from her text, she asked her first to talk aloud about some of the interesting things she'd read. Anna said that she was surprised that Hawaii was really a group of islands rather than just one. Sr. Susan replied, "That's interesting and certainly something worth writing about." As she moved on to another student, Anna began to focus on constructing her text.

Throughout this writing episode Sr. Susan checked on Anna's progress. She knew this was a new, more difficult type of writing for Anna, so she kept in touch with the ongoing process as it developed. She encouraged with smiles and physical touches, rewarded with praise, ensured that Anna was proceeding correctly, and finally congratulated her successful final product. Anna was pleased and energized about her writing.

The Researchers

Since we, the researchers, played a participant observer role in the writing activities of the children in these classrooms, we too contributed to the academic and social context in which writing took place. On some occasions, observation and interaction actually became a source of instruction, albeit indirectly. In October of fourth grade, Anna wrote a story about a cat and a mouse while a researcher sat close by. After Anna finished writing the piece, she read it aloud to the researcher. The researcher asked her if the last sentence made sense. ("Then on they played together and he never played a joke.") Anna read it again and nodded her head yes. The researcher then said, "If I put a *from* at the beginning of the sentence, would it still make sense?" Anna studied the suggestion, said yes and started to add it. But the researcher stopped her and asked if Anna would normally say it this new way (with *from*). She said no, so the researcher went on to talk with Anna about different dialects. They compared notes on how their different dialects allowed different responses and rejected others. In the end Anna decided to leave her sentence the way she originally wrote it.

As the year progressed, we began to interact more with the children during the composing period, usually at the very end of the composing session when the children had completed their own interactions with their compositions. (Although our original intention had been to play a somewhat uninvolved, "fly-on-the-wall" role, we began to realize that certain kinds of interaction, like the one described here, could provoke the use of interesting and otherwise uninitiated activity. It was a way of seeing what children *could* do, even if it was not always what they spontaneously *chose* to do.) One day in November of fourth grade, after Anna had finished her piece, she read it to the researcher and then made several revisions as a result of reading the piece aloud. When she finished, the researcher told Anna that she had used some invented spellings and asked her if she could find them. Anna read carefully, stopping to change FURST to *first* and JIST to *just*. The researcher pointed out that something was wrong with DREMING and asked her if she could figure it out. Anna immediately added the *a* in its appropriate place.

Peers

Peers as well as adults made important contributions to Anna's development as a writer. She often used them as resources for spelling, ideas, and clarification of procedures. One day Anna talked with Mike, one of her class-mates at her table, about the letters they were composing to Mr. and Mrs. Turkey, who had just found out they'd lost their son to a Thanksgiving feast. They discussed appropriate letter format, spelling, and whether their letters made sense given this outrageous event. The interaction was reciprocal, each sharing opinions of the other's work and requesting information from the other. The atmosphere of Linda's classroom with its organization for interaction among the children facilitated this kind of activity.

The fact that Anna asked others' opinions did not necessarily mean she felt obliged to take their advice, however. One day, for example, Anna asked a group of students how to spell *kept*. After she listened attentively to each one's view she decided her original spelling was probably right and left her text the way she first wrote it.

Often throughout the year when characters in her stories needed names, Anna would choose the names of her classmates. Sometimes this naming resulted from collaboration with the others, and sometimes she did it to tease them, creating a game that heightened the social context for writing. One day, for example, when a character needed a name, the aide, Ms. Manuel, got included. Anna played a little game and pretended that she was writing her story about the aide and hid her text from Ms. Manuel (who was trying to observe the writing process).

Sometimes classmates proved to be more of a hindrance than a help to Anna's composing, especially when the writing episode was being videotaped. One day Mike distracted her by sticking his fingers up behind her head and teasing her. His own agenda was to get himself on tape, and he didn't mind that he was interfering with Anna's writing. On another occasion, during the whole 20-minute writing center time, Anna completed only one sentence because she and Mike were comparing their heights, grabbing each other's papers, and talking about things other than their writing.

Occasionally Anna served as arbiter of other classmates' problems. One day, two boys fought over a picture that had been used as a stimulus for writing. One supposedly grabbed the picture from the other one, and a great ruckus arose. They were bothering Anna, so she stepped in, determined what was going on, and immediately solved the problem. Both boys seemed perfectly happy for Anna to settle their dispute.

At times, though, what actually made it onto a student's paper was largely the result of group effort. One day Anna collaborated with several different people while writing her piece. Initially the group at her table helped Anna make a decision about a topic. Then others in the class helped her at different times to spell conventionally and to edit for different kinds of semantic information, such as identifying omitted words or determining whether her story made sense.

COMPOSING OVER TIME IN A COMMUNITY OF WRITERS

I now examine Anna's development over the course of the two years we worked with her, proceeding chronologically from the beginning of third grade to the end of fourth, drawing largely on the field notes that described her behavior over that time period. I present this information in a series of "snapshots" that highlight different aspects of who Anna was as a writer.

Who Am I as a Writer?

By early in third grade, Anna had adapted very well to the social environment of her classroom. Since most of her classmates had lived in the Indian Oasis school district all their lives and were in many cases related, they already knew one another. They had also adapted well to Linda Howard, their teacher. Writing had a high priority in Linda's room, and Anna knew it was valued. She responded with a positive attitude toward writing even when it was difficult. In our first concepts of writing interview with her, Anna indicated that a good writer has the ability to "put words together and make them into a story." That is, meaning making is the main task of writers who are good at what they do. Bad writers, on the other hand, "just kind of sit down. They never do anything. They just play around. They try to write an interesting story and they're not doing that."

Anna had a clear idea of what her own writing was like when she had written well, valuing it "when it's real exciting or something." She also knew what she needed to do when her writing wasn't so good. "When it's boring you want to trade things around so it'd be kind of exciting." At that time she believed that spelling was important in writing because "you get to know words when you write them." It was also important "so you can read what the story says."

Anna's concepts of good and poor writing and the importance of spelling were often evidenced by her behavior during the writing process. She often used outside resources for spelling, but she didn't allow not knowing how to spell a word to interfere with the flow of her thoughts. She often wrote down a real word with a strong sound-symbol relationship to the one she had in mind, such as GET for *got*, WERE for *we're*, SAID for *sad*, or DID for *died*. It was as if she had a pool of linguistic data to choose from and, rather than inventing a completely new spelling, used a word she knew she already controlled. She continually expected her writing to make sense, and when it didn't she showed her dissatisfaction. At this early point in her development, she usually wrote about real events, and she liked for her writing to show what she had experienced. During a December interview, I asked why she liked certain pieces better than others.

Anna: 'Cause I got to see this started and I wrote about it and I didn't get
     to see these.
Researcher: OK, so you wrote about something that you saw that you
     really liked.
Anna: Uh huh [yes].
Researcher: OK . . . do you like to write about things that you've really
     seen, Anna?
Anna: Uh huh [yes].
Researcher: How come?
Anna: 'Cause you see 'em, and you get to tell about them.
Researcher: . . . And why do you like that?
Anna: So they'll know what it's like.

When questioned about the story she liked least, Anna said that she
didn't like the one about a fireman because "I didn't think what I was writing."

Researcher: OK, if you don't think, then what happens?
Anna: Then you just write anything and when you read it to somebody
     you just . . . you . . . you make like . . . like . . . you make mis-
     takes and you didn't do the right thing.

In this early interview, Anna showed that she had a difficult time separat-
ing her affection for her topic from the value she assigned to the quality of her
writing about that topic. If she didn't like the subject she usually ended up not
liking the piece; it wasn't good writing.

Researcher: OK, why don't you like the wolfman story too much?
Anna: Um, 'cause it tells about these people that are always getting
     choked from this man, that when it gets full moon he turns to a wolf-
     man and he kills these people.
Researcher: OK, and why don't you like that?
Anna: 'Cause it's mean.
Researcher: It's mean? OK, what about the story, though. Why did you
     write that if you don't like it?
Anna: Um . . . . [long silence]
Researcher: You don't know?
Anna: [shakes head]

Conversely, if she did like the topic or what happened in the story, then it
was good writing.

Researcher: OK, Anna, what else do you like about this story?
Anna: 'Cause it was a good time.

> *Researcher:* OK. You think that it was a good time and it was fun to write about it. Just looking at this, though, are there things here that you see that you especially like?
> *Anna:* Uh huh [yes].
> *Researcher:* What?
> *Anna:* Um, like at the end . . . That's when they're all singing along.

At other points in the interview Anna indicated that good writing is longer than bad writing, and that she had difficulty creating good writing when she had to write about what was assigned rather than what she wanted to write about.

Anna's writing concepts and writing behavior did not always mesh, however. Even though she believed that rewriting or "trading things around" would improve her writing she rarely did it. She often revised at the word level (to correct spelling or to "make it neater") or at the sentence level to include omitted words or to delete an inappropriate word or phrase. She rarely revised on the global textual level. Once written, a sentence was rarely discarded.

Audience, Story, Syntax, and Punctuation

Early in third grade, Anna wrote two letters, both requiring a stated audience. In both texts her pragmatic decisions were consistently appropriate: Her writing spoke directly to her audience; she made appropriate assumptions about what her audience knew or needed to know; and she showed her control of letter format.

Her narratives were more complex, however. Here she often made inaccurate assumptions about what her audience knew or needed to know about both the plot and the characters she was creating. In "The Wolfman," Anna probably had a clear picture in her own head of a horrible story about a werewolf who attacked innocent men and women. This piece was written on our first day of observation in Anna's classroom. As usual, the teacher had provided information on a general topic, Halloween, from which the students were to generate their own specific individual focus. Anna's story read as follows:

The Wolfman

> A man was going home. A strange man got him. The next morning they did not find him. The police said, "We can't. But we did not find him." Then a lady got killed. Then one night they found out that it was wolfman. They killed it.

She let her audience know that the police were inefficient at first but finally caught the man in the end. We don't get the whole picture, but we do get enough of the details to get a hint of the complicated scary story she must have had in her mind. The potential for an excellent story was tucked away in this and other brief pieces, but Anna's reader might find it difficult to imagine what Anna saw.

Her sense of story as evidenced by each of her narratives in this early phase was well developed, including characters, plot, and setting. What we would expect to see develop in subsequent stories is a fleshing out of each area: more well-defined settings, characters more fully described, and more detail to carry the plot development.

It is interesting to note the variety of sentence structures that occurred early in third grade. Anna introduced dialogue in her first narrative; she used different kinds of dependent clauses; she varied sentence structure order and expanded both noun and verb nodes of sentences with adjectives, adverbs, and prepositional phrases. She also used several different conjunctions (such as *but, then, and*, and *so*) as cohesive devices and either introduced or closed sentences with adverbial phrases acting as connectors.

Anna's stories early in third grade indicated that she controlled an increasing number of periods and other sentence boundary markers, hardly ever inserted inappropriate punctuation marks, and occasionally omitted commas. She seemed not to know how to use quotation marks conventionally yet.

Involvement and Revision

Two other interesting aspects of Anna's writing in third grade were her level of involvement in the writing process and her use of editing and revising. It seemed that when a narrative assignment was first presented to Anna, whether it was a fairy story or legend, she was willing and eager to invest her best energies. She chose a topic readily, wrote without interruptions, and made revisions that would increase the readability of her text. After she had already written on that theme, however, it seemed to be difficult for Anna to remain engaged. Then her behavior became primarily concerned with fulfilling the requirements of the assignment. This seemed to be corroborated by her mother's comment that Anna liked to write and chose to spend some of her free time writing, but she didn't like to rewrite and sometimes left a piece unfinished.

A piece written in January gave a picture of what writing was like for Anna when she wasn't particularly involved in it. This piece, "The State Seal," was part of a unit planned by Linda Howard to emphasize research writing. Each student was required to do some reading in encyclopedias and other reference materials on Arizona and to write separate expository pieces on the Arizona state flag, bird, seal, tree, and flower. Students were instructed first to read the materials (short articles and blurbs that were either in reference books or on the bulletin board), write about each of the major areas in their own words, and then draw a picture to illustrate their writing. Anna's final piece read as follows:

> Behind the seal are some mountains with the sunset coming up. On the side of the mountains there are a storage reservoir and dam. In the middle are irrigated farms.

Anna spent less actual writing time on this piece than she had on others up to this point (about 10 minutes as compared to an average of 20 minutes previously). She used several resources: the bulletin board materials, handouts on procedures for this assignment, and several people, including Linda Howard, the classroom aide, and several classmates. Much of her spelling was copied from the resource material.

When we look at Anna's behavior during these composing episodes, it's easy to see that she was not investing much of herself. When the writing center began, Anna had already begun the piece and had completed the first sentence. She reread that first sentence aloud and then said to the researcher, "I don't know what to write." She talked to her seatmates, wiggled around, played with papers in her folder, and then read the printed text on the state seal from the reference material. She asked the researcher what "storage reservoir" said and what it meant. She read her text again, and then added the sentence. When she finished the piece and tried to read her text aloud to the researcher, she had difficulty with many of the words that had been copied from the reference materials. Usually when Anna took a piece to be edited she remained involved in the editor's decisions about what might need to be revised and why. On this occasion, however, Anna took the piece to Ms. Manuel (the aide) to edit. While Ms. Manuel made the needed corrections, Anna danced around swinging her arms, uninvolved in the editing process. She then got new paper and rewrote, incorporating the changes Ms. Manuel had indicated.

At this point in her development, Anna revised mostly on a surface or local text level, adding punctuation and capitalization, correcting spelling, and adding or deleting words within a sentence, and engaged in very little global (whole-text level) revising. Global revisions seemed to occur only when Anna was highly involved in the task at hand, when she seemed to know what she already wanted to say and how to say it. Rereading and revising then became ways to confirm or to correct her written text to make it more like the text in her head.

What Anna Paid Attention To

It is clear from the evidence provided by Anna's composing behavior and from a description of general classroom activity that many factors interacted to both facilitate and deter Anna's composing. When she had a clear notion of what she wanted to say, external unrelated classroom activity had only a minimal effect. When she was neither enamored of the assignment nor compelled by a message of some sort, however, she was often distracted by others around her or provided the distraction for others. She had learned to incorporate social activity into her work process, though, and made good use of others as a resource for ideas, clarification of procedures, and confirmation of decisions.

In March of third grade, Anna was interviewed for the second time regarding her concepts of writing. It is interesting to note that at this time Anna still saw her own writing in the classroom as relatively mechanical. Even though she believed it was most important for writing to make sense, when asked the question, "What's the first thing you do when you write?" she presented a rather low-level skills picture of writing.

> *Anna:* First I look at the pictures on the board and see what I'm going to write about. Then I start writing about that picture.
> *Researcher:* What do you do when you want to end it?
> *Anna:* I just put an ending, like put "The End" or something.

Nothing in what she said had anything to do with creating stories that made sense, yet that was what was most important to Anna. She often gave indications that she was dissatisfied with stories that didn't make sense or were unclear when she read them back to the researcher at the end of the writing time. Her dissatisfaction was never expressed verbally, at least not in any articulate way, but the message was made clear by her nonverbal language—facial expressions such as frowns and groans, and body language like slumping and head shakes. Sometimes rather than actually making revisions, she would simply point out the problem.

Assignments, Involvement, and Connections Between Them

Two final features of Anna's writing during third grade are important to review: the effect of an assignment on her writing and her personal level of involvement—two apparently separate issues that were actually related.

It seems that the more specific and detailed a topic, the more difficult it was for Anna to "own" it, to become integrally involved in the writing. One day the students were asked to "write about what you see as your spaceship lands on a strange planet and you look out your porthole." Linda Howard had already prepared her own piece responding to this assignment, and she read it to the class as a model for their writing. Anna, however, had a difficult time with what to say. Her final product ended up being only one sentence: "One day I went to Jupiter to see what it's like," and she engaged in a lot of activity unrelated to the story she was trying to tell. It may be she had no story to tell at all. Was it that the activity distracted her attention from writing, or that she engaged in this behavior because she was having difficulty with the narrowly defined topic or her inability to match Linda Howard's model?

Anna's level of involvement in a writing episode related to the issue of assignments because she appeared to control a topic more effectively, exert more energy in the task, and maintain a more intense level of involvement when the topic was general rather than specific or when she ignored the specificity of the assignment and made it more what she wanted it to be. For instance, in an open-ended piece on Switzerland she had the latitude to focus on what she had experienced rather than to write on a specific feature of Switzerland. Her story read:

> When I was in Switzerland in the winter they have a horn that calls the cows home. And they have skiing like us. And they do not have houses like us. Their houses are big and on the top it is big. Their mountains are not like us. They are hilly. They are not like ours. [They are] really something.

In this piece Anna provided a vivid example of how writers bring their knowledge of the world to each episode. If Piaget is right, it must be difficult for a child raised in the desert all her life to imagine what life is like in someplace as different as Switzerland. Since she didn't have firsthand knowledge available, she had to rely on what she did know: her own physical surroundings. Her strategy was to focus on what she experienced vicariously through informational articles and pictures in reference materials and then compare those with her own world. Her text indicated that she was somewhat speechless as she tried to describe some of the features of the Swiss landscape. To Anna they were "really something." Even though this piece was difficult for Anna, she maintained a reasonably high energy level, perhaps because she could choose to say what she had in mind and not directly address an unfamiliar, inaccessible topic.

Commitment to Writing

Early in fourth grade, in the strong classroom community that Sr. Susan Caldwell was creating, we saw Anna beginning to include her classmates in her writing process, calling on them for help in spelling and ideas for writing. Sr. Susan had spent a lot of time discussing the social atmosphere of the room and how important the students all were to one another. Her major objective during this early part of the school year had been to help the children learn to work together and share their work without fear of derision and to help them understand and value all human beings.

In this atmosphere Anna was learning both involvement in and commitment to her writing. Nearly every day the children in Sr. Susan Caldwell's class shared their writing formally with one another. They were encouraged during these sharing times to ask questions of the writer. They asked for clarification and expansion of ideas, and they got ideas for their own writing from others. This new awareness of reader/listener concerns was evidenced in Anna's revisions and in her comments about how good writing makes sense to a reader. In her first concepts of writing interview in fourth grade, she identified Sharon as a good writer not only because she could spell well but because she wrote "long stories that make sense." She also indicated that Sharon and others were always available to read and respond to what she had written.

Even though Anna had learned to do a considerable amount of revising and rewriting during composing, this interview illustrated that she wasn't yet comfortable talking about the process. She hadn't yet developed an overt awareness of the planning and revising that went on when she wrote.

> *Researcher:* When you decide to write what's the first thing you do?
> *Anna:* Decide what I'm going to write.
> *Researcher:* OK, and then what do you do?
> *Anna:* Then I start writing.
> *Researcher:* And then what?
> *Anna:* And then, and then if I forget what, what I want, maybe I'll read it.
> *Researcher:* And when you want to end your writing what do you do?
> *Anna:* Um, I try and put, and put, and end it.
> *Researcher:* Like what?
> *Anna:* Like, um, like what I've got and what I can put in there.
> *Researcher:* If you're writing a story and you want to end it, how do you do it?
> *Anna:* I write different stories. I write "finished" and then if I want to write some more I get through with that one and then I write "The End."

Writing just happened; she seemed not yet consciously aware of how.

Anna was aware of several spelling strategies she used such as sounding out, using the dictionary, and asking other people, but learning to spell was still for the most part a mystery to her. She identified Sharon again as a good speller, although she conceded that even Sharon probably made spelling errors.

> *Researcher:* Do you think Sharon can spell "Halloween"?
> *Anna:* Unh-uh [no].
> *Researcher:* Do you think she will be able to spell it in a couple of weeks?

Anna: Uh-huh [yes].

Researcher: Why?

Anna: Like when she gets, um, if she only hears Halloween and she'll not know how to spell it, she'll probably get used to it and start spelling it.

The first five pieces Anna wrote in fourth grade were in response to some visual stimuli, such as a drawing or a story starter. Anna's texts assumed that the reader had a visual reference to the stimuli, which was accurate given how the writing was shared with readers in the classroom. Since the text was never separated from the visual stimuli, there was no need to explain it in detail. This economy principle of saying only what one needs to say and no more is a principle that guides adults' writing as well; for instance, the text of a cartoon is not expected to stand on its own, without the picture. As writers mature, they come to realize that stories written to be read by classmates who share a common context can be written so that an outsider can make sense of them as well; thus the concept of audience expands.

Variety in Writing

Further into fourth grade, Anna began to attempt a variety of texts: factual, descriptive, and narrative. She was also becoming more adept at getting her personality into her writing. A piece about Mexico was one of her favorites because it had a twist at the end. She had used this strategy before and enjoyed watching her reader's response. The piece read:

One day I went to Mexico. The first thing I did was I went to the ramada. I had so much fun that I did not want to go back to the motel. But I had to go cause it closed. The next day I went to the beach and I met a friend of mine. We went back to the ramada. Then I went back to the motel. The next morning I woke up and I was just dreaming. The end.

Anna called the ending "a joke" and laughed every time she read it. The class responded with praise when she read it aloud to them, liking the ending themselves.

Anna was also beginning to explore her social relationships in her writing. A piece about a spat between two friends appeared to be a realistic picture of friends having problems. This piece was also an interesting one to watch her write. The piece read:

One day I went to Sharon's house. Sharon had company so I went back to my house. I went to sleep. When I woke up I went to Sharon's

house. I did not know that Sharon's company was Geraldine so I
knocked on Sharon's door and she said, "Come in." I said, "O.K . . ."
Then Geraldine got mad and said, "I am going home." The end.

The assignment was creative writing on any topic, which Anna usually
liked. But that day she just couldn't get started. She chatted with others at the
table, read from a copy of *The Guinness Book of World Records*, folded paper
she needed for work in another center, and chatted again, all for nearly 15
minutes before she began to write. Even then she had difficulty coming up
with an interesting topic. She began in her usual way, "One day I went," and
interrupted herself to tell the researcher about surprises that Sr. Susan had
given the class and to ask Sharon how to spell her name. She finished the sentence, then stopped again to listen to conversation at the next table. Throughout the piece she stopped frequently to chat with classmates about several topics seemingly unrelated to her writing. The interesting point is that the
finished product did not provide any evidence of lack of engagement. In fact,
no measure of the piece's quality, such as syntax, mechanics, or semantics,
reflects Anna's halting progress in creating this text. In spite of all the interruptions, ten lengthy ones, she managed to maintain a sense of story, to write
syntactic structures that compared in complexity to others she had written
during the year, and to keep levels of conventional spelling and punctuation
within her own norm.

The key to how that could happen may be in her rereadings, either silent
or subvocalized, and in her revisions. Anna appeared to use each interruption
as a time to reread and/or revise her text. At one point when the class was
interrupted by a knock at the door, Anna included the knock in her text: "So I
knocked on Sharon's door and she said come in." It may have been that she
could incorporate these interruptions into her text because the topic was such
a familiar one. Sr. Susan commented that children often wrote about such
friendship quarrels and their resolutions.

New Sophistication as a Writer

By the second half of fourth grade, Anna had grown as a writer in many
areas: syntax, spelling, punctuation, semantics, and pragmatics. Her stories
were generally longer, more complex semantically, and more sophisticated
syntactically than before. With only a few exceptions, Anna's written product
demonstrated a growing control over most tasks. Our observations of her revealed more revisions and rereadings, often occurring together, and a sophisticated use of a variety of resources. Even though her composing process was
often interrupted by various events, she seemed not to be distracted much
unless she was struggling with a topic of little interest or a form that was new
and difficult.

A piece written in February illustrated her new sophistication:

The Mountain

One night Elaine was at the mountain. She was trying to fall down so she could go to the hospital. But her mother heard her and said, "Get down from there." So Elaine had to come down from the mountain. Elaine said, "I wanted to hurt myself!" Her mother said that if she did that she would have to stay in the hospital. So Elaine said, "OK, I will never go up the mountain." So Elaine never went to the mountain. But one day Elaine went up to the mountain and she fell down from the top. And her mother heard her fall down from the top. So they rushed her to the hospital. The doctor said that she would have to stay at the hospital for a week. When Elaine got out of the hospital her mother gave her a spanking. Now Elaine does not go the mountain.

Even though Anna wrote this story with hardly a pause, it was very complex. In the first few sentences she used adverbial phrases, prepositional phrases, embedded nominal clauses, an inferential connector that introduces an embedded adverbial clause ("if she did that"), a disjunctive inter-t-unit connector, conjoined verbs, and dialogue. Semantically the piece includes several relatively complex ideas: a child who wants to hurt herself so she can go to the hospital, a protective yet angry mother, and punishment for the child who disobeys. It isn't always clear what motives direct the actions of characters, but it is clear that for the most part Anna told a complicated story very well. In an interview, she rated this piece second in a group of stories, even though she couldn't say why. Perhaps she was enjoying the writer's prerogative to deal with miscreants any way she pleased.

A piece written in April, describing a visit to Tucson with classmates, is a good example of how far Anna had come as a writer in two years. (This text can be contrasted to her "wolfman" piece, seen earlier, which was the first story we saw her write.) After Anna had returned to her classroom from her overnight trip, she could hardly wait to write her story. She sat down quickly, got her writing materials together, and wrote this account of her adventure:

Tucson

One day I went to Tucson to stay with some people. We went to the Planetarium and then to the Museum of Arizona. Then we went to the arcade. We had lots of fun. After that we went to Miss Vaughan's house to put our clothes and sleeping bags away. Then we went to Miss Kasten's house to have the cookout. Michael and Gordon and Vincent and Dana were swimming already. After Michael was cooking the hot dogs. Then we ate. After that we had ice cream for dessert. Then me and Miss Vaughan and Elaine and Rachel went to the Tucson Mall. We went on the escalator and looked at the records and clothes and Miss Vaughan bought herself something. Then we went to the YMCA to swim. We stopped swimming at 9:00. Then we went back to Miss Vaughan's house and had cereal with bananas. Then we watched a little t.v. and then went to bed. In the morning we got ready and had cereal with bananas and strawberries and milk and donuts. We went to go pick up those Michael, Gordon, Vincent, Dana and Miss Kasten. We met them at the university and then we came to school. The End.

Anna, in a change from what we had seen on other occasions, did not choose words because they were easy to spell nor did she avoid difficult ones. She invented the spellings PLANA TEREUM (planetarium), ESKLADER (escalator), and UNESTE (university), as well as spellings for proper names. She kept all the events in their correct order and even remembered what she had to eat.

This composing activity was a delight to observe. Anna stopped only occasionally to confirm a detail with the researcher. She was driven by her message and the need to communicate it with the others in her room. It seemed that telling it was almost as much fun as being there, a fun that was not daunted by necessary revisions and rereadings.

ANNA'S USE OF LINGUISTIC SYSTEMS

In this section I summarize some aspects of Anna's use of language systems (syntax, spelling and punctuation, and semantic/pragmatic features) over the two-year period of the study. In doing so, I demonstrate the use of categories of data that may help teachers understand their own students' writing development. To help our students grow more proficient in using written language for its myriad possible functions, we need to consider carefully both how to look at and how to describe what we see. Not only do we need to describe this development so we can provide useful instruction, we need to help others understand it as well: the student, other teachers, parents, and school administrators interested in a more valid description of language growth than standardized testing allows.

Syntax

Figure 7.1 shows the varying lengths (expressed as words per story) of Anna's pieces of writing across third and fourth grades. It is clear that as third grade progressed, Anna's story length fluctuated greatly. Her longest story of the year and her shortest were produced close together, on April 20 (story

Third Grade

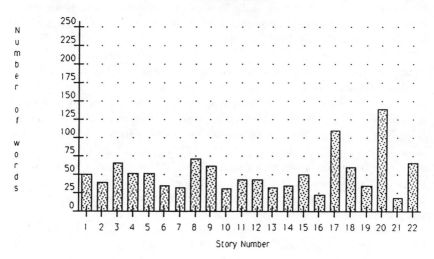

Fourth Grade

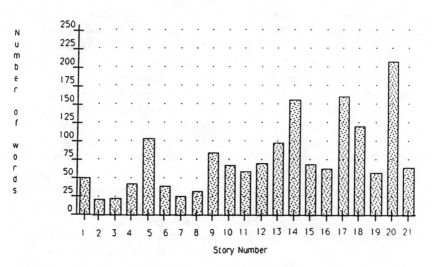

FIGURE 7.1: Anna—Words per Story

number 20) and May 5 (story number 21). Many factors, of course, interact to determine both the extent and the quality of a writer's performance across time. However, over the two-year period, Anna's texts gradually increased in length, particularly during the second half of fourth grade.

Figure 7.2 similarly shows the length of Anna's sentences (more technically, words per t-unit; see Chapter 2) across the two years. (This words per t-unit measure is a commonly accepted index of syntactic growth.) The graph illustrates that Anna's sentence length across two years did not follow any sort of linear developmental trend but rather varied widely from story to story, although the pattern appeared somewhat more stable by fourth grade. Since many factors (social, academic, and personal) interact within any writing episode, one is not likely to see a straight line of development revealed in any measure of performance in a context like this one. Because of such variability, no single piece of writing can ever be a definitive statement about a child's writing. The pattern of development over time is the key.

Spelling and Punctuation

Figure 7.3 illustrates the percentage of words that Anna spelled correctly in each story we collected over the two years we observed her. The same variability occurs here as in her syntax, although there is a general trend toward increasingly appropriate spelling. It is important to note that neither teacher had a formal spelling program; Anna's progress resulted from her own growing knowledge of the English spelling system, supported by the use of human and physical resources (peers, teachers, aides, researchers, dictionaries, wall charts, and bulletin board materials) as they were needed in the functional context of producing text. Anna used many of those resources during any given composing episode, with some types taking precedence over others depending on what words needed to be spelled, who she sat with, her particular mood and inclination of the day, and what other classmates were doing.

When Anna's spelling patterns are examined more closely, several interesting patterns emerge. First, as mentioned earlier, when Anna wasn't sure how to spell a word she often substituted a similar real word, perhaps pulling words from a preexisting linguistic data pool rather than producing new words (or nonwords). In many instances word length was identical, and one vowel might be substituted for another (e.g., BET for *but*).

Second, there were only a few words for which Anna invented spellings more than twice. Some of these were spelled the same way every time, in a single story each. Anna also spelled the word *when* the same way (WHAN) every time—a fairly stable pattern, since it occurred in March and May of third grade and December and March of fourth grade. This shows how rare it is for a writer to stay with a consistent invented spelling; with the exception of

Third Grade

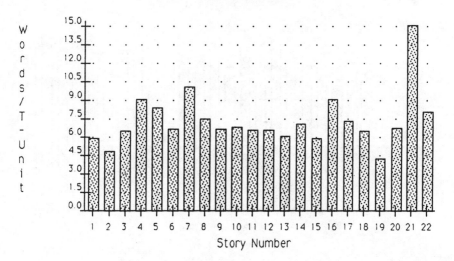

Fourth Grade

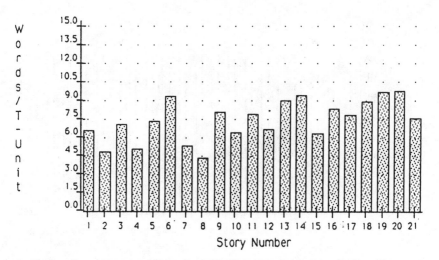

FIGURE 7.2: Anna—Words per T-Unit (Sentence Length)

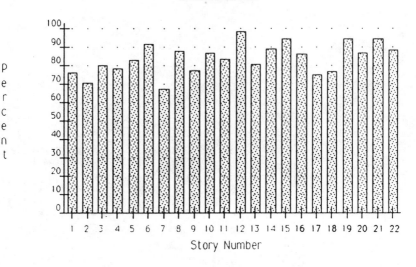

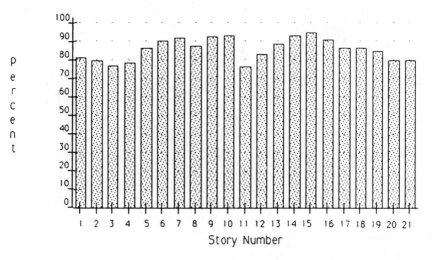

FIGURE 7.3: Anna—Percent Appropriate Spelling

this case, if Anna used invented spellings more than once or twice for the same word over time they tended to be reinventions (i.e., different invented spellings). For instance, *never* was spelled NERV in April of third grade; in fourth grade, it was spelled NARE in October, and appeared both correctly and as NAVER in February, with a recurrence of NAVER in March.

Most of Anna's invented spellings made sense, such as STORES for *stories*, GOST for *ghost*, and HERT for *hurt*. Only a few were more unusual, such as UETPET for *Kitt Peak* and SCORDY for *scary*. However, Anna's problems with spelling were minimal and indicated active attempts to apply hypotheses about how to represent familiar words in written form. For the words Anna used most, standard spelling was the rule.

Moving on to punctuation, Figure 7.4 shows the percentage of correct punctuation in Anna's stories. The pattern is so uneven as to suggest that Anna's use of punctuation was probably dependent on many factors such as the type of punctuation required by the story content, her control over that punctuation type, other cognitive and linguistic demands, and the constraints of the context of each writing episode. Her pieces in which punctuation was 100 percent appropriate tended to be short ones with simple declarative sentences; her piece with the least successful use of punctuation was a long one with a good deal of dialogue, including questions and exclamations.

Anna was most successful in her use of periods, supplying them 73.5 percent of the time they were needed in third grade and 87.1 percent in fourth. Question marks (although of course less frequent than periods) were supplied appropriately about a quarter of the time in third grade and in every case in fourth. She rarely used commas or quotation marks, using only one of each in all of third grade, but supplying them appropriately somewhat more often (33 percent and 19 percent of the time, respectively) in fourth grade.

Semantics and Pragmatics

The two aspects of the semantic and pragmatic systems of language that I focus on here are Anna's choices of literary genre and of the topics and content of her writing.

Genre. I define genre here in terms of four different kinds of texts that Anna produced: narrative, expository, letters, and an "other" category used primarily for pieces written about drawings or as continuations of story starters. In third grade the genre of a particular piece was, for the most part, stipulated by an assignment from the teacher. On only one occasion when we were present during that year were students allowed unassigned writing. (On that occasion, Anna wrote a letter to the classroom aide who was in the hospital.) Genre, like topic, was self-selected in fourth grade. Over two years, Anna

Third Grade

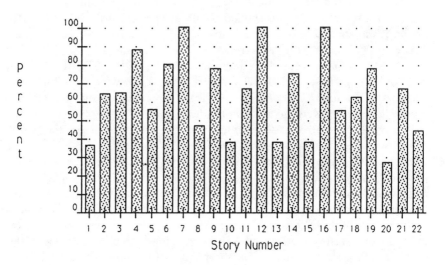

Fourth Grade

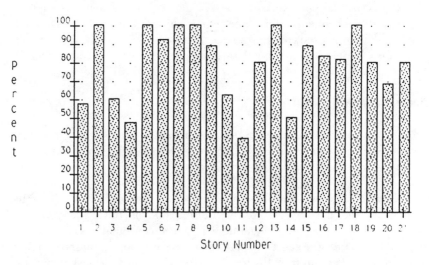

FIGURE 7.4: Anna—Percent Appropriate Punctuation

wrote 29 narratives, 4 expository pieces, 3 letters, and 7 pieces in the "other" category.

The differences between these genres as Anna used them are clear. The narratives, perhaps because there were so many of them, represented a wide variety of quality of performance. Anna clearly knew how to produce an effective narrative, but whether she controlled story structure or not on any given occasion was dependent on a complex combination of social and personal factors.

Anna's expository pieces were not particularly successful as written products. Our observations of her indicated that she wasn't yet sure how to get information from a textual resource into her own composition. She wrote expository pieces only rarely, and it is likely that much more of her reading material had been narrative than expository, so she probably had no clear schema for expository text. Her state seal piece (seen earlier) was copied almost verbatim from resource material, so the elements usually used to evaluate an expository piece—purpose, content, structure, and audience awareness—weren't given much attention. However, the end product was probably not what mattered most in Anna's expository writing. Linda Howard indicated to us that she assigned a research unit because she wanted her students to begin to investigate different kinds of resource texts and learn that a different kind of writing results from research on a topic. Linda could have done more to help her students go from reference books to their own written text, and to discern a purpose for their investigation.

Letters, in contrast, were a much more comfortable genre for Anna, both real letters and those written as imaginative exercises. In one case, the class had just returned from watching a scary movie and a special program by the fourth graders, who were all decked out in Halloween costumes. As soon as Anna's class arrived back in their classroom, their assignment was to write a thank-you letter to the fourth graders for presenting the program. Anna wrote:

> Dear Ghouls,
> I really liked it. Our class was scared, real scared. It's good. It was fun but when you came in, it really was scary. I liked the program.

(Pronoun use in this piece was discussed in Chapter 5.) Anna was excited, delighted, and scared all at once, and all of that comes through in this piece. She wrote directly to a specific audience, and although she didn't provide specifics of what elicited this particular emotion, the emotion was clear. Function existed and the text that resulted was meaningful. Therefore, even though the form was not fully conventional, this did not seriously hamper the communication of Anna's intended meaning.

A fictional letter Anna wrote to Mr. and Mrs. Turkey (discussed earlier in this chapter, as well as in Chapter 5) was in response to the assignment: "Send a sympathy letter to Mr. and Mrs. Turkey. They have just lost their son to a Thanksgiving dinner. Use correct letter form. Don't forget the date." Even though this letter wasn't written to a real person and surely wasn't mailed, some function was obviously being met, perhaps that of eliciting imagination. Anna's stories across the two years suggested that she had a vivid sense of humor. It was just this kind of activity, writing a letter to turkey parents whose son was eaten on Thanksgiving, that Anna seemed to enjoy. Our observations suggest that Anna's level of involvement was high on this piece, and her final product confirms it:

> Dear Mr. and Mrs. Turkey,
> I am sorry that your son died in a dinner. I felt sad for you. I think the next Thanksgiving you should hide. But on Thanksgiving I will not eat you because I think you are nice people. I am sorry your son Bob died.

The pieces categorized as "other" in terms of genre are those Anna produced in response to drawings or to story starters. As for quality of text, these pieces are decidedly more constrained than Anna's usual narratives. The pragmatics of producing these pieces were quite different from the narrative situations in that the drawing itself, the visual aspect, seemed to stand for or represent ideas that needed no further comment. To describe the picture would be redundant, since the audience never read the text without the accompanying drawing. Furthermore, the artistic element of the communication seemed to be valued at least as much as the text, by both the teacher and the other students. To compare this "other" category with either the narratives or the expository pieces would be like evaluating Picasso by Faulkner's standards. Even though Anna was neither a Faulkner nor a Picasso, we cannot gain much insight into her writing development by lumping these pieces together. The aspect of genre in semantic evaluation clearly illustrates why writing development must be examined within a context that includes all the relevant elements of each composing event.

In general, Anna's choice of genres seems to support Halliday's (1975) contention that form follows function and that meaning-making that originates from energy supplied by that function is crucial to the success of both the process and the product of written language.

Topic and Content.   The topics of the stories Anna wrote in third grade were almost exclusively determined by the teacher's assignments, but in fourth grade, her topics were self-selected. (Anna sometimes chose story starters as one of many possible options provided for those who needed some help selecting a topic.) Even in third grade, however, the specific content of what

Anna wrote was always her own choice and often reflected events occurring in her life both inside and outside the classroom.

During October of third grade the major topic for writing was Halloween, including ghosts, goblins, ghouls, and werewolves. Anna chose to write a story about a wolfman who she said she didn't like because "he was mean." She said she had seen a similar story on television; popular media clearly influenced the content of some of Anna's stories.

The only story of Anna's we collected in December was one about a Christmas elf who got hurt, was rushed to the hospital, and mysteriously died. Anna's mother indicated that Anna's grandfather had been taken to the hospital and died about the same time that Anna wrote this story.

In February, Anna wrote a story about a queen who was poisoned when something was added to her food. The topic was fairy tales, but Anna said she got the idea for her story from a salt fight that morning in the cafeteria during breakfast when some students surreptitiously put salt in other students' food. Putting something in someone's food made its way into Anna's fairy tale.

In a February story about an Indian boy, the main character was given the name Warrior. She indicated that she got the idea for that particular name from the high school sports team, the Baboquivari Warriors.

An elaborate story in March about a puppy getting run over by a car and ending up in a circus came from a cartoon Anna saw on television, and another piece, "I kissed the earth goodbye," was influenced by a story the teacher read to the class that had a mouse as the main character.

Throughout fourth grade, some of Anna's topics were repeat performers: visiting with friends, animal tales, and stories growing out of real events such as the trips to Tucson and to Rocky Point, Mexico. Anna indicated that she liked to make her readers laugh or show surprise when they read or listened to her pieces. She especially liked a piece about winning the lottery because she felt that it was exciting to win money and go to places like Hawaii and Mexico. It is here we see the dreamer in Anna.

One interesting piece of information about the content of Anna's stories came up in an interview in April. I pointed out to Anna that she always ranked her make-believe narratives higher on her preference list than narratives about real events. Anna replied by saying that it was always easier to write a made-up story "because your ideas just come and you can just write them down instead of remembering what you did." Anna didn't yet fully appreciate her talent for having ideas "just come," which many adult writers would envy.

CONCLUSION

Without realizing it, the Anna I had come to know and appreciate gave me a treasured gift. For two years I was permitted to sit next to her on various occasions as she shared her ideas, her thinking processes, and her evolving notions about how language could serve to bring her thoughts to others. Anna taught me that a complex combination of events interact to create both the writing process and the product that results. Every writer comes to the writing event with a set of social, academic, and personal experiences and beliefs that provide a unique setting for each composing activity. Because of that uniqueness, only by looking at writing over time can we discover a particular writer's strengths and challenges in composing.

Anna showed me what becoming a writer was like for her. Sharing that information with her teachers helped them provide instruction that was more likely to aid her progress. Further, it helped me understand my own writing process as well. Looking at Anna's composing process was a little like holding up a mirror to my own. The same factors that influenced Anna's process—social, academic, and personal—affect mine as well. In that sense, Anna's examined writing life was a prototype of all writer's lives. Anna's gift, then, to me and to you is both professional and personal. For that, Anna, I thank you.

CHAPTER 8

Parrots, Soldiers, and Deer-Hunting

GORDON GROWS AND CHANGES

Sandra Wilde

GORDON WAS A DELIGHTFUL CHILD we all enjoyed working with; although he was not seen by the school as particularly strong academically, he enjoyed writing and thought of himself as a writer. This case study describes some of his characteristics as a writer and some elements of his growth as a writer during the third and fourth grades. (See Chapter 2 for a further description of Gordon as a person and a student.)

GORDON WRITING: THIRD GRADE

In the work of any writer, many linguistic and personal factors are interacting at once; these need to be examined to get a sense of all the influences going into a single composition. In the sections that follow I describe some major features of Gordon's writing processes, looking at his writing from multiple perspectives and going from global concerns, such as concepts of writing, to narrower ones, such as spelling and punctuation.

Concepts of Writing

During writing concept interviews in October and March, as well as in three periodic interviews about his stories, Gordon revealed a good deal about how he conceived of writing. To him, writing was a fairly straightforward, uncomplicated matter: "I just sit there, and then I think and then I write it." This was reflected in his composing behavior; he never agonized over what to write about but just plunged right in. When asked why he chose some of his stories as better than others, he usually referred only to the content, saying, for instance, that a story was good "because we found some eggs," or "because it's how the parrot got to talk." He could also give a very global assessment of why he liked a story: "it's the words, and the letters, and how it sounds." Also, he said that a good writer is someone whose stories are sometimes funny and sometimes sad. He also felt that surface aspects of writing were important; he said consistently that a good writer was one who had good handwriting, "writes straight . . . and never makes no mistakes." A good writer doesn't write "sloppy or crooked," in contrast to bad writers who have messy papers when they erase, which "makes black marks and tears the paper." He also felt that his teacher would prefer his longer stories, that length was an important measure of a piece's worth. He saw these surface aspects of writing as important for success in the adult world. Spelling is important because if you're "a police" you have to write well on the job. Other adults get forms where "they have to fill out all the blanks," and if words are misspelled, "he'll give it back to you." In contrast, Gordon felt that when writing a personal letter to another adult, spelling didn't matter because "it's your writing."

In general, these interviews revealed a writer who was relatively un-sophisticated about the process, who liked a story if it was about something interesting, and who was aware of the impression made by surface aspects such as spelling and handwriting. He was not yet able to talk about his stories or the writing process in a more detailed way.

Interaction

Gordon was a very active, sociable child who could not easily sit still while he wrote. For instance, during a story that he wrote in November of third grade, which was only 26 words long, Gordon stopped 14 times to talk to peo-ple. Some of these occasions were related to the writing, such as asking other children how to spell a word or asking for an eraser. Others were purely social: talking about bingo games (as he wrote); asking the researchers if they were married; talking about a Thanksgiving song; or teasing a classmate. An ob-server sitting with him got a feeling of a fairly constant stream of interaction; even when he was writing silently, Gordon was often following a conversation elsewhere at the table and joined in when he had a comment to make.

While writing another piece, in March, Gordon showed that he was inter-ested in anything and everything. As he wrote the story, he talked to a number of fellow students and to the researcher observing him about a range of topics totally unrelated to his written text. He said that his mother had more money than she used to; went to see what his friend Vincent was reading; asked what the researcher and Charlie were talking about; asked his seatmates if anyone liked to watch the television show "Facts of Life" and discussed television in general with them; told the researcher about a story Phyllis wrote; sang; teased Mark; and asked Diane if she was Mark's cousin. Gordon was able to carry on these multiple conversations while continuing to write his story and to keep up his train of thought, producing a story that his teacher called "super-imaginative." The piece read:

> One day some soldiers were hunting for old, old men and the soldiers did find some old, old men. When they found old, old men they whipped them with a black whip. One day two old, old men heard about the soldiers. When the two old, old men were talking about the soldiers the soldiers were hiding by some nearby trees. So they could hear them.

Although his stories were perhaps shorter than they could have been because he spent so much time talking, the interaction didn't appear to interfere with his concentration. Many writers find it frustrating to try to write while people are talking around them, but Gordon appeared to thrive on it. Although he was not this active every time he wrote, it was certainly a common mode of behavior for him. In an interview in May, he admitted that he liked to be active while he wrote and that he chose to do so most of the time. He recognized that there were children in the class who preferred to sit and write without stopping, and that both of these personal styles were valid.

Assignments

During third grade, most of the writing the children did was to some extent assigned. They often had a choice among several topics, pictures, or story starters. All the children's writing was influenced in different ways and to a different extent by these constraints. The imaginary diary of a pilgrim on the *Mayflower* that Gordon wrote (described in Chapter 2) is an example of how the students worked within such constraints. Similarly, in January, the class worked on a research unit on Arizona. One of the assignments was to produce stories about the state bird, flag, and tree, using encyclopedias as reference sources. Two pieces by Gordon reflect two different approaches to such an assignment. The first one read:

> The green field stands for the forests. It was named for George Washington. The seal was adopted in 1889 and the flag was adopted in 1925. The state was named on the date 1889.

Gordon produced a text that contained, to a great extent, the kind of information his teacher wanted, but that was largely copied from the encyclopedia. He spent a fair amount of the writing period arguing with a classmate over whose turn it was to use the "A" volume of the *World Book* (which was, of course, much in demand). The resulting text was very flat in tone and unlike his usual writing style. Two days later, he wrote about the state flag. His incomplete piece read:

> The State Flag is the American Flag because [word unclear] likes the State Flag. Even Ms. Kasten and Ms. Vaughan and Ms. Wilde and Ms. Bird likes.

This piece was a very different approach to the topic than the earlier one. Rather than writing a report, he personalized the topic by writing about people liking the flag and including the names of all the researchers. Linda Howard was very dissatisfied with the research unit as a whole, feeling that she had asked the children to do something too difficult. When faced with an assignment that was beyond his capabilities (i.e., a true research paper), Gordon attempted one day to produce the kind of product his teacher wanted and another day to write in his usual way. One can't really determine from the available evidence which he preferred doing; he did, however, seem more serious while writing the first piece and more playful during the second one.

In February, the class began a unit on folktales. They had read some together, and their writing assignment was to do a story along the lines of how the leopard got its spots or how the rattlesnake got its rattle. Gordon chose to write about how the parrot got to talk:

How the Parrot Got to Talk

Once there was a parrot named Draw Two and every morning and night Draw Two would sing his very best song. It goes like this: "LALALALALA," to me. And everybody would wake up and say, "That's incredible." In the morning Draw Two would sing his very best song again: "LALALALALA" to me.

After writing the title, Gordon didn't really stick to the topic at all, but wrote the beginnings of a personal fantasy about having a parrot who would sing to him. He used the assignment only as an idea source, and then went off in his own direction. His teacher liked the story, saying that it sounded like the way he talked and thought.

In general, Gordon was able to handle the constraints of assignments because he took control of the process and decided how much he would let himself be influenced by the assignment. The stories described here illustrate a range of choices, from paying only minimal attention to the assignment to trying to produce just what was expected. Gordon often went in his own direction on an assignment, and it was important that his teacher allowed this to happen.

Topic Development and Style

Gordon's stories were for the most part imaginative narratives with a lot of action. He wrote in both first and third person, but none of his pieces were factual accounts of his own life. He often put a special imaginative twist on a fairly ordinary topic. A story Gordon wrote about a turkey is a fairly typical piece from early in third grade:

One day a turkey got out of his home. His mother was worried about him. He was walking in the woods and he got eaten up.

This very short and simple story has a clear beginning, middle, and end, demonstrating that Gordon already had a basic sense of story when we began observing him. Although many of his stories (such as the one about the old, old men and the soldiers seen earlier) didn't have real endings, this was probably due to the limited time allowed for writing (usually 20 minutes) rather then to his lacking a sense of how plots develop.

In January, Gordon wrote about a picture of the Grand Canyon, producing the following text:

> One day I went with some people to the Grand Canyon. And we went with some horses. And when we got there we went down to the canyon. When we got down the canyon we climbed some hills. When we were climbing the hills a volcano exploded. And we almost fell down into the water.

Gordon often spent time at the beginning setting the scene and then added action later as ideas occurred to him. He typically did little planning before he wrote, preferring to construct meaning as he went along. In this case, he began writing immediately, made comments to the researchers only about spelling and other surface features, and never discussed what he was going to write about. The last sentence of this story added a typical Gordon twist; where another child might have stuck to a hiking story, Gordon added an exploding volcano.

In March, the students were asked to write about what circus act they would like to be. Again, Gordon added a typically vibrant touch:

> One day when I was at the circus a man was whipping the lions so they would jump through the circle that's on fire. After the circus was over the lion's trainer asked me if I wanted to be a trainer like him. I said, "O.K."

This was a very short story, no more than a vignette really, but it created an image very effectively.

Another interesting feature of Gordon's writing is that the majority of his narratives began with the words "One day" (along with variations such as "One Christmas night" and "Once upon a time"). This was another index of his straightforward, relaxed approach to writing. When he was ready to write, he sat down and began in the most convenient way, confident that once he started writing, the ideas would develop. Many adult writers who are terrified at the sight of a blank piece of paper could learn from Gordon.

Syntax

Gordon used a variety of syntactic structures in third grade. His simple turkey story, written in November, was made up of four relatively short t-units (i.e., independent clauses) with an average length of 6.5 words, with no subordinate clauses. In contrast, his lion-tamer piece and a story about Switzerland, both written in March, were relatively complex syntactically. Two of the sentences in the story about the lion tamer were quite long, one of them 24 words (4 clauses) in length and the other 19 words (5 clauses). Similarly, one of the sentences in the Switzerland story was 29 words long and contained 4 clauses. Looking at two of the sentences illustrates the type of syntactic complexity that Gordon was able to handle. The first one, seen earlier, reads, "One day when I was at the circus a man was whipping the lions so they would jump through the circle that's on fire." In this sentence, a main clause ("One day . . . a man was whipping the lions") is modified by an adverbial clause of time ("when I was at the circus") and another one of intention ("so they would jump through the circle"), which itself is modified by a nominal clause ("that's on fire").

The long sentence from the Switzerland story reads, "One day when I went to Switzerland and saw a lot of houses and buildings, as I was walking down the street a man said, 'Do you live here?'" This sentence contains a main clause ("One day . . . a man said") and a direct question ("Do you live here?"), as well as adverbial clauses of time ("when I went . . .") and manner ("as I was walking . . ."). These two sentences are so complex because they each modify a main clause in more than one way. Although syntactic complexity of this type occurred only occasionally in Gordon's writing, it certainly indicates what he was capable of doing.

Spelling and Punctuation

Gordon's spelling and punctuation varied a good deal from story to story, and it was interesting to look at the types of invented spelling he used and the linguistic systems he was drawing on. Two pieces are used to illustrate this, shown here with invented spellings in upper-case letters.

Gordon's Christmas Piece

One Christmas night Santa didn't show up for Christmas. BU'T [but] not OLLE [only] that HAPPED [happened] when Santa didn't show up for Christmas. The KIS [kids] were CRIY [crying] to THERE [their] moms and dads. When they did the moms WOD [would] say, "DONT [don't] WEA [worry]. Santa will come and give you presents."

Gordon's Outer Space Piece

One day I was on a SIUP [ship] and the SIUP went KURSA [crazy]. Then I LANDA [landed] on a planet called Uze. Then KUEL [quickly] I UN HUT [unhooked] my CEBCLEBAT [seatbelt] and I looked out the WIDE [window] AN [and] I opened the door AN [and] I SPED [stepped] outside.

With the Christmas piece, Gordon was very involved in his writing, with few distractions of any kind. With the outer space piece he was quite restless; Linda Howard described it as being a day in which "he was very nervous and upset and climbing the walls." These occasions were thus very different for him, but on both of them he chose not to ask for help with spelling or to look up words. As a result, both of these stories contained a number of invented spellings (nine different ones each).

Several linguistic features can be seen operating in these invented spellings. Some examples are:

Phonetic

AN/and
KIS/kids
WEA/worry
WOD/would

The term "phonetic influence" is used here to describe cases in which a child was attempting to spell the word more or less the way it sounded. Even WEA and KIS are not implausible phonetic spellings in light of Gordon's dialectal variant of English.

Orthographic Patterns

KURSA/crazy
KUEL/quickly
CEBCLEBAT/seatbelt

In these examples, Gordon began each word with an incorrect but plausible letter. The sound that is spelled with a *c* in *crazy* and a *q* in *quickly* is of course spelled phonetically with *k*, the letter Gordon used. *Seatbelt* begins with the letter *s* and the phoneme /s/, but in this case Gordon chose an alternative, but equally common, spelling of the phoneme.

Real-Word Substitutions

AN/and
SPED/stepped
THERE/their
WIDE/window

When children aren't sure of how to spell a word, they may substitute a real word, which may be a homophone as in THERE for *their*.

Suffixes

CRIY/crying
LANDA/landed
KUEL/quickly
UN HUT/unhooked

An important aspect of spelling for children to gain control over is inflectional (e.g., past tense) and adverbial suffixes. These examples illustrate that Gordon had not yet completely learned to abstract these out, although he did spell *-ed* conventionally in other words in these two stories, as well as *-ing* in other pieces. (He used no other *-ly* adverbs in third grade.)

Punctuation Related

BU'T/but
DONT/don't
UN HUT/unhooked

Gordon had learned that some words ending in *t* have apostrophes in them; he just hadn't completely learned which ones (although *but* is the only word he ever inserted one in inappropriately). Similarly, children take a while to learn exactly where some word boundaries fall. (In other stories Gordon wrote "cowboy rustler" as one word and "nearby" as two.)

Handwriting

Stories from November 24 (Figure 8.1), March 9 (Figure 8.2), and March 30 (Figure 8.3) provide a sense of Gordon's handwriting at three different points in the year. Early in the year, handwriting was a relatively slow and labored process for him. He was left-handed, and on November 24 the researcher noticed that he made many of his letters unusually; for instance, he started his *s*'s at the bottom rather than the top. There was almost a sense that he was drawing each letter individually; that is, that handwriting was not yet very automatic for him. His handwriting was large and he fit only about five words on a line. By March 9, manuscript printing had become far easier for Gordon. He was faster, his letters were smaller and more regularly formed, and he did not have to devote much conscious effort to details of handwriting. Not all of his stories were written as neatly as the March 9 piece, but this one indicates what he was capable of when he chose neatness as one of his goals for a story. It should be noted that Linda Howard did not provide any penmanship instruction to the students; this change in Gordon seemed to come about primarily through time spent on writing. By March 30, Gordon had begun writing some stories in cursive script, which Linda Howard had suggested that the

One day a turkey got
Out of his home his mother
was weda abbite hem.
he was walkingin the Woods
and he got eat ain up.

FIGURE 8.1: Gordon's Handwriting (November 24)

One day when I Was at the Circus
a man was Weaping the Lions so
they Could jump therre the Corse thes
or frie. after the Circus was ofor' the
tringermr akeders me If I Wantan to be
a tringermr liKe he I said," ok.

FIGURE 8.2: Gordon's Handwriting (March 9)

One day when I went to Switzerland
and saw a lout of houses & bidings
as I was walking down the seet
a man said do you live here. I
said no he said oh.

FIGURE 8.3: Gordon's Handwriting (March 30)

students do. Since this was a new process for him, he returned to making his letters slowly and carefully at least some of the time. He had a little trouble forming some of the letters (e.g., *k* in "walking"; *s* in "seet"), but was eager to write in cursive and persevered. In a May interview, he mentioned that he preferred cursive and wrote with it most of the time now that he had learned it. He even said that he found cursive easier than manuscript.

Developmental Trends in Third Grade

Any single piece of Gordon's writing involved many factors interacting at once. It is instructive to look at some of these aspects across time, particularly those aspects that can be quantified. An early piece such as the turkey story is clearly different in many ways from a later one such as the story about the soldiers and the old, old men. Can these differences be characterized? As with Anna (see Figures 7.1 through 7.4), looking at various aspects of Gordon's development across the 20 stories that were collected in third grade reveals a great deal of variability; these measures indicate not a gradual change from story to story but extreme shifts between stories. These shifts are, of course, due to the variability of writing situations: the topic, the child's mood, choices about whether to try to spell conventionally or not, amount of social interaction, and other factors that combine to produce texts that differ in these quantifiable ways as well as more impressionistic ones. However, cognitive development is also likely to be a factor; one can perhaps get some sense of it by comparing groups of stories. Gordon's 20 stories for the year were divided in half chronologically for comparative purposes and various features of his writing were measured, as seen in Table 8.1.

Gordon's stories stayed within a fairly narrow range of length throughout the year (from 11 to 66 words, with a mean of 37.6 and a standard deviation of 11.2). Although he was able to write faster later in the year as he gained more control over his penmanship, his stories in the second half of the year were only slightly longer on average than those in the first half.

Gordon's number of words per t-unit (i.e., sentence length) varied quite a

TABLE 8.1: Gordon—Third Grade, First and Second Half

	First Half	Second Half	Overall
Words per story	35.9	39.3	37.6
Words per t-unit	8.75	8.93	8.84
Clauses per t-unit	1.48	1.72	1.61
Appropriate spelling	81.9%	77.1%	79.4%
Appropriate punctuation	47.6%	27.9%	35.0%

bit, ranging from 5.85 to 19.0 (the latter was a one t-unit story), with a mean of 8.84 and a slight increase from the first to the second half of the year. Clauses per t-unit varied from 1.0 to 3.66, with a mean for the year of 1.61, comparable to an eighth-grade mean of 1.68 reported by Hunt (1965). The means for the two halves of the year were 1.48 for the first half and 1.72 for the second half; clauses per t-unit typically grow in fairly small increments, usually only about 0.1 clause per year (Hunt, 1965). In the first half of the year, only one story out of ten had more than two clauses per t-unit; this was a very short story with only one t-unit. In the second half of the year, six out of ten pieces had two or more clauses per t-unit.

Gordon's percentage of appropriate spelling ranged from 68 percent in the story about the soldiers and the old, old men to 100 percent, with a mean of 79.4 percent. There was a slight drop from the first to the second half of the year, but it is small when considered in terms of the overall variability. Of the 20 words Gordon used most frequently, which made up 39.7 percent of his total words, 97.1 percent of their occurrences were appropriately spelled. There was a floor of about 70 percent conventional spelling below which Gordon rarely fell. The 20 most frequent words accounted for a little more than half of this, but the 70 percent floor also meant that Gordon was quite successful in spelling words he used less often (i.e., six or fewer times during the year).

Gordon's percentage of conventional punctuation varied even more than his spelling did, ranging from 0 to 100 percent, with a mean of 35.0 percent. For the most part, periods were the only punctuation marks that Gordon used, and he omitted them about half the time. He had begun to use dialogue in his stories but used quotation marks only once, omitting nine pairs of them. His only problem with punctuation was omitting it; he never inserted extraneous punctuation or substituted one mark for another. From the first to the second half of the year, there was a drop from 47.6 percent to 27.9 percent conventional punctuation. Of the 49 omitted punctuation marks in the second half of the year, 16 were quotation marks, reflecting his need for a new feature that he had only begun to learn how to use. His other omissions were mainly periods. It is unlikely that he forgot how to use them (since he still did so effectively in some stories); presumably, he merely forgot or did not bother to include them. Rather than calling this a developmental regression, it is more accurately described as a context-induced variability.

GORDON WRITING: FOURTH GRADE

Gordon had a successful year in Sr. Susan Caldwell's fourth-grade class, where he continued to explore a variety of aspects of writing. One can again get a sense of him as a writer by examining several of these areas.

Concepts of Writing

Interviews in October and April about various aspects of writing as well as periodic interviews about his stories revealed the nature of Gordon's explicit knowledge and attitudes about writing. He continued, as in third grade, to mention both global aspects of writing and surface-level ones. He felt a story of his was a good one because of "how it sounds" or "what it's about." Good writers, according to Gordon, are those who "write straight . . . it seems like they use a ruler . . . they keep their hands straight." A good writer he knew "writes fast and she doesn't make no mistakes." Bad writers "write sloppy and they keep erasing and they make like a black stain." However, he had also begun to be able to specify more about the qualities that make a story "sound good." He said that one of his stories was good because of a little surprise twist in the plot, and that his teacher, who was a nun, would like one of his stories because "it's talking about God." Good writers, according to Gordon, are those who write funny stories and stories with "interesting stuff put in." When asked why he liked one of his stories less than some others, he said, "It's just about going in somebody's house! I mean it sounds boring like." When discussing why his teacher would like some of his stories better than others, he talked both about how interesting they were and about surface features (e.g., a story where "I spelled the letters right this time" was better than one where "my lines are crooked"). However, when pressed about whether Sr. Susan would prefer an interesting messy story over a boring neat one, he chose the former because "I [could] just copy it over" to make it neater.

Gordon also showed that he was beginning to take a slightly broader perspective on each piece of writing. In October, he said that the first thing he did when he wrote a story was, "Sometimes I always put 'one day,'" and that at the end he put a period, and "if I don't feel like writing any more I can just write the ending." By April he said that the first thing he did was to think of a title, and that the last thing he did was to "read it over and see if it makes sense." These comments don't necessarily reflect a change in his actual behavior, but they do suggest that he may have been thinking of a story more holistically and less as a linear string.

Interaction

During fourth grade, Gordon continued to spend a good deal of time interacting with other people and using the physical resources of his classroom. One day in September, he wrote a fairly short story during which he kept up a steady stream of talk and activity. His short piece read:

One day some little boys were trying to catch some butterflies. But they didn't catch any butterflies. All they found was just bees.

Much of his activity was related to the writing of the story: At different points he read the story starter aloud; said, "How do you spell *catch?*" to the researcher (who he knew wouldn't tell him), then looked at a word list on the wall and said, "I remember how to spell it"; looked at a dictionary Anna was using; got another dictionary but couldn't find *butterfly* in it; went to get another dictionary, looked at it while standing by the shelf, then brought it back; said "butterflies" as he wrote, adding an *s*; and looked for three more words on the wall chart.

Some interaction involved other children's writing: Gordon gave Anna an eraser; told Anna how to spell *dragon;* helped David find a word; and helped Mark spell something. Children came to learn that Gordon was a good person to ask for help with spelling and dictionary use, but on this occasion most of his assistance to others occurred because he was both tuned in to their needs and eager to help with spelling because he enjoyed it intellectually.

Some of his activity was also purely social or self-expressive: He talked with David about drums; sang "butterfly, butterfly" as he brought a dictionary back to his seat; and chatted with the researcher.

As he did in third grade, Gordon was able to maintain adequate concentration on his writing as he talked and moved about the room. In one sense, this behavior interrupted his writing, since he wasn't sitting focused on his paper at all times. But in another sense, there was no evidence of the actual writing *process* being interrupted, since he was able to stop and do something every few words but still maintain his train of thought.

One day in November, Gordon wrote a story twice as long as the butterfly piece, which he was able to do even though he was engaged in a constant stream of activity, much of it totally unrelated to the story he was writing. The story read:

> One night when I was coming home from a football game something
> threw a rock at me and the rock hit me very hard on the head. I
> stopped to see what hit me on the head and it was a monster. The monster had sharp teeth and had a hairy body.

The following examples of activity give a feel for Gordon's personality and his wide range of interests:

- Gordon got up to change the date on the calendar, then spent two or three minutes putting the cards with the days on them in order.
- He asked, "Does coming home from the football game mean that you were going home from the football game?"
- He asked, "Does football game go together?" (i.e., should it be written as one word). He decided that there should be a space between "foot"

and "ball," but smaller than the usual one between words because "they're together."

- Gordon looked up and whistled (trying to get the researcher's attention to show her he'd used a hyphen, which they'd discussed previously).
- He looked at *The Guinness Book of World Records* with classmates Gary and Susan.
- Gordon told Gary that he had just made a period (which he later erased) in the shape of a diamond.
- He talked with Gary about Elvis Presley, and they sang bits from favorite songs and talked about the movie *The Wall*.
- He asked Gary about his story, then sang a line from *The Wall*—"Hey teacher, leave those kids alone"—and talked about the movie some more.
- Gordon spent five minutes talking about the carnival and rodeo and movies with Gary.
- He asked the researcher if she "smoke[d] weed" and talked about people he knew who did.
- Gary asked the researcher if any words start with *x*. Gordon said "exorcist," and he and Gary talked about *The Exorcist* and other scary movies.
- Gordon ripped his paper while erasing, pretended to cry, looked to see if the researcher wrote that down, looked for tape, fixed the rip, and talked about his fingerprints on the tape.
- Gordon said to the researcher, who he knew wouldn't tell him how to spell words, "How do you spell *sharp?* Just spell me it once" (said in a pleading tone).

This level of activity was probably unique to Gordon among the children we studied, and not all his writing episodes were as frantic as this one. Many writers might need to be much quieter in order to concentrate, but the important point here is that writing can at least in some cases go on successfully in the presence of an extensive amount of social interaction.

Meaning Creation

In Sr. Susan Caldwell's classroom, writing was virtually always unassigned. There were often subjects that the class as a whole was learning about that emerged as themes for writing, but the children always had the option of choosing their own topics. There were usually story starters available, but they were presented in a low-key way, as a source of ideas for children who didn't know what to write about, a problem Gordon rarely had. During the year, Gordon wrote stories that touched on a wide range of topics, genres, and elements of his culture. Several of these stories are discussed here to illustrate the variety of ways in which Gordon created meaning. They are presented in chronological order to give a feel for his development over time.

Popular Culture. In the fall of fourth grade, a PacMan craze swept through Sr. Susan Caldwell's room. The video game was at the height of its popularity, and the television cartoon show based on the character had just begun. At this point in the school year, Sr. Susan had her students begin the morning by drawing a picture that their writing was then based on. There was a period of a week or two when PacMan was the most popular subject for pictures and stories, not least because he was so simple to draw. A piece that Gordon wrote in October (with his accompanying picture shown in Figure 8.4) read:

> PacMan is eating the ghost. Baby PacMan is helping PacMan. The
> ghosts are saying "Help us." The other ghost is saying "I can't." Mrs.
> PacMan is looking for Baby PacMan. The sun is burning the tree. The

FIGURE 8.4: Gordon's PacMan Picture

tree is saying "ouch." The next day PacMan took Baby PacMan for a walk in the park. Then the ghosts were chasing PacMan and Baby Pac-Man. But PacMan and Baby PacMan ate the ghosts up.

Much of Gordon's creation of meaning for this story took place while he was drawing his picture. The first half of the story, up to "ouch," was clearly based on the picture. He wrote that much fairly quickly after he had finished drawing, then went to talk to his teacher and came back and wrote the rest, which was not about the picture but described later events. When Gordon read his story to the class during sharing time, the children noticed how long it was, since they were asked to write only four lines to go with their pictures. Sr. Susan told the class that because he had finished early she had told him he could write chapter two, and suggested that other children could do the same if they finished early. The other important point about this story is what it suggests about cultural influences. As Lois Bird described in Chapter 3, the cultures that these Tohono O'odham children lived in included not only elements of traditional and modern Native American culture but also many elements of North American fourth-grade culture such as PacMan.

Tohono O'odham Culture. On November 9, many of the children were writing rodeo stories, since it was around the time of the annual O'odham rodeo and carnival. Gordon wrote a piece that read:

> One day when I was at the rodeo a man was riding a bull. It was a big bull. Then the man fell off. Then the bull was trying to kill the rider but the man jumped on the fence as fast as he could. Then the clowns came out to chase the bull away.

Although an outsider might not recognize this story as being particularly Native American in content, the rodeo experience is a major cultural event in the lives of present-day O'odham children. We don't know whether Gordon based this story directly on an incident he saw, but he certainly could have. His teacher commented that it was less imaginative than some of his other pieces, because "it's usually what happens at the rodeo. . . . It could be almost factual." However, what this story lacked in imagination it made up for in plot structure. It had a clear, interesting sequence of events, which Gordon recognized himself when discussing this story in an interview. He said that it was a good story because the rider jumped on the fence "so he could be safe," and because "it also has the clowns in it, chasing the bull away." Perhaps when Gordon was writing a story based on real events, he could structure the plot more tightly since he already knew more specifically what the sequence of events was going to be.

Horror Stories.   Most children around fourth grade like horror movies and stories, and Gordon was particularly fond of them. He wrote quite a few "scary stories" in fourth grade. In his football game story (seen earlier), he began with a real incident and extrapolated from it to the supernatural. When asked how he got the idea for the story, he said, "When my father took me to a football game I just decided to write about it and the monster." (He said that in real life it wasn't at all scary when he came home from the football game, and he didn't see any monsters.) His teacher commented that it began with a realistic incident of being hit on the head with a rock and then went in the direction of fantasy. She felt that it was just an introduction to a story and wished he'd gone further with it, but she appreciated the plot twist, the way it "could be taken from [a real incident] and then changed into a creative figure." It was typical of Gordon to start a story in a low-key uneventful way in order to set a scene and provide a context for his imagination to work on. His ideas often came not before he began to write but during the process of writing.

Christmas Stories.   The children we observed often wrote stories about Christmas and other holidays. On December 2, Gordon wrote a highly episodic Christmas story. It is made up of several events: leaving cookies for Santa but having them stolen by a friend, meeting Santa and talking about being good and getting millions and millions of presents as a result, and getting a big bike and falling off. Although he knew the story was fictional, in that he didn't really bake cookies for Santa, he felt that one part was somewhat realistic: "It was for real. . . . I know Darnell would take the cookies." The story effectively combined traditional elements of the Santa-story genre and Gordon's own personal touches. He was very pleased with it; later that afternoon he was editing it to turn it into a book, which primarily involved correcting his spelling. When asked by the researcher if he was going to change the content, he said (jokingly), "No, I think it's perfect."

Religion.   Gordon on occasion chose to write about religious themes, and these were some of his favorite stories. On February 3, he wrote about an avalanche in, of all places, Bethlehem:

Avalanche in Bethlehem

There was once a high mountain and over that high mountain lived a little town called Bethlehem. In one of the houses lived a lady and a boy named Mary and Jesus. One day when Mary was cooking she saw a bundle of snow falling from the mountain. Then Mary said, "Jesus, do something." Jesus said, "I will put a ring around the earth." When Jesus put a ring around the earth the snow just melted and all the people in Bethlehem started to sing, "God is our Father." After

they got through singing they all said, "God and the sisters are the spir-
it of Bethlehem." The End

When asked how he got the idea, he said that he had first thought of just writing an avalanche story but then got the idea of making it religious: "I was going
to write a regular story, and then I thought about Jesus and Mary, and I just
writed 'an avalanche,' and then I wrote it in Bethlehem." The story has the
flavor of Sunday-school stories, but with Gordon's special touches, such as his
unusual vocabulary choice in "a bundle of snow" and his very realistic piece of
dialogue, "Jesus, do something."

Folktales.   In February, Sr. Susan Caldwell's class spent time reading
and listening to tall tales about Paul Bunyan, John Henry, and other similar
heroes. Gordon decided to write about Paul Bunyan and to draw a picture
(Figure 8.5) to get ideas for the story, which ended up reading:

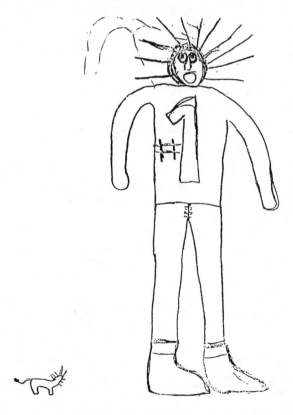

FIGURE 8.5: Gordon's Paul Bunyan Picture

> One day when Paul Bunyan was going to play baseball, he forgot to comb his hair. Then Paul Bunyan went back and combed his hair. Then Paul Bunyan went back to play baseball. But when Paul Bunyan was walking to the baseball field, he saw a mouse, and Paul Bunyan's hair flew up in the air and Paul Bunyan ran home and he never combed his hair.

At the beginning of the writing time, he worked on his picture, talking with other children as he did so, and also stopped from time to time to write the first few words of his story. (The researcher had discussed with him previously how he often started his stories with "One day." After writing the first word of this story, he commented, "I started with 'One' again, huh?") Eventually he decided he was going to draw and write about Paul Bunyan being scared by a mouse. This Paul Bunyan story was different from the traditional ones; he was not a giant logger but instead a fellow in jeans and a baseball shirt who got scared by a mouse. Sr. Susan Caldwell mentioned that the part about the mouse may have come from a story they read as a class, but the baseball part was original. Gordon liked this story a lot, because of the humor of the hair flying up.

Integration of Themes.   On March 24, Gordon wrote a story that integrated several of his interests:

The Day the Indian Got Power from God

> There was once a boy named Little Knife. Little Knife was brave and fast but he was not strong. One day Little Knife's father said, "Little Knife, come with me. We are going hunting. You can help me carry the deer." Little Knife got scared when his father said that he could carry the deer with him. Little Knife said, "Father, I am not strong." "Little Knife," said his father, "don't worry. When you pick up that deer God will give you power." When Little Knife picked up the deer God gave him powers. Little Knife was so happy he carried the deer all by himself. He said, "From now on I am going to carry the animals we catch for you." When Little Knife got home his mother said, "Little Knife, go get some more wood for the fire." And he brang [*sic*] lots of wood for the fire.

This story drew elements from his identity as a Native American and his interest in religion. Gordon also had a very strong relationship with his father, which came out in this story. He drew as well on a "storybook" conceptualization of Native Americans. Deer hunting is not a part of Tohono O'odham culture, and Gordon took a moment to decide whether to call his character "Little

Knife," "Little Fire," or "Little Fox," which are the kinds of Indian names often found in picture books. When asked how he got his idea for what to write about, he said, "I thought about Indians, I was going to write about Indians, then I saw 'power'" (on the cover of a book that was lying on a nearby table). He seemed to have decided on his general topic when he wrote the title and then developed the details as he went along. It was probably his most effective story, with a strong plot, a meaningful theme, and real character development. This story was a special favorite of Sr. Susan Caldwell's. She commented, "I think this is one of the most neat stories I've ever read in my whole life . . . and not just because I'm a nun!" She found it fascinating that someone as young as Gordon would come up with the idea of getting strength from God, and saw parallels with "the old Indian ways of . . . [having] a dream and getting power from the dream, and once you have the power, you have the power to use." She also remarked that "he's using the power to be helpful; I thought that was really neat."

Summary.   Gordon was clearly able to write about a large variety of topics and to maintain a strong story sense through them all. Sr. Susan Caldwell commented that he seemed "to have a story line right from the beginning" of the year, and that he usually stuck to one topic: "He doesn't seem to just go to one thing and then skip and then come back like some kids do." When asked if he would write different kinds of stories when he was older (e.g., in sixth grade), Gordon said that he would write about buildings and skyscrapers then, and that when he was in first grade he had written about sheep and plants. When asked what he mostly wrote about in fourth grade, he replied "interesting stuff"; the reader of his stories is compelled to agree.

Syntax

An early story of Gordon's from fourth grade shows him operating at a relative simple syntactic level:

> One day my rabbit ran away from me because I got mad at him. He was
> hungry. He wanted a carrot. I ran after him. His name was Timmy.
> Timmy was a good rabbit. He always was a good rabbit. I liked Timmy.
> He was my great pet.

This story is made up of short sentences, with an average of only 5.33 words each, and only the first sentence has more than one clause. However, later in the year, as the ideas Gordon expressed became more complex, he used more sophisticated syntactic structures. The story about the avalanche in Bethlehem seen earlier is a prime example. It has an average of 11.77 words per t-unit and 2.11 clauses per t-unit. Looking at some of the sentences involved shows what this complexity looks like.

"There was once a high mountain, and over that high mountain lived a little town called Bethlehem." This sentence is made up of a simple one-clause t-unit followed by a complex one. The second t-unit is introduced by a prepositional phrase and has a main clause with the subject and verb inverted, followed by a nominal clause modifying the subject ("called Bethlehem"). The repetition of the phrase "high mountain" and the subject-verb inversion produce a strongly literary effect.

"In one of the houses lived a lady and a boy named Mary and Jesus." This sentence also has subject-verb inversion followed by a nominal clause ("named Mary and Jesus"). The pairing up of a compound noun and its modifier is a particularly sophisticated structure. The literary flavor of this sentence can be especially appreciated when contrasted with the same meaning arranged more conventionally: "A lady named Mary and a boy named Jesus lived in one of the houses."

"One day when Mary was cooking she saw a bundle of snow falling from the mountain." A main clause ("[One day] she saw a bundle of snow") is modified by an adverbial one of time and a nominal one modifying the object "bundle of snow." When Gordon was writing at this level of syntactic complexity, he was approaching the style of much older writers, both in the length of his sentences (twelfth-grade writers average 14.4 words per t-unit and 1.68 clauses per t-unit, Hunt, 1965) and in the variety of syntactic structures he used.

Spelling and Punctuation

Many aspects of Gordon's spelling and punctuation continued to develop during fourth grade, as can be seen in his behavior as he wrote and in the stories themselves.

Resource Use.   Gordon used a variety of strategies for spelling words. When asked in interviews what he did when he didn't know how to spell a word, his answers included: sound it out, look in the dictionary, and look in your desk and see if you spelled it already (i.e., on another paper). Gordon consulted the dictionary a good deal as he wrote; a few examples show the range of his spelling strategies.

In one story, also mentioned in Chapter 6, he needed to spell *surrounded* and *gang;* the piece read:

The Cross and Switchblade

One day a man was surrounded by a gang of other men. The men had bats, blades, chains, and axes to kill people. Then the man tried to jump over a fence, but the gang just pulled the man down and started to hit him and stick him, and the man died. The men that killed the other man had to go to court.

In looking for *surrounded,* he commented, "I know how to spell it—it's *s, r, round,* then *e-d.*" He couldn't find it in the dictionary and decided to just write it the way he had stated it, but then got an easier dictionary to confirm the spelling of *round.* Next he got a harder dictionary to look for *gang.* His search strategy wasn't very systematic once he had found the initial letter. Although he was able to figure out what the second and third letters were likely to be, he didn't use this information to direct his search. After he found *gang* he copied it down, then made a note of the page number it was on in case he needed the word again. When the researcher kidded him about this, he realized that he didn't need the page number now that he had the word. He was sensitive about which dictionary was likely to have the words he was looking for, using a harder dictionary for *gang* and *surrounded* and an easy picture one for *stick.* Gordon was not yet fully proficient in all the abilities a dictionary user needed to have, but he was well under way; his ownership of the process and eagerness to learn more were a big part of this.

Knowledge of and Attitudes About Spelling.   Gordon mentioned in an April interview that he tried to spell all words correctly if possible. He revealed that there were two ways for him to know a word was misspelled when he reread a story. They might have been words that he remembered not taking the time to spell accurately, "if I just wrote it any way, any kind of letters"; or he may have noticed the errors through applying orthographic knowledge as he reread: "if it sounds right then you know it's spelled right . . . or [if it] looks right." Gordon continued to see spelling as important not intrinsically but as a means to success. He said that if you were "police ladies or men, you have to write nice so they can understand" and that spelling is especially important if you're a teacher. A sign painter has to spell correctly "because if they don't they might not even get hardly any money" (i.e., a store's sign must be legible in order to draw customers). Spelling is important for children for "your report card." However, his motivation for correct spelling in his own writing certainly didn't seem to be report card oriented; his focus seemed to be a more general one of doing the best work that he could.

Invented Spellings.   As in third grade, Gordon's linguistic knowledge can be inferred by looking at the variety of invented spellings he used. Examples have been chosen from two stories that have a variety of them, "The Cross and the Switchblade" and the story about Little Knife, both seen earlier. (This discussion includes most of the invented spellings from these two pieces.)

One can see the following processes going on in Gordon's spellings (it should be noted that these are suggested influences, not an attempt to categorize each spelling):

Phonetic

CORT/court
NIFE/knife
SWICH BLADE/switchblade
STARED/started
SROUNDED/surrounded

For some of these words (*court, knife, switchblade*), Gordon's spelling was a more direct phonetic representation of the word than the standard spelling is. In *surrounded*, the reduced vowel in the first syllable was eliminated. STARED for *started* may represent an influence from Gordon's dialect of English, in which stop consonants are sometimes replaced by a glottal stop (the closing of the throat occurring in the middle of "uh-oh"), which is not represented by any letter in English spelling.

Orthographic Patterns

MOUTHER/mother
OUTHER/other
AXS/axes
TRYED/tried
CARYED/carried

In these spellings, Gordon did not fully control patterns for adding suffixes and for alternative spellings of certain phonemes. (His spellings of *mother* and *other* may involve an analogy with the vowel spellings in words like *touch* and *rough*.)

Real-Word Substitution

FARTHER/father
WEREY/worry

Gordon's spelling of *father* is a real word; in his spelling of *worry*, he appeared to be writing *were* and adding a *y* as a final marker.

Punctuation Related

DONT/don't
HIS SLFE/himself
SWICH BLADE/switchblade

As in third grade, Gordon didn't fully control apostrophe use and one-word–two-word patterns.

Punctuation.   Gordon for the most part controlled sentence-boundary punctuation, and during fourth grade he began to be aware of and to use other forms of punctuation as well. The two most interesting were the hyphen and quotation marks. Gordon was very proud one day to show the researcher that he knew how to use a hyphen when he ran out of room at the end of a line; he mentioned that his sister had taught it to him. In "Avalanche in Bethlehem," he hyphenated as follows: *g-/ot*, *sn-/ow*, and *some-/thing* (the slashes represent line breaks). Interestingly, he hyphenated one-syllable words whenever he ran out of room but two-syllable words at the syllable boundary, even though in the case of *something* he had plenty of room to fit more letters in. He was not able to articulate why he did this, which suggested that his knowledge about hyphen use was tacit as well as explicit. In one story, he used a hyphen in the middle of the word *cup-cakes* because "they go together." The week previously he had put a small space between the two parts of *football* for the same reason; when questioned, he said that either option was allowable.

Gordon began to use quotation marks quite a bit in fourth grade. Sr. Susan mentioned in an interview that she told him about them when he began to use dialogue a lot, and that when he remembered, he usually included them. His story about Little Knife, seen earlier, has an interesting example that shows how he conceptualized quotation marks. One of his sentences was punctuated as follows (spelling has been conventionalized): Little Knife said "his father don't worry when you pick up that deer God will give you power." What he really intended was: "Little Knife," said his father, "don't worry. When you pick up that deer God will give you power." In an interview, Gordon made it clear what strategy he was following. The first quotation mark went after *said*; the second went after the person was done talking. This served him surprisingly well in most cases, except for indirect quotations and divided ones like the one above.

Developmental Trends in Fourth Grade

As in third grade, quantifiable aspects of Gordon's development showed a variable pattern. Patterns of change from the first half to the second half of fourth grade are illustrated and compared to third grade in Table 8.2. In the first three measures seen, Gordon showed dramatic changes from the first to the second half of the year. His stories in the first half of the year were not much longer than those he wrote in third grade, but in the second half of the year most stories were 50 words or longer. In both words per t-unit and clauses per t-unit, Gordon's averages were lower than in third grade, but both showed

TABLE 8.2: Gordon—Fourth Grade, First and Second Half, with Comparison to Third Grade

	First Half	Second Half	Overall	Grade 3
Words per story	42.0	73.1	58.2	37.6
Words per t-unit	6.5	9.74	8.31	8.84
Clauses per t-unit	1.29	1.81	1.58	1.61
Appropriate spelling	88.9%	89.2%	89.1%	79.4%
Appropriate punctuation	42.1%	48.9%	46.1%	35.0%

an upward trend from the first to the second half of the year. The uncharacteristically low figures for the first half of the year may reflect assignment constraints; writing four sentences about pictures may have resulted in less complex structures than the broader scope of more fully unassigned writing found later. By the second half of the year, Gordon had hit his stride; most of his stories had more than nine words per t-unit and more than 1.5 clauses per t-unit.

Gordon's percentage of appropriate spelling was high for all stories, dropping below 80 percent only once, and was similar in the first and second halves of the year. The 20 words Gordon used most frequently, which made up 40.4 percent of his total words, were always correctly spelled. Gordon's percentage of conventional punctuation varied from 25 percent to 100 percent, but improved throughout the year and was on the average higher than in third grade. He omitted periods sometimes and commas often, and had partial control of quotation marks. (Many of the omitted commas were those that obligatorily precede quotation marks.)

Over the two years of the study, Gordon showed both his ability to express himself through writing and his active interest in gaining control over the linguistic systems of written language. An observer's impressions of the lively inquiring nature of his mind are confirmed by both the stories themselves and the summary data derived from them. Gordon was clearly on his way to becoming an involved and competent adult writer.

CHAPTER 9

Process Data

CAN I DO ANYTHING REAL WITH THIS STUFF?

Sherry Vaughan

WHATEVER CURRENT PROFESSIONAL LITERATURE you've read lately, I'd be willing to bet that the author considered data about process to be vital evidence for insights about learning and recommendations for instruction. Everywhere there is evidence that the learning process is central to effective instruction, not only in writing but in other traditional content areas such as reading, mathematics, and science. Writing research may have pointed us in that direction. Since the mid-1970s, teachers and researchers intrigued by the complex process occurring when pen meets paper have been asking questions about why some students find the activity fun and fulfilling but others find it pure drudgery or, even worse, eminently painful (Emig, 1977; Britton et al., 1975; Graves, 1975). Once the observation of process began, insights essential for effective instruction emerged, and there was no turning back. The romance with observing and documenting writers at work had begun.

Since that time, other researchers interested in the writing process have focused on the development of the process-product relationship from the youngest child (Ferreiro & Teberosky, 1982; Harste, Woodward & Burke, 1984) to junior high, high school, and adult (Flower & Hayes, 1979; Odell, Goswami & Herrington, 1983; Perl, 1979).)

Reading research has also considered process data to be vital to understanding text comprehension. Meaning making is viewed not as a mere transmission of ideas from the author to the reader but as a transaction—a reciprocal, two-way street in which a unique meaning arises as a text is constructed by the reader (K. Goodman & Y. Goodman, 1978; F. Smith 1973, 1982). The Goodmans, Smith, and others have pointed out that different interpretations can occur not only across several readers reading the same text but within one reader over several occasions (Rosenblatt, 1978). Psycholinguists like Smith and the Goodmans have held this view of the reading process for some time. With the added contribution of cognitive psychologists, sociologists, and linguists, the portrait of the learner now includes the constructive nature of the reading process, scores of snapshots of transactions between the reader and other vital influences and constraints in the reading process, and even insights into how texts themselves may lead readers astray (Anderson, Spiro & Montague, 1977; Garner, Gillingham & White, 1989; Heath, 1983; Hymes, 1981).

Classroom research, involving collaboration between teachers and researchers to describe the context in which reading and writing occur, reveals that when we look at process and product simultaneously, we get quite a different view of meaning making than if we look at the product alone (Y. Goodman, 1984; Vaughan, 1983/1984). Process data reveal both strengths and weaknesses in several areas: risk taking, level of engagement, ownership, composing/comprehending strategies, and appropriate use of resources and contextual elements—all essential activities in literacy development. When we broaden our lens to include process information alongside the developing written product and view composing events over time, we begin to compose a movie of the learner's meaning-making activity.

And yet, although many teachers and researchers continue to develop strong instructional programs built on their observations of learning in the classroom context, others may not. Several explanations are possible. First, documenting process takes time—blocks of time during which teachers can carefully observe and document cognitive process in action. Some schooling contexts may make it difficult for teachers to create those blocks of time, to free themselves from "teaching" a required program, or to release children from program constraints so they may write for extended periods of time on topics of their choice. Others may be unsure of how to provide for that time in the day's already too busy schedule or within the ethos set by other professionals in the school. Those issues are more political than academic; that is, they have to do with who decides what goes on in classrooms. Although political issues are vital to development for both teachers and children, I focus primarily on academics in this chapter.

For those simply unaccustomed to observing and documenting learning in process, that information may appear inaccessible during regular classroom activity and unwieldy when it is finally gathered. Teachers may feel they don't know how to organize, synthesize, or interpret information about process. Additionally, and here the issue is often both political and academic, teachers need to provide verifiable evidence of students' progress in literacy development. They may often find it difficult to determine how this slippery mass of information could be translated into marks in a grade book.

In this chapter I address each of those concerns, beginning with an example of process data collected during a single composing activity by Anna and continuing with several suggested forms for organizing and synthesizing the information obtained. Finally, I suggest some methods for assigning a performance level to various kinds of process information, information that can then be translated into a score for grades when they are required. Although this may seem like a complicated way to evaluate students, we learned during our two years with these children that the more we worked with process information, the more likely we were to feel comfortable with its unfamiliar characteristics and to appreciate the benefits it offers.

ANNA: WRITING IN PROCESS

The text to be analyzed was produced by Anna in her fourth-grade year. Remember that her class was labeled "pre-fourth grade." Although she and her classmates had finished third grade the year before, they were not considered quite ready to move on to the fourth grade, which was housed in a separate upper elementary school and where certain competencies were assumed to be firmly in place. Anna's group was held back in order to provide more time for and assistance in reading and writing skill development. The significance of this piece of background information becomes more evident as we use process data to view Anna's strengths in meaning making. If we look only at product, Anna's weaknesses are clearly evident, but if we look at information from Anna's composing episode as it unfolds, we see her considerable strengths as a developing reader and writer.

On February 16, Anna produced the piece of informational writing seen in Figure 9.1, the first piece of this type she had attempted that school year. Both the expository mode and the topic were self-selected. The piece was written during science time, with her peers and the teacher as primary audience. Since it was a first draft, Anna may not yet have known herself what the purpose of the piece was, except to explore a topic of her own interest within the general subject area of science selected by the teacher.

At first glance the piece seems uneventful, to say the least. Her syntax is neatly patterned around a few basic structures (which are curiously numbered in the left margin). The first few sentences present some basic facts about the planet Saturn, but also reveal that Anna had run into trouble with accuracy. On line 4 she wrote that Saturn has 9 moons, but by line 6 the number had changed to 10, and by line 9 the moons had grown in number to 15! What in the world was going on? What can account for this discrepancy, and why did Anna allow this inaccuracy to remain in her piece? The product appears to suggest that Anna was unaware of or unconcerned with a striking semantic discrepancy and perhaps with some basic usage conventions as well. However, a look at process data, another type of information altogether, broadens our base for making hypotheses about Anna's composing competencies.

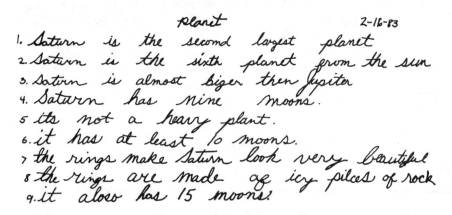

FIGURE 9.1: Anna's Saturn Piece

While Anna wrote this piece an observer sat next to her, recording not only what she wrote but what she did while writing—the resources she used, her movement about the classroom, and her interactions with other people, as well as verbatim transcriptions of comments she made to others as she wrote. During our visits to the school, I often observed Anna's writing myself since I had taken primary responsibility for studying her, but on this particular occasion I was not the one observing her. The nature of process data, however, enables me to read another's remarks and note important details about Anna's writing episode. Even though I was not physically there, I can relive the dynamic, holistic nature of this composing session, learning about the kinds of decisions Anna made that resulted in this final product.

Anna began the piece by referring to an article about Saturn in a *World Book Encyclopedia*. The first sentence was written immediately after she read a portion of the Saturn entry. At the beginning of the second sentence, she wrote "Space," erased it, and then wrote the whole sentence quickly before pausing for a few moments. Before she put pencil to paper again, several events occurred. She reread the sentence she had just produced, referred again to the encyclopedia, and then was interrupted by a classmate who asked for a piece of paper. She then went back to her writing, reread her previous text, and paused for a minute or two. Sandra Wilde, the observer on this occasion, wrote: "She seems stuck. We talk about ways she could use the article, whether to pick out bits or read through. She decides to read through." At that point Anna was interrupted by another classmate who wanted to chat for a bit. When this brief conversation ended, Anna went back to the encyclopedia. After a few moments she stopped reading, talked to another classmate, got a drink of water, and then returned to browse through the encyclopedia, looking for her place until she came to the section on snakes, which she skimmed. At that point she commented that the encyclopedia was "too hard" and went to get another reference book, an informational book about space, from a classmate. She browsed through this new book, found the section on Saturn, read the first sentence of the section, and started to copy it. She wrote the first word, "Saturn," and then stopped to talk to a classmate, David, nearby. The rest of the sentence was written not by copying but by paraphrasing what she remembered reading before her conversation with David. When she got to the word *Jupiter*, she stopped to wonder aloud, "Is Jupiter a capital [letter]?" Not waiting for a response, she checked the reference book for spelling. She began sentence 4 with "Saturn" but wasn't sure she'd spelled the word right. She erased it, read two sentences from the book, and asked aloud how to spell Saturn. She found it in the book and then wrote sentence 4. Sentence 5 was written after several references to the same source.

Composing activities related to sentence 6 were particularly interesting for several reasons. First, Anna began what appeared to be an interesting idea by writing "people say if they put Saturn on," but then stopped to chat with a classmate. When she came back to her text, she reread her incomplete sentence and said, "It's too long," and erased it. She then wrote "people say with," stopped to think for 30 seconds or so, and then went back to read from her reference book. She wrote "with" again and then erased the whole structure, saying, "It's too long." She then skimmed through the book, selected and reviewed another book on the universe, talked to yet another classmate, went back to the source she was presently using, and quickly found the page on Saturn.

At that point something very interesting occurred. She read from this new reference book that Saturn has ten moons! She pointed out to Sandra that the previous reference said Saturn had nine. She made a comment that this second book was probably right, although when Sandra asked why that was so, Anna replied that she wasn't sure. She stopped to point out this problem to a classmate and then wrote sentence 6, "it has at least 10 moons."

Anna then went back to the reference material, ignoring other information on the Saturn page as she skipped ahead to skim the rest of the book. She finished the book, selected another one, got a cough drop from her desk, and turned again to the section on Saturn, using the information there to write sentence 7, "the rings make Saturn look very beautiful."

Having used as much of that book as she saw fit, she got yet another book, making the comment, "I like to use these books, *Let's Discover*." With this text, she referred to the table of contents, selected the section on Saturn, and read, "It is the farthest planet we can see without a telescope." From that, she selected "it is the far" but then erased her incomplete sentence. Reading ahead, she noticed that this book said something different about what the rings are made of. She went back to the previous book and checked it out, resolving the conflict by shrugging her shoulders and commenting that the *Let's Discover* book was actually the accurate one. When Sandra probed, Anna said she wasn't sure why. She went on to write sentence 8.

After stopping her own reading and writing to help a classmate spell a word, she read on to discover that this text said Saturn has 15 moons! By that time she realized something weird was going on and tried to get the teacher's help. The teacher was busy, however, and Anna was left to deal with this conflict on her own. She checked out another reference, found it didn't shed any light on the issue, and quickly put it away. By that time the period was about to end, and Anna was left with a difficult decision: what to do about the moon problem. With a glance at the clock, she quickly wrote sentence 9, "it also has 15 moons," and offered the explanation, "I like that book best." So much for resolving conflicts in accuracy of information! The complete composing episode consumed 17 minutes.

SO WHAT DOES IT MEAN?

When introduced to this sort of process data, teachers often comment that they see their own experiences with classroom composing reflected in the activities young writers such as Anna exhibit. Students' decisions about what they will write, how to get complex thoughts best represented in linear fashion across the page, and how best to manage conventions required by the task stand out in high relief, offering insight about why writing is often difficult and suggesting hints for how the teacher might help.

A quick review of Anna's writing episode reveals competencies required of successful writers. She was willing to take risks; she was interested enough to stay with a difficult task; and she knew how to use available resources. In this piece, Anna chose to use a mode of composing totally new for her, the expository mode. She was also willing to invest in a difficult topic—astronomy—one she had shown interest in earlier in the week during a science lesson. Perhaps she had seen Saturn through a telescope on one of her many visits to the observatory on Kitt Peak. Whatever the reason, her decision to pursue this interest during an extended writing period is important to note, since it indicates both an interest in further exploration of a science topic and an awareness that to do so required a mode unlike the narrative she usually chose. Anna was willing to juggle two new constraints simultaneously—information on a relatively unfamiliar topic and composing in the expository mode. It's important that she get credit for this difficult feat.

Other noteworthy information involves Anna's use of resources. If readers and writers are to become independent and self-directed they must learn to "live off the land," as Graves (1983) says. Anna made repeated and varied uses of both human and textual reference sources for different purposes. She used an encyclopedia (*World Book*), textbooks (*Space* and *Let's Discover*), and people (Sandra, the researcher, and Sr. Susan Caldwell, the teacher) for obtaining information, checking accuracy of information, and confirming guesses about content and spelling. In looking at what Anna did during a 17-minute period, we've learned vital information about what she could already do at this time and what kind of instruction was likely to be helpful.

Although it's easy to recognize the value of this information, it's more difficult to see it as accessible for instructional and evaluation purposes. Learning to use process information takes time, support, encouragement, and experience—commodities often not readily available. At least part of the solution to this dilemma lies in learning to critically evaluate our own teaching—to bring our "walk" and our "talk" together.

It is true that teachers' values, attitudes, and knowledge affect not only *what* but *how* students learn. Since that is the case, what is actually evaluated is not only the students' performance but our own as well. The context in which we evaluate students' progress includes two major groups of influences—one relating to teachers and one relating to students—as well as the interaction of those influences.

First, teachers' values, attitudes, and knowledge are fundamental to the specific identity of the classroom as a place to learn. If we value writing and reading, we include adequate time for those activities in daily schedules. If we regard learners as active agents in the learning experience, we provide opportunities and encouragement for students to offer topics, materials, and questions to be pursued, as well as legitimate methods for answering those questions. And finally, if we characterize learners' responses as a unique reflection of learners' worldviews, we predict diverse responses to questions and see our role primarily as respondent, negotiator, and collaborator rather than transmitter and evaluator.

Second, students' values, attitudes, and knowledge about the world and about the role of language in finding out more about the world are important as well. Because learners have different home lives, school experiences, and biological makeup, they respond differently to the experiences we provide in the classroom. When cognitive process, with all its complex elements interacting freely, becomes a value we support and nourish, students can also begin to trust its value and respond to activities with a willingness to take risks. Only when students take risks can they try new methods of solving problems, experience creative energy, and develop a positive attitude toward literacy and learning in general.

So, if process is as important as we think it is, then valuing it, providing time for it, responding to it, encouraging others to respond to it, even making sure that grade books reflect that value, bring our talk and our walk together. As Applebee (1984) reminds us, students tend to trust more what we *do* than what we *say*.

HOW EXACTLY ARE WE TO DO ALL THIS?

First, how can we manage classroom activity so that we have time to spend 17 minutes with one child and still get through the day's work? If we actually manage to get comments written, how do we get this essentially holistic information into a format that can be recorded in a grade book or documented as evidence of meeting our own carefully specified objectives? I would like to illustrate some viable ways of doing just that.

Providing both the time and opportunity to observe and interact with students as they engage in composing activities is not as difficult as it may sound. Atwell (1987), Calkins (1983), and Graves (1983) have shown us that it is possible. It does require working out classroom management strategies and organizational plans consistent with the objectives stated above: providing time for reading and writing; allowing students to choose topics that are meaningful to them; designing open-ended activities that encourage diverse, creative responses; and supporting a feeling of ownership of learning that fosters willingness to take risks. All these activities require school personnel, teachers and administrators alike, to provide the opportunity and perhaps even active support for students to control their own learning. It means that teachers become guides rather than directors, collaborators rather than authoritarians, and negotiators rather than evaluators. Graves (1983), Calkins (1983), and Kirby and Liner (1981) illustrate how these process-oriented activities can be managed in classrooms at all grade levels.

Those of us who support these educational values devise our own creative methods for managing them in our own classrooms. The important criteria include providing a clear message to students, to parents, and to other teachers about how development is proceeding. Some teachers, those with a manageable class size, find that they can usually make time to evaluate a composing session with each student (like the one with Anna) about once every ten days. Other teachers use these very detailed observations only with students who are having difficulties of one kind or another. One teacher I know wears a smock with two pockets on the front, one filled with blank file cards, the other pocket empty. As the day progresses she observes and interacts with students about their work. When she recognizes significant process information, she takes out a card, records the student's initials and the date along with brief documentation, and files the card in the empty pocket. Later she files all the note cards in a box, organized alphabetically by students' names. That information is then incorporated into profile forms (examples to follow). If she gets busy or engaged with the moment and forgets, students remind her by asking her to share with them what she has written that day. In this sort of environment, students collaborate with teachers in their own instruction.

Information about which peers a student chooses to work with, how much and what kind of interaction results, and how a student manages time during long blocks of uninterrupted work, when carefully recorded throughout the day, reveals how effectively students work in a particular classroom context. A clipboard with unlined paper travels easily with me around the room as I visit with individuals and small groups in my own role as a classroom-based researcher. Statements with the student's initials and brief relevant comments are easily dated, cut apart, and filed chronologically in students' files. A first-grade teacher taught me the value of adhesive-backed labels of various sizes that transfer easily onto plain paper in the students' files.

Periodic analysis of student-selected samples from writing folders provides information on progress with writing conventions, use of various literacy modes, variety of topic choice, use of writing strategies, and evidence of sentence development. A final developmental profile, then, is not based simply on product analysis but becomes a holistic, chronological, documented record of a student's written language development within a classroom context, ready to provide further questions to explore as well as instructional suggestions and quantifiable evidence of development.

Difficult and frustrating as it may be, most teachers are required to present normative grades of some sort, so the issue of how to synthesize and quantify process information is also important. The crucial point is to view the grading requirement as an opportunity to construct an accurate description of how students progress as they learn to diversify language use. The following examples of process evaluation forms illustrate how those objectives might be met. Anna's composing episode described above is used to illustrate how these forms might document her progress toward important literacy objectives. The forms have been filled out after the fact, with information drawn from the observational notes on her writing episode, and serve to highlight selected areas of behavior or knowledge. The forms are only suggested examples of how process information may be codified and quantified. Other topics and themes may be explored with similar procedures.

Form A (Figure 9.2) was designed to both identify and describe instances of Anna's risk-taking activity. It's important to point out here that the form actually provides a heuristic function; that is, it was a learning tool for me. I didn't appreciate the extent to which Anna was willing to stick her neck out on this piece until I began to chart the instances in which she ventured out onto new ground.

Other noteworthy information mentioned in the description of Anna's writing episode involves her use of external resources. One piece of evidence that Anna was learning to "live off the land" was her repeated and varied uses of both human and textual reference sources. Form B (Figure 9.3) documents the type, purpose, and result of those uses of textual references. Completing this form served the same heuristic function as that on risk taking; listing the resources Anna used led to discovering their multiple uses and the results thereof. As Anna explored each text, her strengths in manipulating a resource for her own purpose stood out clearly. She reread, skimmed, used the table of contents, ignored irrelevant information, and began to paraphrase what she had read. It is evident that she read for meaning, since she was clearly cognizant of the moon problem, although she didn't yet know what to do about it. With this information, valuable instructional clues emerge, revealing that Anna is ready to explore the issue of scientific data that continually evolves because of our rapidly advancing technological knowledge.

Another topic emerges as relevant in this episode—the apparent interruptions to Anna's composing task. On the surface it appears that Anna was off-

Student	Date	Observation
Anna	2/16	1. Chose expository mode for first time. 2. Selected relatively unfamiliar science topic for writing during Language Arts period.

FIGURE 9.2: Form A—Evidence of Risk Taking

Student **Anna**   Date   **2/16**

Text	Purpose	Results/Comments
1. World Book Encyclopedia (WB)	Info	Writes Sentence 1.
2. WB	Info	Rereads; writes 2nd & 3rd sentences; pauses.
3. WB	Info	Solicits interruption; skims; distracted; says WB is too hard.
4. Space (SP)	Sentence structure	Begins to copy; solicits interruption; paraphrases.
5. SP	Spelling	Writes sentences 4 & 5
6. SP	Info	Phrases; rephrases; dissatisfied; skims text.
7. SP	Info	Finds info that conflicts with other reference; writes Sentence.
8. SP	Info	Skims; ignores irrelevant info.
9. Unidentified Ref. (UR)	Info	Finds Saturn section; writes sentence 7.
10. Let's Discover (LD)	Info	Expresses positive attitude; refers to table of contents; reads; notices conflicting info.
11. UR	Confirm	Chooses LD as authority
12. LD	Info	Writes Sentence 8.
13. LD	Info	Finds conflicting info again.
14. Additional Ref.	Confirm	Gets no help.
15. LD	Info	Writes sentence 9.

FIGURE 9.3: Form B—Evidence of Resource Use

task a lot. Perhaps that could explain why she allowed the factual discrepancy to remain in her finished product. But when observations of Anna's work and interactions are carefully documented, at least two interesting patterns emerge. When she used a reference book she determined to be too difficult, she interrupted her work often. With a reference she favored, however, or ones she felt were particularly useful, interruptions seemingly unrelated to

Student _____ Anna _____   Date ___ 2/16 ___

Ref.	Source	Purpose	Result
WB	Peer	Peer wants paper	Rereads to find place.
WB	Researcher	Procedural request.	Decides to read through first.
WB	Peer	Peer wants to chat.	Returns to task.
WB	Peer	A. wants to chat. Gets drink.	Gets distracted by section on snakes.
SP	Peer	A. and D. chat.	Paraphrases what was read before.
SP	Peer	Chatting	Erases incomplete sentence. Writes one acceptable to her.
UR	Researcher	A. points out conflicting info.	Decides present text is right.
UR	Peer	A. points out info. problem.	Writes.
LD	Peer	A. helps spell a word.	Reads on.

FIGURE 9.4: Form C—Apparent Interruptions during Composing

the task were reduced. I certainly recognize my own trips to the refrigerator and pauses to cuddle the cat during difficult writing sessions reflected here.

Form C (Figure 9.4) illustrates that what may appear to be behavior unrelated to the task at hand is often directly related to the composing activity and indicative of involvement, however painful, rather than distraction. Of course, this is only a tentative observation that would need to be followed up during later sessions. By organizing information developed across several composing sessions, I was able to recognize Anna's significant effort to use references and learned how her involvement in her own composing process reflected the particular resources she consulted. These insights could now be introduced in mini-lessons either with Anna alone or in a group of others ready for the same information.

Further documentation of Anna's composing activities and attitudes might be achieved via an open-ended form for documenting self-evaluation like that in Form D (Figure 9.5). Completing a form like this one would also give Anna an opportunity to reflect on the reference information problem and a chance to ask the teacher for some help. Her first experiences with such an open-ended form would probably require some consulting with the teacher in order to clarify what kind of information would be helpful.

Opportunities to self-monitor during specific composing sessions may contribute to the quality of Anna's evaluation, appreciation, and ownership of her own writing development. But how would this information be recorded in

NAME: Anna	DATE: 2/16
Today in writing I:	
I learned that:	
I still want to know:	
Here is my plan for finding out more:	

FIGURE 9.5: Form D—Student Self-Evaluation

a grade book? The answer lies in something mentioned earlier, identification of patterns of development. Any one piece of information is not very helpful in itself, but that single piece of data becomes extremely valuable when combined with others collected over time, carefully dated to reveal a chronological picture of a student's developing competencies. Patterns can be identified holistically and assigned performance levels. It is that performance level that makes its way into a grade book.

For instance, several issues were identified in the research cited above as indications of progress: time spent reading and writing; student selection of topics and methods; diverse, creative responses to open-ended activities; and willingness to take risks. Each of these behaviors can be observed, recorded, quantified if appropriate, and then assigned a performance level appropriate for that child. A plus (+) may designate excellence; a zero (0) may indicate effectiveness; a minus (−) may flag potential problems and need for improvement. No commercially prepared test or worksheet could provide such valuable information on students' progress in reading and writing development because the information here is gleaned from pieces in which the student made individual choices about what to say and how to say it. Although it may be easier or at least more familiar to assign an "objective" score based on the percentage of items correct on worksheets, that score tells little of students' performance in the context in which meaningful learning is both occurring and being displayed. A code such as that above for scoring process data more accurately reflects the learner's strengths and weaknesses and at the same time provides helpful information to the teacher about what help the child needs next. Quantifying the code is not difficult. Counting pluses, minuses, and zeros and assigning a letter grade within the context of the learner's whole performance fulfills the formal requirement of a letter grade. The important issue is that relevant processes and attitudes, when they are assigned performance levels and compiled chronologically, provide feedback to all concerned about progress in cognitive activity that may have been left unaccounted for without insights gained from process data. These "snapshots" of actual performance can then be combined to reveal a dynamic picture of development over time. The teacher is not misled by overemphasis on easily tested elements, and instructional decisions are fortified by many evidences of a student's performance over several sessions.

WHAT DOES THIS MEAN FOR TEACHERS?

At least one topic in the area of valuing and applying process data remains unaddressed. Just as students need time, support, and encouragement for development, so do teachers. And, although we would like that support from administrators and parents, we must sometimes be satisfied with getting it solely from one another. To grow as teachers, we too must take risks, become engaged, try solutions we haven't fully worked out yet, and generally rush in even when wise others might not, given the dangers ahead. Perhaps Anna and her peers have helped you see that the dangers may be even greater if students and teachers decide in favor of comfort rather than growth.

CHAPTER 10

The End

Yetta M. Goodman

THE TITLE OF THIS CHAPTER is in keeping with our observations during our study of Tohono O'odham children's writing. So many narratives were concluded with these two important words: "The End." Yet in no way does anyone expect "The End" to refer to the final point of an author's writing about a particular subject. In a similar vein, we do not want to imply that this is the end of the story of our research. In fact, this chapter is as much a beginning of our story as it is an ending. Any researcher who has collected as many examples, texts, field notes, observations, and interviews as we have knows that we have just begun to analyze our data, to share our conclusions, and to tell our story.

I always like to acknowledge that *everything we know about writing we have learned from kids.* We are indebted to the theorists and researchers on writing who informed the important questions we tried to answer. However, we cannot underestimate the impact that observing and interacting with Anna, Dana, Elaine, Gordon, Rachel, and Vincent had on our knowledge about writing in schools and the writing process. It is through observations of and interactions with young authors in their school environment and through further interaction with their written work that we have been able to verify the work of scholars in the field of composition, to confirm or reject beliefs about the composing process and its place in the elementary school curriculum, and to consider new questions and their answers.

In this last chapter I want to present reflections and ideas not shared earlier in the book. There is no attempt to summarize or to conclude. We've made summaries at the appropriate points in our narrative. Rather, I want to present some ideas about the implications of our study for the classroom and for further research.

THE SOCIAL CONTEXT FOR WRITING

In this study we focused on writing in the classroom, the social context in which writing in school takes place. We were fortunate to have the opportunity to spend two years in these classrooms, and we chose to work in these particular schools because of their Native American population of children. We believe that, by providing evidence about the knowledge these children had about language generally and about written language specifically, we have dispelled some prevalent but unfortunate myths about the deficits of non-mainstream populations in our schools. As Dr. Ofelia Zepeda (the Tohono O'odham linguist from the University of Arizona who consulted with us about certain language features in the writing of the children and who wrote the foreword for this volume) said as she responded to our reports of this research, "It's good to find out that our kids are doing okay."

We're grateful to the teachers who were willing to allow outsiders to visit their classrooms on a regular basis for two years. Although we were not always in agreement with the kinds of writing instruction we observed, we appreciated finding teachers who believed that writing was important and agreed to have their students write regularly and to interact with us about writing in the elementary school curriculum. There is no doubt that whenever students write, they learn to write, they learn about writing, and they learn through writing about themselves and the world (Halliday, 1980).

The discussion of the literacy event in Chapter 1 stressed the importance of the writer's social community in the evolution of text. Through this study we learned to appreciate the dynamic interactions of students, teachers, paraprofessionals, and researchers as written language was created. We also began to understand the many forces, including many that are not even overtly present at the moment writing occurs, that influence writers and their compositions. These include parental, cultural, and community values about writing; attitudes of the larger society toward the young author as a learner; personal relationships in the classroom (both teacher-learner and learner-learner); and the personal life history of the writer. As we began to understand the influence of socially agreed-upon conventions of writing, we observed the children's continual inventions of the forms and uses of written language, influenced by the classroom and home communities. All these factors have important impacts on how writers view themselves as writers as well as on what they choose to write about and how they express themselves in written form. We came away from this study with a healthy respect for the roles of collaboration and cooperation between teacher and student and among the students themselves. Vygotsky (1978, 1986) developed the concept of the zone of proximal development, Bruner (1978) and Cazden (1983) discuss scaffolding, and Halliday (1980) uses the term *tracking:* All of them indicate the role that others, significant adults or peers, play in learning. These concepts relate to the power the social community has on the development of the learner. As writers play the role of audience, as they cooperate, listen, argue, and offer suggestions during writing, their own writing shows greater complexity in form. At the same time their writing shows greater concern for communicative meaning, for sharing with an audience the important things that must be said.

Significant adults in the school community must also become aware of their own impact on the writing and overall language learning of their students. Assignments, comments, the tone of conferences and discussions, and the degree of significance placed on the process of writing and/or the finished written products by teachers, tutors, researchers, resource personnel, and peers all leave their mark on the seriousness with which young authors assume responsibility for their writing. As researchers we were often amazed at how interested the children were in the field notes and observations we made about their writing. They helped us, corrected us, and reminded us, and their writing often reflected their belief that their work was important to us.

Three years after the completion of the study, I returned to interview some of the students once again. They remembered that we had been interested in their writing and they asked me about the other researchers they had worked with. They loved seeing the reports we had written about their work and reread their compositions. Vincent told the school principal that we had driven all the way from Tucson each week because we wanted to see their writing and wanted to know more about how they wrote. He told me that he still remembered how we "*really* read" and responded in detail and with enthusiasm to anything he had written.

The significance of the social organization of a writing community (which is part of a larger literacy community in which reading and other symbolic representations such as oral language, art, music, drama, and dance are also involved) needs to be a focus of teacher education. Teacher education programs must organize environments so that both pre-service and in-service teachers can experience a rich literacy community in their own educational settings (i.e., the ones in which they are the learners rather than the teachers). In such environments they can examine their own roles and the roles of others as collaborating members of a literacy community. They can become sensitive to the concept of people reading and writing for real purposes, to solve real problems, or to answer real questions. As teachers have personal reading and writing experiences and as they come to appreciate the role of their own peers as an interested audience, they will build new models of literacy communities. They will not continue to teach as they remember having been taught, with a focus on surface features such as perfect spelling, neat handwriting, and "proper" grammar.

The National Writing Project and various teacher support groups where teachers write for each other and read with each other—expressing ideas, sharing narratives and professional writing—are evidence of teachers' need to write in social communities. Teachers play a major role in creating the social context in which a literacy community develops in their classrooms. Through programs in which teachers experience the power of writing and reading communities, they begin to realize how exciting the classroom can be when authors, whether adults or children, are encouraged to assume ownership of their own learning through their own writing and their own reading. In such classrooms everyone becomes a member of a learning community. Reading and writing are used to solve problems, to answer questions, to respond to wonderings and worries, to critique one another's views, and to challenge one another's truths. Members of such a community respond to one another's writing (and to reading as well) with interest and involvement.

REVISION AND THE NATURE OF ERROR

In the classroom settings in which we were involved, we did not see the kinds of revision processes through teacher-student conferences that have been advocated by Graves (1982) and Calkins (1983). We support these authors' conclusions, however, about the importance of students' being involved in monitoring their own writing. We have shown, unequivocally, that the students with whom we worked were always involved in self-correcting as they wrote, but that their editing and revising reflected what *they* primarily believed was demanded of good writers, namely neatness, good handwriting, correct spelling, and appropriate length. They were more concerned with editing for good form than with revising for appropriate communication and self-expression.

Many cautions about an excessive focus on editing and revising have been expressed by others. I wish to focus here on the issue of error or miscue in writing because of my 30 years of involvement in miscue analysis research as it applies to the reading process (Y. Goodman, Watson & Burke, 1987). Miscues are unexpected responses observed by a teacher or researcher during reading. Errors in writing can also be called miscues: unexpected or unconventional responses from the point of view of an observer. In much of the literature on miscue analysis, miscues are referred to as unexpected responses or observed responses, suggesting that the miscue is not necessarily wrong from the point of view of the reader or writer who produced it. Whether a particular response is to be categorized as a miscue is determined on the basis of the expectations and interpretation of the observer, although the response may be quite logical to the student. Many miscues can be considered inventions by readers and writers; these miscues represent learners' personal knowledge at a particular point in time. By examining the kinds of miscues students produce as they write and observing how they monitor their own composing, we learn a great deal not only about the writing process but about the knowledge, beliefs, and personal history of the student.

In previous research on the reading process (K. Goodman & Burke, 1968, 1973; K. Goodman & Y. Goodman, 1978), the notion of the confirmation process, readers' self-monitoring for the purpose of making sense, has been well established. It is obvious that readers constantly question themselves about the degree to which their reading sounds like language and has meaning. We have evidence in the present research that writers are similarly confirming as they write. The children we observed often monitored their writing, rereading before they continued to write, wondering whether their writing made sense, whether it read like written language. These conclusions are supported by our detailed recordings of their errors, inventions, or miscues; their editing, revisions, and rereadings; and the concerns the students shared with us about their writing.

It is absolutely necessary to understand the significance of writers' being in control of monitoring their own expression of meaning through written language. The errors children generate are not only a necessary part of writing but are actually part of the dynamic developmental process that allows meaning to grow and to be expressed in varied and complex ways. Many teachers, specialists from various fields of education, and researchers, in their application of behavioral psychology, have for too long disseminated the myth that if teachers do not immediately correct and then reinforce the correct form in their students, there will be a long-range negative impact on the learner. This is an outmoded notion not supported by current research in writing. It has also been rejected by the years of miscue research in reading. In fact, miscue research provides evidence that the more the teacher responds with corrective feedback, the less likely it is that learners will monitor their own language use and the more likely they are to rely on the teacher as the source of all knowledge (Board, 1982/1983).

Error is a necessary and intrinsic part of development. Teachers and researchers often have culturally influenced views and assumptions about the nature of error that are not based on insights from careful observation of writers and readers. As teachers and researchers come to understand the nature of error in writing in relation to self-monitoring, they begin to trust that error (miscuing), monitoring, and self-correcting are integral to all language learning. At such a point it becomes difficult to conceive of error as negative, and a term like *miscue* seems more appropriate. Ethnographic techniques may help researchers provide additional insights for understanding these phenomena. Kidwatching (Y. Goodman, 1978), anecdotal record keeping, periodic interviews, and collections of selected compositions for student portfolios can help teachers deepen their understandings about development in student writing and discuss a student's development with the student, subsequent teachers, parents, and administrators.

We need additional information about the nature of rereading and revision and their influence on miscues and the evolution of written texts. We need to help teachers know what kinds of questions encourage children in their self-expression through writing and what kinds of questions and statements may actually inhibit children's writing. We need to build strong teacher education programs in which teachers learn how they can interact with children about their writing through both thought-provoking questioning techniques and spontaneous and organized conferencing.

Teachers who observe children with a perspective based on the latest knowledge and theories about language, who question children in ways that support their development, who know the significance of the nature of error or miscue, and who organize the kind of environment in which children are willing to take control of their learning, willing to take risks in writing, and willing to "learn how to mean" (in Halliday's phrase) through written language are professionals who promote writing development in classroom settings. Professionals who understand the power of their ability to observe development in students become tuned in to the power of research. They begin to realize that they are building professional responses to children's writing. They become teacher researchers who know how to ask questions based on a continual examination of their theories of teaching, learning, and language. They also begin to find ways to answer their own questions and begin to solve their own problems through reading of professional literature, involvement with other professionals, careful evaluation of the writing of their students, and continual self-evaluation of their literacy curriculum.

RELATIONSHIPS BETWEEN RESEARCHERS AND SCHOOL PERSONNEL

Not only has our research story explored how children learn to write and its implications for teachers and for classroom organization, it has also revealed a good deal about how researchers and the members of a school community interact to learn more about human writing development. During the two years we spent in three classrooms and two different schools on a regular basis, we learned a good deal about the significance of a strong and supportive relationship among the many people involved in classroom research.

In classroom research, everyone involved must know the purposes for the research. This research was suggested by Ann Francisco, the principal of the primary school where we worked. She was involved in the planning of the research proposal and made suggestions and raised concerns throughout the project from the writing of the proposal through the final written report.

The agenda for school research must be carefully presented to all those involved. We discussed our objectives with the school board, with the administrators of each school, with the teachers and paraprofessionals, and with the children with whom we would be involved most closely. We were honest about what we wanted to observe, why we were conducting the research, and what our research questions were. We made ourselves available on a regular basis to school personnel to discuss individual children and issues of curriculum and to respond to any requests. We set up interviews with the parents of the young authors, which provided opportunities for them to question us as well as for us to gain greater insight into the students and the community. We interacted with the children in our study and answered their questions, which helped us learn more about them and their views of writing.

There were some aspects of communication that we were not as successful in achieving, for a variety of reasons. We were not in the school as often as we would have liked because of the distance from our research center and limited funding. As a result we did not discuss the writing curriculum with the teachers as much as we wanted to, but the teachers were interested in and responsive to what we were learning. More interaction about what we were learning would have been helpful to the teachers and might have led to our having a greater impact on curriculum than we did. Although we followed through on all the planned formal interviews and responded immediately to any serious concerns raised by the teachers and administrators, we seldom had extended periods of time to interact about impressions, concerns, and feelings.

We had hoped to give the teachers and children ongoing information about the results of the study as we were analyzing data. Unfortunately our data analysis did not keep pace with data collection. We tried to analyze data during the data-collection period but, for the most part, we were behind in our schedule for analysis and most of the data were analyzed over the summers or after the children had moved on to other classrooms. Organizing our research to provide for continuous analysis of data with a quicker turnaround time would have been useful not only for the teachers and students but also to inform our continuing data-collection procedures. We would have been able to ask both the students and the teachers more informed questions and to organize specific writing experiences with the teachers and the students had we known specifics about the research analysis more immediately. This would have taken more financial support and a larger research staff. We were all involved in both data collection and data analysis. It might have been better to have more people involved in ongoing data analysis.

FUNDAMENTAL PRINCIPLES FOR A WRITING CURRICULUM

Our research story has been a long and complicated one, involving characters who learned and benefited from the experiences and an extensive plot with a long chronology of events, crises, problems, and successes. One of the themes we've explored is how this work can inform teachers and those responsible for building writing programs in schools, in order to promote environments in which writing development is best supported. And so we've come to "The End" of the research narrative. In closing, we recommend a set of principles that are fundamental to informing a sound curriculum in writing.

We hope that they provide opportunities for some new beginnings. These principles are strongly influenced by our research conclusions, by beliefs about language, learning, teaching, and curriculum that we have expanded through our research history, and by other scholars, researchers, and teachers concerned with the writing process and whole language programs.

- Children learn to write by writing.
- Children learn to write in a social environment that encourages and supports writing.
- Children learn to write as they know their audiences and use writing for a variety of purposes of communication.
- Children learn to write as they express themselves through many varieties, modes, and genres of writing.
- Children learn to write as they read a wide range of different kinds and genres of reading materials.
- Children learn to write as they make personal choices and decisions about what to write and what to read.
- Children learn to write as they experiment, take risks, and invent new forms of writing while they try to express their meanings through writing.
- Children learn to write as they talk about and critique their own compositions with others and as they discuss and critique the compositions of others with them.
- Children learn to write when they share with others through writing what they've learned about specific content in social studies, science, math, or other areas of the curriculum that they care about and are interested in.
- Children learn to write when they have important ideas or concerns to share with others.
- Children learn to write as they make miscues (errors) and inventions and self-monitor and self-correct their own writing.
- Children learn to write with teachers who understand the factors that influence writing and can organize rich literacy environments that support children's learning.

As each of the above principles is turned into real experiences in the classroom, children not only learn to write but their writing develops. The opportunities to use writing in these many ways allow students to experiment with and experience writing in ways that continue to impact writing development.

Opportunities to use writing, to talk about it, to reread writing, and to rewrite when it is appropriate to do so allow children to focus on writing as an abstract symbol system. In this way children learn how writing works, what it is used for, how people learn to write, and the conventions of the writing system. Teachers play a significant role in helping children learn to write. This role is a positive one when teachers know enough about writing, language, learning, and teaching to organize a rich literacy community in which writing, learning to write, and learning about writing are daily experiences for all learners.

References

Altwerger, Bess, & Flores, Barbara. (1991). The theme cycle: An overview. In Kenneth S. Goodman, Lois B. Bird & Yetta M. Goodman (Eds.), *The whole language catalog* (p. 295). Santa Rosa, CA: American School Publishers.

Anderson, Richard C., Spiro, Rand, & Montague, William E. (1977). *Schooling and the acquisition of knowledge*. Hillsdale, NJ: Erlbaum.

Applebee, Arthur. (1978). *The child's concept of story: Ages two to seventeen*. Chicago: University of Chicago Press.

Applebee, Arthur. (1984). *Contexts for learning to write: Studies of secondary school instruction*. Norwood, NJ: Ablex.

Atwell, Nancie. (1987). *In the middle: Writing, reading and learning with adolescents*. Portsmouth, NH: Heinemann.

Atwell, Nancie (Ed.). (1990). *Coming to know: Writing to learn in the intermediate grades*. Portsmouth, NH: Heinemann.

Baker, Robert D. (1980). Orthographic awareness. In Uta Frith (Ed.), *Cognitive processes in spelling* (pp. 51–82). London: Academic Press.

Barnitz, J. G. (1979). *Reading comprehension of pronoun-referent structures by children in grades two, four and six* (Technical Report No. 117). Urbana, IL: University of Illinois, Center for the Study of Reading.

Bartlett, Elsa J., & Scribner, Sylvia. (1981). Text and context: An investigation of referential organization in children's writing narrative. In Carl H. Frederiksen & Joseph F. Dominic (Eds.), *Writing: the nature, development and teaching of written communication: Vol. 2. Writing: Process, development, and communication* (pp. 153–67). Hillsdale, NJ: Erlbaum.

Bauman, James F., & Stevenson, Judith. (1986). Teaching students to comprehend anaphoric relations. In Jennifer A. Irwin (Ed.), *Understanding and teaching cohesion comprehension* (pp. 95–124). Newark, DE: International Reading Association.

Beers, James W., & Henderson, Edmund H. (1977). A study of developing orthographic concepts among first graders. *Research in the Teaching of English, 11*, 133–148.

Berko, Jean. (1958). The child's learning of English morphology. *Word, 14*, 150–177.

Bird, Lois B. (1986). The reflection of personal experience in the writing of Papago Indian children (doctoral dissertation, University of Arizona, 1985). *Dissertation Abstracts International, 46*, 2950A.

Bird, Lois, & Gollasch, Inta. (1979). *Language arts manual*. Sells, AZ: Indian Oasis School District.

Bissex, Glenda. (1980). *Gnys at wrk: A child learns to read and write*. Cambridge, MA: Harvard University Press.

Blaine, P., Sr. as told to M. S. Adams. (1981). *Papago and politics*. Tucson: Arizona Historical Society.

Board, Peter. (1983). Toward a theory of instructional influence: Aspects of the instructional environment and their influnece on children's acquisition of reading (doctoral dissertation, University of Toronto, 1982). *Dissertation Abstracts International, 44*, 717A.

Bolinger, Dwight L. (1946). Visual morphemes. *Language, 22*, 333–340.

Bormuth, John R., Carr, J., Manning, John, & Pearson, P. David. (1970). Children's comprehension of between-and-within-sentence syntactic structures. *Journal of Educational Psychology, 61*, 349–357.

Bradley, Henry. (1919). *On the relations between spoken and written language: With special reference to English.* London: Oxford University Press.

Britton, James. (1970a). *Language and learning.* Coral Gables, FL: University of Miami Press.

Britton, James L. (1970b). The student's writing. In Eldonna L. Evertts (Ed.), *Explorations in children's writing* (pp. 21–76). Urbana, IL: National Council of Teachers of English.

Britton, James L., Burgess, Tony, Martin, Nancy, McLeod, Alex, & Rosen, Harold. (1975). *The development of writing abilities: Eleven to eighteen.* London: Macmillan Educational, for the Schools Council.

Brown, Hazel, & Cambourne, Brian. (1989). *Read and retell.* Portsmouth, NH: Heinemann.

Bruner, Jerome. (1978). The role of dialogue in language acquisition. In A. Sinclair, R. J. Jarvelle & W. J. M. Levelt (Eds.), *The child's conception of language* (pp. 241–256). New York: Springer-Verlag.

Bullough, Edward. (1912). "Psychical distance" as a factor in art and an aesthetic principle. *British Journal of Psychology, 5*, 87–118.

Calkins, Lucy M. (1983). *Lessons from a child: On the teaching and learning of writing.* Exeter, NH: Heinemann.

Calkins, Lucy M. (1986). *The art of teaching writing.* Portsmouth, NH: Heinemann.

Calkins, Lucy M. (1991). *Living between the lines.* Portsmouth, NH: Heinemann.

Cazden, Courtney. (1983). Adult assistance to language development: Scaffolds, models and direct instruction. In Robert P. Parker & Frances A. Davis (Eds.), *Developing literacy: Young children's use of language* (pp. 3–18). Newark, DE: International Reading Association.

Chao, Yuen R. (1968). *Language and symbolic systems.* London: Cambridge University Press..

Chapman, L. John. (1981, May). *The comprehension of anaphora.* Paper presented at the meeting of the International Reading Association, New Orleans. (ERIC Document Reproduction Service No. ED 205 897)

Chodorow, Nancy. (1974). Family structure and feminine personality. In Michelle Z. Rosaldo & Louise Lamphere (Eds.), *Women, culture, and society* (pp. 43–66). Stanford, CA: Stanford University Press.

Chomsky, Carol. (1970). Reading, writing, and phonology. *Harvard Educational Review, 40*, 287–309.

Chomsky, Noam. (1970). Phonology and reading. In Harry Levin & Joanna P. Williams (Eds.), *Basic studies on reading.* New York: Basic Books.

Chomsky, Noam, & Halle, Morris. (1968). *The sound pattern of English*. New York: Harper & Row.

Clark, Pamela. (1991, June). *Principal/teacher collaboration*. Paper presented at San Jose Whole Language Conference, San Jose, CA.

Clay, Marie. (1975). *What did I write?* London: Heinemann.

Durkin, Dolores. (1976). *Teaching young children to read* (2d ed.). Boston: Allyn & Bacon.

Edelsky, Carole, Altwerger, Bess, & Flores, Barbara. (1990). *Whole language: What's the difference?* Portsmouth, NH: Heinemann.

Emig, Janet. (1977). Writing as a mode of learning. *College Composition and Communication, 28*, 122–128.

Ferreiro, Emilia, & Teberosky, Ana. (1982). *Literacy before schooling*. Exeter, NH: Heinemann.

Flower, Linda, & Hayes, John. (1979). *A process model of composition* (Technical Report No. 1). Pittsburgh: Carnegie-Mellon University. (ERIC Document Reproduction Service No. ED 218 661)

Fontana, B. L. (1981). *Of earth and little rain: The Papago Indians*. Flagstaff, AZ: Northland Press.

Forester, Anne D. (1980). Learning to spell by spelling. *Theory into Practice, 19*, 186–193.

Freeman, David. (1986). Use of pragmatic cohesion cues to resolve degrees of pronoun reference ambiguity in reading (doctoral dissertation, University of Arizona, 1986). *Dissertation Abstracts International, 47*, 1306A.

Freeman, David. (1988). Assignment of pronoun reference: Evidence that young readers control cohesion. *Linguistics and Education, 1*, 153–176.

Frith, Uta. (1971). Why do children reverse letters? *British Journal of Psychology, 62*, 459–468.

Gamberg, Ruth, Kwak, Winniefred, Hutchings, Meredith, & Altheim, Judy. (1988). *Learning and loving it: Theme studies in the classroom*. Portsmouth, NH: Heinemann.

Garner, Ruth, Gillingham, Mark G., & White, C. Stephen. (1989). Effects of "seductive details" on macroprocessing and microprocessing in adults and children. *Cognition and Instruction, 6*, 41–57.

Gentry, J. Richard. (1978). Early spelling strategies. *The Elementary School Journal, 79*, 88–92.

Gespass, Suzanne. (1990). Control and use of pronouns in the writing of Native American children (doctoral dissertation, University of Arizona, 1989). *Dissertation Abstracts International, 51*, 410A.

Gibson, Eleanor J., & Levin, Harry. (1975). *The psychology of reading*. Cambridge, MA: MIT Press.

Gill, Charlene E. (1980). An analysis of spelling errors in French (doctoral dissertation, University of Virginia). *Dissertation Abstracts International, 41*, 3924A.

Goldstone, Bette. (1983). *Seeing is believing: Applications from naturalistic research*. Unpublished paper.

Goodenough, Ward H. (1976). Multiculturalism as the normal human experience. [Council on] *Anthropology and Education Quarterly, 7*, 4–7.

Goodman, Kenneth S. (1984). Unity in reading. In Alan C. Purves & Olive Niles

(Eds.), *Becoming readers in a complex society: Eighty-third yearbook of the National Society for the Study of Education, Part I* (pp. 79–114). Chicago: University of Chicago Press.

Goodman, Kenneth S., & Burke, Carolyn. (1968). *A study of oral reading miscues that result in grammatical re-transformations* (Office of Education Final Report Project No. 7-E-219, Contract No. OEG-O-8-070219-2806-010). Detroit: Wayne State University. (ERIC Document Reproduction Service No. ED 039 101)

Goodman, Kenneth S., & Burke, Carolyn. (1973). *Theoretically based studies of patterns of miscues in oral reading performance* (Office of Education Final Report, Project No. OEG-0-9-32075-4269). Detroit: Wayne State University. (ERIC Document Reproduction Service No. ED 079 708)

Goodman, Kenneth S., & Gespass, Suzanne. (1983a). *Analysis of text structures as they relate to patterns of oral reading miscues* (Final Report, Project NIE-G-80-0057). Tucson: University of Arizona, College of Education, Program in Language and Literacy.

Goodman, Kenneth S., & Gespass, Suzanne. (1983b). *Text features as they relate to miscues: Pronouns* (Occasional Paper No. 7). Tucson: University of Arizona, College of Education, Program in Language and Literacy.

Goodman, Kenneth S., & Goodman, Yetta M. (1978). *Reading of American children whose language is a stable rural dialect of English or a language other than English* (National Institute of Education Final Report NIE-C-00-3-0087). Detroit: Wayne State University, College of Education. (ERIC Document Reproduction Service No. ED 173 754)

Goodman, Yetta M. (1978). Kid watching: An alternative to testing. *National Elementary Principal, 57,* 41–45.

Goodman, Yetta M. (1984). *A two-year case study observing the development of third and fourth grade Native American children's writing processes* (National Institute of Education Final Report NIE-G-81-0127). Tucson: University of Arizona, College of Education, Program in Language and Literacy. (ERIC Document Reproduction Service No. ED 241 240)

Goodman, Yetta M., & Goodman, Kenneth S. (1990). Vygotsky in a whole-language perspective. In Luis C. Moll (Ed.), *Vygotsky and education: Instructional implications and applications of sociohistorical psychology* (pp. 223–250). Cambridge: Cambridge University Press.

Goodman, Yetta M., Watson, Dorothy J., & Burke, Carolyn L. (1987). *Reading miscue inventory: Alternative procedures.* Katonah, NY: Richard C. Owen.

Goodman, Yetta M., & Wilde, Sandra. (1985). *Writing development in third and fourth grade Native American students: Social context, linguistic systems, and creation of meaning* (Occasional Paper No. 14). Tucson: University of Arizona, College of Education, Program in Language and Literacy. (ERIC Document Reproduction Service No. ED 278 017)

Graves, Donald H. (1974). Children's writing: Research directions and hypotheses based upon an examination of the writing processes of seven year old children (doctoral dissertation, State University of New York at Buffalo, 1973). *Dissertation Abstracts International, 34,* 6255A.

Graves, Donald. (1975). An examination of the writing processes of seven-year-old children. *Research in the Teaching of English, 9,* 225–241.

Graves, Donald H. (1982). *A case study observing the development of primary children's composing, spelling, and motor behaviors during the writing process* (National Institute of Education Final Report No. G-78-0174). Durham, NH: University of New Hampshire, Department of Education. (ERIC Document Reproduction Service No. ED 218 653)

Graves, Donald H. (1983). *Writing: Teachers and children at work.* Exeter, NH: Heinemann.

Grice, H. Paul. (1975). Logic and conversation. In Peter Cole & Jerry L. Morgan (Eds.), *Syntax and semantics* (vol. 3: Speech acts) (pp. 41–58). New York: Academic Press.

Guba, Egon. (1978). *Toward a methodology of naturalistic inquiry in educational evaluation* (CSE Monograph Series in Evaluation No. 8). Los Angeles: UCLA, Graduate School of Education, Center for the Study of Evaluation.

Halliday, M. A. K. (1977). *Learning how to mean: Explorations in the development of language.* New York: Elsevier.

Halliday, M. A. K. (1980). Three aspects of children's language development: Learning language, learning through language, learning about language. In Yetta M. Goodman, Myna Haussler & Dorothy Strickland (Eds.), *Oral and written language development research: Impact on the schools* (Proceedings from the 1979 and 1980 IMPACT Conferences, National Council of Teachers of English) (pp. 7–19). Newark, DE & Urbana, IL: International Reading Association & National Council of Teachers of English. (ERIC Document Reproduction Service No. ED 214 184)

Halliday, M. A. K., & Hasan, Ruqaiya. (1976). *Cohesion in English.* London: Longman.

Hanna, Paul R., Hanna, Jean S., Hodges, Richard E., & Rudorf, Erwin H., Jr. (1966). *Phoneme-grapheme correspondences as cues to spelling improvement.* Washington, DC: U.S. Office of Education. (ERIC Document Reproduction Service No. ED 128 835)

Hardy, Barbara. (1968). Towards a poetic of fiction: 3) An approach through narrative. *Novel: A Forum on Fiction, 2,* 5–14.

Harste, Jerome C., Woodward, Virginia, & Burke, Carolyn. (1984). *Language stories and literacy lessons.* Exeter, NH: Heinemann.

Heald-Taylor, B. Gail. (1984). Scribble in first grade writing. *Reading Teacher, 38,* 4–8.

Heath, Shirley B. (1983). *Ways with words: Language, life, and work in communities and classroom.* New York: Cambridge University Press.

Hildreth, Gertrude. (1936). Developmental sequences in name writing. *Child Development, 7,* 291–303.

Hodges, Richard E. (1982). Research update: On the development of spelling ability. *Language Arts, 59,* 284–290.

Holmes, E. E. (1936). Writing experiences of elementary children. *The Elementary English Review, 13,* 107–111.

Horn, Ernest. (1957). Phonetics and spelling. *The Elementary School Journal, 57,* 424–432.

Hunt, Kellogg W. (1965). *Grammatical sturctures written at three grade levels* (National Council of Teachers of English Research Report No. 3). Champaign, IL: National Council of Teachers of English.

Hunt, Kellogg W. (1966). Recent measures in syntactic development. *Elementary English, 43*, 732–739.

Hymes, Dell. (1981). *Ethnographic monitoring of children's acquisition of reading/language arts skills in and out of the classroom* (National Institute of Education Final Report G-79-0124). Philadelphia: University of Pennsylvania Graduate School of Education. (ERIC Document Reproduction Service No. ED 208 096)

Kasten, Wendy C. (1985). The behaviors accompanying the writing process in selected third and fourth grade Native American children (doctoral dissertation, University of Arizona, 1984). *Dissertation Abstracts International, 45*, 2389A.

Kasten, Wendy C. (1990). Oral language during the writing process of native American students. *English Quarterly, 22*, 149–156.

Kasten, Wendy C., & Clarke, Barbara K. (1987). A study of third and fifth grade students' oral language during the writing process. *Research Bulletin, 19*(4), Florida Educational Research and Development Council. (ERIC Document Reproduction Service No. ED 294 180)

Kirby, Dan, & Liner, Tom. (1981). *Inside out: Developmental strategies for teaching writing*. Portsmouth, NH: Heinemann.

Lancaster, William, Nelson, Laurie, & Morris, Darrell. (1982). Invented spellings in Room 112: A writing program for low-reading second graders. *Reading Teacher, 35*, 906–911.

Langer, Susanne K. (1942). *Philosophy in a new key: A study in the symbolism of reason, rite, and art*. Cambridge: Cambridge University Press.

Lashley, K. S. (1951). The problem of serial order in behavior. In L. A. Jeffress (Ed.), *Cerebral mechanisms in behavior*. New York: John Wiley.

Lindfors, Judith W. (1987). *Children's language and learning* (2d ed.). Englewood Cliffs, NJ: Prentice-Hall.

Little, Jean. (1987). *Little by little*. Markham, Ontario: Viking.

Marek, Ann, & Goodman, Kenneth. (1985). *Annotated bibliography of miscue analysis* (Occasional Paper No. 16). Tucson: University of Arizona, College of Education, Program in Language and Literacy.

Marino, Jacqueline L. (1979). *Children's use of phonetic, graphemic, and morphemic cues in a spelling task*. Unpublished paper. (ERIC Document Reproduction Service No. ED 188 235).

Marsh, George, Friedman, Morton, Welch, Veronica, & Desberg, Peter. (1980). The development of strategies in spelling. In Uta Frith (Ed.), *Cognitive processes in spelling*. London: Academic Press.

Mayher, John S., Lester, Nancy B., & Pradl, Gordon M. (1983). *Learning to write/Writing to learn*. Portsmouth, NH: Boynton/Cook.

Miles, Miska. (1971). *Annie and the old one*. Boston: Little, Brown.

Miller, George A., Bartlett, Elsa, & Hirst, William. (1982). *Anaphora: A theory and its applications to developmental research* (Final Report, Project NIE-G-78-0171).

New York: Rockefeller Foundation. (ERIC Document Reproduction Service No. ED 213 042)

Milz, Vera E. (1984). A psycholinguistic description of the development of writing in selected first grade students (ethnography, composition, spelling) (doctoral dissertation, University of Arizona, 1983). *Dissertation Abstracts International, 44,* 3279A.

Moll, Luis C., Vélez-Ibáñez, Carlos, Greenberg, James, Whitmore, Kathy, Saavedra, Elizabeth, Dworin, Joel, and Andrade, Rosi (1990). *Community knowledge and classroom practice: Combining resources for literacy instruction* (OBEMLA Contract No. 300-87-0131). Tucson: University of Arizona, College of Education and Bureau of Applied Research in Anthropology.

Momaday, N. Scott. (1975). A note on contemporary Native American poetry. In Duane Niatum (Ed.), *Carriers of the dream wheel: Contemporary Native American poetry* (pp. xix–xx). New York: Harper & Row.

Murray, Donald M. (1982). *Learning by teaching: Selected articles on writing and teaching.* Montclair, NJ: Boynton/Cook.

Murray, Donald. (1985). *A writer teaches writing.* Boston: Houghton Mifflin.

Murray, Donald M. (1989). *Expecting the unexpected: Teaching myself—and others—to read and write.* Portsmouth, NH: Heinemann.

Murray, Michele. (1980). Creating oneself from scratch. In Janet Sternberg (Ed.), *The writer on her work* (pp. 71–94). New York: Norton.

Nabhan, Gary P. (1982). *The desert smells like rain.* San Francisco: North Point Press.

Neisser, Ulric. (1976). *Cognition and reality.* San Francisco: W. H. Freeman.

Nolen, Patricia, & McCartin, Rosemarie. (1984). Spelling strategies on the Wide Range Achievement Test. *The Reading Teacher, 38,* 148–157.

O'Donnell, R. C., Griffin, W. J., & Norris, R. C. (1967). Syntax of kindergarten and elementary school children: A transformational analysis (Research Report No. 8). Urbana, IL: National Council of Teachers of English.

Odell, Lee, Goswami, Dixie, & Herrington, A. (1983). The discourse-based interview: A procedure for exploring the tacit knowledge of writers in non-academic settings. In Peter Mosenthal, Lynne Tamor & Sean M. Walmsley (Eds.), *Research on writing* (pp. 220–236). New York: Longman.

Paley, Vivian G. (1981). *Wally's stories.* Cambridge, MA.: Harvard University Press.

Papago Education Committee. (1982). *Comprehensive education plan for the O'odham tribe.* Sells, AZ: Papago Education Department.

Perl, Sondra. (1979). The composing processes of unskilled college writers. *Research in the Teaching of English, 13,* 317–336.

Pitcher, Evelyn G., & Prelinger, Ernst. (1963). *Children tell stories: An analysis of fantasy.* New York: International Universities Press.

Polanyi, Michael. (1966). *The tacit dimension.* Garden City, NY: Doubleday.

Pollock. John F. (1986). A psycholinguistic analysis of oral reading miscues involving pronoun-referent structures among selected second, fourth, and sixth grade children (doctoral dissertation, University of Arizona, 1985). *Dissertation Abstracts International, 46,* 3306A.

Read, Charles. (1975). *Children's categorization of speech sounds in English* (Research Report No. 17). Urbana, IL: National Council of Teachers of English.

Read, Charles. (1986). *Children's creative spelling*. London: Routledge & Kegan Paul.

Richek, Margaret A. (1976–77). Reading comprehension of anaphoric forms in varying linguistic contexts. *Reading Research Quarterly, 12*, 145–165.

Rosen, Harold. (1983). *Stories and meanings*. London: National Association for the Teaching of English.

Rosenblatt, Louise. (1978). *The reader, the text, the poem*. Carbondale, IL: Southern Illinois University Press.

Rupley, W. H. (1976). Teaching and evaluating creative writing in the elementary grades. *Language Arts, 58*, 586–590.

Schwartz, Sybil, & Doehring, Donald G. (1977). A developmental study of children's ability to acquire knowledge of spelling pattern. *Developmental Psychology, 13*, 419–420.

Scragg, D. G. (1974). *A history of English spelling*. Manchester, England: Manchester University Press.

Smith, Frank. (1973). *Psycholinguistics and reading*. New York: Holt, Rinehart & Winston.

Smith, Frank. (1982). *Understanding reading* (3d ed.). New York: Holt, Rinehart & Winston.

Smith, Philip T. (1980). In defence or conservatism in English orthography. *Visible Language, 14*, 122–136.

Sutton-Smith, Brian. (1975). The importance of the storytaker: An investigation of the imaginative life. *The Urban Review, 8*, 82–95.

Templeton, Shane. (1979). Spelling first, sound later: The relationship between orthography and higher order phonological knowledge in older students. *Research in the Teaching of English, 13*, 255–264.

Thomas, Valerie. (1982). *Learning to spell: The way children make use of morphemic information* (Research Report 1/82). Carlton, Victoria, Australia: Education Department of Victoria. (ERIC Document Reproduction Service No. ED 230 933)

Vallins, G. H. (1965). *Spelling* (revised by D. G. Scragg). London: Andre Deutsch.

Vaughan, Sherry C. (1984). *The effect of megacognitive strategies on children's writing* (doctoral dissertation, University of Arizona, 1983). *Dissertation Abstracts International, 44*, 3645A.

Venezky, Richard L. (1970). *The structure of English orthography*. The Hague: Mouton.

Volavková, Hana (Ed.). (1978). *I never saw another butterfly: Children's drawings and poems from Terezin Concentration Camp, 1942–1944*. New York: Schocken Books.

Vygotsky, Lev. (1978). *Mind in society: The development of higher psychological processes*. Cambridge, MA: Harvard University Press.

Vygotsky, Lev. (1986) *Thought and language*. Cambridge, MA: MIT Press.

Ward, Daniel C. (1975). The relationship between rated quality and selected syntactic variables in written compositions of second, fourth, and sixth graders (doctoral dissertation, University of Georgia, 1974). *Dissertation Abstracts International, 35*, 6376A.

Wells, Gordon. (1986). *The meaning makers*. Portsmouth, NH: Heinemann.

Werner, Heinz, & Caplan, Edith. (1950). The acquisition of word meaning. *Monographs of the Society for Research in Child Development, 15* (Serial No. 51, No. 1).

Wilde, Jack. (1988). The written report: Old wine in new bottles. In Thomas Newkirk & Nancie Atwell (Eds.), *Understanding writing* (2nd Ed.) (pp. 179–90). Portsmouth, NH: Heinemann.

Wilde, Sandra. (1987). An analysis of the development of spelling and punctuation in selected third and fourth grade children (doctoral dissertation, University of Arizona, 1986). *Dissertation Abstracts International, 47,* 2452A.

Wilde, Sandra. (1989). Looking at invented spelling: A kid-watcher's guide to spelling, part 1. In Kenneth Goodman, Yetta Goodman & Wendy Hood (Eds.), *The whole language evaluation book* (pp. 213–226). Portsmouth, NH: Heinemann.

Wilde, Sandra. (1992). *You kan red this! Spelling and punctuation for whole language classrooms, K–6*. Portsmouth, NH: Heinemann.

Wilkinson, Andrew, Bornsley, Gillian, Hanna, Peter, & Swan, Margaret. (1980). *Assessing language development*. Oxford: Oxford University Press.

Williams, Vera B. (1990). *More more more said the baby*. New York: Scholastic.

Witty, Paul A. (1941). Creative writing climates. *Childhood Education, 17,* 253–257.

Wolcott, Harry. (1991). Propriospect and the acquisition of culture. *Anthropology and Education Quarterly, 22,* 251–73.

Zepeda, Ofelia, & Hill, Jane. (1986). *A sociolinguistic study of regional dialects in O'odham (Papago)*. Unpublished project proposal.

Zutell, Jerry. (1979). Spelling strategies of primary school children and their relationship to Piaget's concept of decentration. *Research in the Teaching of English, 13,* 69–80.

About the Editors and Contributors

Lois Bridges Bird is an instructor at San Jose State University, a whole language consultant, and coeditor of *The Whole Language Catalog* and *The Whole Language Catalog Supplement on Authentic Assessment*.

Suzanne Gespass is an Assistant Professor at Rider College and is interested in issues relating to teacher education. She has researched the role of pronouns in basal texts and in children's writing. She also works with several groups of teachers in New Jersey.

Yetta M. Goodman is Regents Professor of Language, Reading, and Culture at the University of Arizona and is the coauthor of *Reading Miscue Inventory: Alternative Procedures* and coeditor of *The Whole Language Evaluation Book* and *Organizing for Whole Language*.

Wendy C. Kasten is an Associate Professor at the University of South Florida in Sarasota, where she teaches courses in language arts and children's literature and conducts research in whole language. She has published articles about the Tohono O'odham children discussed in this book in *English Quarterly* (1990), *The Whole Idea* (1991), and *Anthropology and Education Quarterly* (1992).

Sherry Vaughan, an Associate Professor at Washington State University, teaches courses in language development, writing, and language arts and serves as the Associate Dean of the College of Education. Her most recent activities include restructuring the university's teacher education program and working with professional development partners across the state of Washington.

Sandra Wilde is an Assistant Professor at Portland State University (Oregon). She is the author of *You Kan Red This! Spelling and Punctuation for Whole-Language Classrooms, K–6* and coauthor of *Read Any Good Math Lately? Children's Books for Mathematical Learning, K–6* (with David Whitin), both published by Heinemann.

Ofelia Zepeda is a member of the Tohono O'odham tribe and is currently an Associate Professor in the Department of Linguistics at the University of Arizona. She is involved in several research projects on the Tohono O'odham language: developing materials suitable for studying and teaching the language, conducting a comprehensive dialect survey, and creating a living Tohono O'odham literature. She has published *A Papago Grammar* (1983) and *When it Rains: Pima and Papago Poetry*.

Index